P9-APC-315

MOZOS

A DECADE RUNNING WITH THE BULLS OF SPAIN

BILL HILLMANN

 CURBSIDE SPLENDOR

CURBSIDE SPLENDOR PUBLISHING

All rights reserved. No part of this book may be reproduced in any form or by any electronic or mechanical means, including information storage and retrieval systems, without permission in writing from the publisher, except in the case of short passages quoted in reviews.

The stories contained herein are works of fiction. All incidents, situations, institutions, governments, and people are fictional and any similarity to characters or persons living or dead is strictly coincidental.

Published by Curbside Splendor Publishing, Inc., Chicago, Illinois in 2015.

First Edition
Copyright © 2015 by Bill Hillmann
Library of Congress Control Number: 2015934177
ISBN 978-194043053-9
Cover image © Foto Mena
Designed by Alban Fischer

Manufactured in the United States of America.

www.curbsidesplendor.com

PRAISE FOR BILL HILLMANN

"Bill Hillmann is courageous. I'm very happy that there have been many aficionados in the United States like Hemingway and Hillmann."

—MARIO VARGAS LLOSA, 2010 Noble Laureate

"A choose your own adventure story like no other."

—GLENN WASHINGTON, NPR

"Hillmann is one of the last and most serious Hemingwayites."

—*CUARTO PODER* (Spain)

"Bill Hillmann is one of the few who can articulate the chaotic scramble of runners, the icy chill of being gored, and the healing power of nearly bleeding to death on a filthy street in Spain."

—*ESQUIRE*

Ann,

Glad you finished the race! Hope you enjoy!
-Bill

Will Smith

ACKNOWLEDGMENTS

My father instilled a love of adventure in me. My mother showed me what stubbornness could accomplish. Da taught me about compassion. My brothers and sisters strengthened me. Enid, I don't exist without your love. I'm sorry for all the pain my passion for the encierro causes you. If it weren't for David McGrath and his Hemingway class at College of DuPage I may have never developed a love of reading. Ron Wiginton and Elmhurst College taught me to write and believe in myself. John Schultz's Story Workshop at Columbia College showed me how to write a how-to. Irvine Welsh has given me so many opportunities and such great advice, but most importantly his unparalleled work ethic has inspired me to push beyond my limits as a writer. The Local 2 laborers in Brookfield and unionized labor in general have supported me and afforded me the luxury to work intensely for months and then take time to pursue my passions. I am very grateful for Spain and all its wonderful traditions. The encierro has forever changed me and I am eternally grateful. Juan Pedro Lecuona, *usted es el corazón de Pamplona. Nunca he conocido a una mejor persona en mi vida. Gracias por todos sus maravillosos regalos.* I'm grateful for all the Spanish mozos who inspire me so much: Julen Madina, Miguel Angel Perez, Miguel Angel Castander, Chema Esparza, Jose Manuel Pereira, David Rodriguez, David Ubeda, and so many others, especially the budding legend Aitor Aristregui. Dyango Velasco, *ha abierto las puertas de su magnífica ciudad y la tradición, gracias.* I am grateful for the long foreign tradition begun by Matt Carney, which is still very much alive today. Joe Distler, maestro, your guidance is pure gold; thank you from the bottom of my heart. Bomber, you touched my soul, brother, when I take it to the limit, it's for you. Graeme, Gary, John, and Gus—you're my Posse for life. Dennis Clancy, thank you so much, brother. Mikel and Itxaso, thank you for your generosity and friendship.

Many people came to my aid when I was in financial troubles to help me finish the research for this book. Nick Hansen, Jeremy Pard, Deirdre Carney, Declan Flannery, Gordan MacDonald, Bob Mutter, Patrick Salem, Nik Hillmann, Shaun Dmonte, James Garner, Harold Moore, John Ribble, and Jim Hollander, and those who I could not find the names of, thank you from the bottom of my heart.

MOZOS

I fell to the zigzag bricks flat on my back—astonished at how the glory unraveled so quickly. A mozo dropped his knee into my chest and my leg popped up in recoil. The 1,200-pound bull swooped in, his foreleg collapsed as he swung his head low and graceful. The point of his horn struck my inner thigh. I felt a needle prick then a vast universe of nothing. He lifted me in a majestic lunge. My leg sailed between the planks of the barricades. No pain. I grabbed my crotch and thought, *Thank god it's not my balls. I want to have kids.* The horn slid out. I fell to the coarse bricks again. I scampered out on my backside, then the medics pulled me through and for a moment I was alone.

I looked down at the baseball-sized fleshy wound—half expecting it to not be there. *What have you done to yourself?*

Mid thigh, a deep gouge gaped open with the skin torn in three triangular ribbons like undone wrapping paper. Blood streaked down the backside of my calf from a second hole and filled my shoe.

I peered into the deep, mangled flesh—like a concave bloody eye—and a voice inside me calmly said: *Accept it. You knew this day would come.*

CHAPTER ONE:
THAT FIRST TIME
2005

IMMERSION

I was a complete mess before I started running with the bulls. I'm still a mess today but then I was complete.

Authorities jailed me at the age of twenty for the crime of defending myself against three rich kids who'd just humiliated my girlfriend. I hurt one of them very badly and received three months in county jail. There were two guards molesting the prisoners there. That experience angered me and drove me away from society. I'm surprised that I was ever able to return.

In the winter of 2005 I was selling cocaine out of my studio apartment in the Edgewater neighborhood on Chicago's North Side and working on my first novel. The Latin Kings of Little Village were fronting me half ounces every couple weeks. It was like writing on a grant.

I met novelist Irvine Welsh (of *Trainspotting* fame) outside a White Sox game on Chicago's South Side through a mutual friend in Chicago boxing named Marty Tunney. Irvine and I became good friends. He invited me to his wedding in Dublin. When one of the greatest writers in the world invites you to his wedding—you go.

I worked my ass off and raised the funds to fly to Dublin. Irvine was getting married at the end of June. *The Sun Also Rises* was the first novel I'd ever read cover to cover. I remembered the running of the bulls in Pamplona took place in the middle of the summer. I found a $60 flight from Dublin to Madrid.

Twenty-three years old, I was ready for an adventure to sow my wild oats. I considered myself a real cocksman. In reality, I was mostly failing at getting laid, though I would have tremendous weeklong stretches of a different woman every night then be marred with six-month dry spells where I became extremely intimate with my right palm.

Everything fell into place. I sat in a terminal at O'Hare International waiting on my flight. A foxy little brunette sat across from me. We made eyes a few times. When I went out for a smoke she followed. We sparked a conversation. She was French and had a bad attitude. I started to tease her. She liked it. She had light-brown eyes and a nice ass. We boarded the plane together. She sat a couple rows behind me. It was one of those nine-seat getups—five seats in the center and two at the windows. I sat at a window seat and nobody sat down next to me.

After everybody settled into their seats, a stern-faced stewardess appeared, walking this old obese lady my way. They scanned the rows for an open seat. I turned and waved the French girl over and she hurried to sit next to me. We got to talking and giggling. It was a ten-hour flight. We drank a couple of those little bottles of red wine and then things got interesting.

Somewhere over the Atlantic we joined the Mile High Club, but this mean stewardess put a stop to it and threatened to separate us. She was just jealous. We gave up and snuggled the rest of the way. I actually started to fall for her. She had a real nice scent and got kinda sweet after it all. I invited her to the wedding. Then she ditched my ass at the Dublin airport. I walked around the terminal for an hour lovesick before I gave up on the tramp.

Ran around Dublin with Irvine and met his best man, Johny Brown, a radio host, poet, and lead singer of The Band of Holy Joy. I spilled some Guinness on his shirt. He told me to get a rag. I brought him one, but he held a pint in both hands and told me to wipe his shirt. I laughed and did it. We became quick friends. He told me I had to come read some of my stories on his radio show in London. I didn't believe him but said sure.

Irvine's wedding was a blast. They held it at the governor's house or something. It was a big, high-ceilinged ballroom with a balcony terrace. I met a bunch of the characters straight out of Irvine's books, a couple of legendary Edinburgh hooligans; one guy was about 300 pounds of bulk with an enormous head and a big scar on his face. He wore a glass eye in place of one he'd lost in a little underworld misunderstanding involving a samurai sword.

I gave Irvine a draft of my book as a wedding present: a pretty stupid-ass, cocky thing to do. The book was complete garbage. I trashed it a few months later and apologized.

I'll never forget seeing my friend dancing with his new wife Beth well into the night. At one point, everyone crowded around in a big circle. Irvine and a few friends held hands and just leaped up and down. Irvine's Bic'd scalp radiated wild joy; a huge grin streaked across his face. Everybody clapped and cheered around them. That man has a way of experiencing pure joy like no other individual I've ever come across.

I'd been making eyes with one of Beth's friends; she was the hottest one of the bunch. This slimy guy with long, straight, dirty-blond hair started hitting on her and her friends. I didn't sweat it 'cause he was Irvine's age and these girls were in their twenties and he wasn't Irvine Welsh. He bickered back and forth with them a little as I walked off to the bathroom. Next thing you know there he is beside me as I'm washing my hands. He calls me a *poof*. I knew what it meant.

Didn't want to start no trouble with one of Irvine's mates, but I was thinking about cracking him when he starts telling me about all the beautiful women he's fucked in his lifetime. Models, millionaires, celebrities, royalty, you name it. That's when I realize, looking into his weathered good looks and greasy hair, *he's got to be fuckin' Sick Boy, or one of the main inspirations for him anyway*. It was like he was trying to intimidate me away from the girls. I just grinned, maybe he was fucking princesses back in the eighties, but there was no way this British guido was gonna bag a chick who was making eyes with me all night. I ended up heading to a bar with her and a few friends. Sick Boy showed up but he stopped with all the competitive crap. He was actually a cool, friendly guy once that stuff ended. I really liked him. I took the girl back to my hostel as Sick Boy was hitting it off with her friends. I wished him luck and he winked at me as I headed out.

Said goodbye to the girl with a kiss early the next morning and jumped on a Madrid-bound plane.

Got lucky on the sixth of July and I boarded the last seat on a Pamplona-bound bus. As we entered Navarra, a police roadblock halted us. A cop with a black M16 hanging from his neck boarded the bus. Everybody'd been singing before and now they fell silent. The cop walked slowly down the aisle in his blue uniform, eyeballing everybody behind his dark glasses. All the passengers looked down and away. He had the face of a sadist. I decided to stare him down. He walked right up to me and asked for my passport. I felt around for it and realized it was in my bag stored underneath the bus. Somebody asked him something and he turned. I went to tell him about my passport and a Spanish guy hushed me urgently. The officer walked off the bus. The ETA, an acronym roughly translated to Basque Homeland and Freedom, is still very active in Navarra. This Basque separatist militant movement believes Navarra is a sovereign nation. The ETA has a long history of terrorist activity and are firmly aligned with other separatist militants like the Irish Republican Army and the Zapatistas. The ETA historically uses the fiesta de San Fermín as a staging ground for small revolts, none more infamous than the riots in 1979 that put an end to fiesta that year. The singing kicked back up as the bus eased out of the roadblock. Everybody cheered as we rolled into the old Pamplona bus station.

The entire city pulsed electric. It was a few hours after the Chupinazo, the fiesta's raucous opening ceremony. I wandered the narrow cobblestone streets. Balconies rose up five and six stories on either side. I'd been to Mardi Gras in New Orleans a few times. Pamplona during fiesta is ten times wilder than Mardi Gras, and the old section is five times bigger, older, and more beautiful than the French Quarter. There's much less of the stale "been there, done that" spring break vibe. There's also a tenth of the violence. Fiesta is a peaceful insanity. There's a sense that the culture of this ancient city is alive and intact. Impromptu Peña marching bands parade down busy streets. They don't expect you to step aside and observe; they want to encompass you and swallow you into them. They will feast on you and you become one with them, marching and dancing through the garbage-strewn streets.

Searched the town for a place to stay, which is hopeless. Every room in the city is booked six months in advance, unless you know people. I didn't know a soul in the entire country.

I found out about a college that would lock and store your bag for five euros. Chose to keep all my cash on me, figuring that the guys checking the bags might rob me. I took to the street and immersed. Bought a plastic jug of sangria and I wandered the avenues. The epically beautiful northern Spanish women dumbfounded me—their porcelain skin and dark eyes floated through the madness like crystalline ghosts. Pushed and squeezed my way through a tight-packed street that opened onto the immense courtyard called Plaza de Castillo. Thousands of revelers clad in sharp-red scarves and waist sashes filled the plaza. Hazy sangria-red clouds soaked into their bright white shirts and pants from the raucous Chupinazo.

I got lost—like you should in fiesta that first time. Sink into that dark circular maze of streets. Let the music carry you. Follow it and bright eyes and laughter. Enjoy the splash of sangria on your drunken head. Take drinks from anyone who's giving. Kiss and dance with any girl who's willing. Don't fear loud booms and glass bursts; they are not sounds of violence. Here they are background noise pollution, punctuations on joyful sentences. The only foul you can commit at fiesta is to get angry for any reason, and the only repercussion is shameful *ohhh-hhs* and being ignored and left behind. But it's only momentary, 'cause when you smile you are welcomed back into fiesta without hesitation. Over the years I'd learn that you must give and give and give to fiesta and that it will never take from you. But that would be later. Then, I drank for ten hours straight. Realized I should sleep for a while so I could run, but I was afraid of pickpockets, so I tried to sleep up in a tree but a scuffle below woke me. I met an American who was going to school in Pamplona. He told me he'd help me get to the run. We walked across the city to the *ayuntamiento*, (town hall). The city workers began setting up the barricades. I tried to help them. Hoisted up a plank but a cop ran me off. Then I waited on the street, wobbly and dreary. Someone said the run started in two. I took a nap.

Fell asleep on the side of a building and I didn't wake up for a very long time. I arose to an enormous cheer and three guys pissing on the wall way too close to me. Morning light peered down at me over the roofs of the buildings. I ran toward the packed barricades, knifed through the people, and climbed them in time to see four sweeper steers thrust past. I remember saying "those are just cows" disgustedly as I tried to climb over the top plank. A female police officer reeled back and rapped her nightstick with all her might an inch from where my hand gripped the plank.

I froze. The animals vanished and the run was over.

I'd failed to run, and that misery is something I hope to never feel again.

Fell asleep in a doorway and I woke without a single euro in my pocket. I stumbled to the Plaza de Castillo and lay down in the bright afternoon light. The sound of two Spanish guys goofily heckling passersby kept waking me up. I could barely understand their commentary but something in their inflection reminded me of the Mexican construction workers I'd spent years with on work sites in Chicago. I was penniless in a foreign land and I had the worst hangover of my entire life. Still, I found myself laughing. Fiesta has a way of doing that to people, making a joke of their absolute despair. I started talking with two guys and a girl from Madrid. We fumbled our way through introductions and I told them what'd happened. They took me in, and soon I was drunk again and stumbling around the city with them. They took me all over to big fields with stages set up among trees and grass in the shadow of these tall, white stone fortress walls.

The next morning I woke in a strange car knifing through these epic green rounded mountain peaks. The sunlight cascaded through boulder-like clouds. The small car soared through the Pyrenees. I slowly worked out that my new friends had devised a plan that I accompany them to San Sebastian, then they would take me to their home in Madrid where I would stay until my flight left. This instant solution to my plight overwhelmed me with gratitude. The Spanish are a generous people. As I sobered up on the shore of the Atlantic, I realized I couldn't go to Madrid. I bit the bullet and called home. My father said he'd send me money. Picked the money order up in town and I bid farewell to my dear new friends and boarded a Pamplona-bound bus.

It was my first attempt at staying sober in fiesta. It was motherfuckin' difficult. I wandered the area looking for a quiet place to sleep. Slept in doorways, on curbs and benches. It gets chilly in Pamplona at night, even in July. I got really cold. Cops would wake me and move me along. Other times, partiers would offer me a drink and try to pull me to my feet. In my tired wanderings I stumbled across the Hemingway statue outside the arena. He looked stoic, full-bearded and happy. There's a curved brick slope at the foot of the statue. It made for a comfortable bed. Surprisingly no one bothered me, and I slept well there at the foot of Papa Hemingway as fiesta rambled on a half block away.

Ernest Hemingway's writing changed my life. I grew up in the Edgewater neighborhood in Chicago where drugs and violence were commonplace. My parents dropped out of school at thirteen and fourteen years old. They were well-read and self-educated but excelling in school definitely wasn't a priority in my home. Ma even used to bribe my teachers to pass me to the next grade level. My brother was a heroin addict and gang member who ended up in prison for armed robbery. A stray bullet from a drive-by struck my sister and nearly killed her. People I loved died in gangland murders. My parents got us out of the city, but my city sensibilities went to the suburbs with me. They kicked me out of school a bunch, and I even booted a teacher in the nuts then hit him over the head with a chair. I hated school and I could barely read. Midway through high school my history teacher, Brother Peter Hannon, got me into boxing in the Golden Gloves and I turned things around. Still, I needed to go to junior college to get into a four-year school. I took Professor David McGrath's class on Ernest Hemingway there. Up until then I hadn't ever read a novel beginning to end in my whole life. My dad urged me to read Hemingway because he wrote about people like us, but I resisted. When I found out Hemingway won the Nobel Prize writing about fishermen, soldiers, and fist fighters, it piqued my interest. Professor McGrath laid out this whole religious metaphor in *The Old Man and the Sea* that blew me away. I decided to sit down and read a full book. The magnitude of what I was doing hovered in my mind as I strolled the halls of the Elmhurst College Library. I found Hemingway's debut novel, *The Sun Also Rises,* and thought I'd start there. I sat down and immersed myself in the story. He instantly wrapped me up with his characters. I felt like Hemingway himself was oozing from the pages and speaking directly to me. At nineteen years old, it was such a pivotal time in my life and perfect time to read that book. I read it in one sitting, enthralled with the grand adventure, the wild fiesta, and the mystical bulls. When I finished that book after six or seven hours of intense reading I knew it forever changed me. I knew I had to devote my life to literature and that I had to travel to Spain, experience fiesta, and run with the bulls. Like those choose-your-own-adventure stories, I was going to set out on my own adventure, except I was going to actually live it and write it.

I woke at dawn when an officer kicked my foot and walked away laughing. Laborers finished standing and securing the barricades fifty yards away. I wandered to Telefónica. Beautiful young Spanish women swept past by the hundreds. I stood in the center of the street as they passed. I met eyes with them, told them *bonita*. Some stopped and smiled. Others giggled. One took me by the hand and tried to lead me away, but I stayed. I waited and readied for the run. I had no idea I was standing in the wrong place. As 6:00 a.m. approached, the crowds along the barricades thickened and photographers took their posts in peek holes in the boarded-up shops. I moved up Estafeta Street. Hundreds of hopeful runners scattered all over the narrow passageway.

Suddenly a police line the width of the street formed. It moved toward me. They herded everyone up the street. At the first intersection on Estafeta the barricade swung open. I couldn't believe it. *Why are they pushing us off the course? I did everything right! I'm here an hour early, sober!* Some of the would-be runners up front resisted. A tall officer with gray stubble on his cheeks cracked a runner over the head with his nightstick. The police line heaved and shoved every single one of us out onto the side street.

We all panicked. I ran down side streets asking urgently, "Where do we have to go to run?!" People pointed different directions. Sprinted all the way down one long street, found no entry at the barricades, and ran back. I cut down another alley that wrapped around a tall building, praying that I would find a way in. Exhausted, I sat down in a doorway and quit. *Maybe running with the bulls just isn't in my destiny.* My heart ached heavily, and I wanted to go home. Something swooped up to me and whispered urgently. "Listen . . . Just listen." As my breathing slowed I heard a tremendous, tense chatter and a voice on a loudspeaker that switched languages every few seconds.

Curious, I followed the noise around a corner and found a long barricade with many people all perched on the top row with others strung along it straining to see over. I pushed forward. A few people ducked under and onto the course—police stopped another and pushed him out. The nearest officer turned his back and I slipped through the barricades deftly, like stepping through the ropes into a boxing ring. As I passed through the second barricade I smashed into a dense mob of bodies. Tons of body-to-body pressure squeezed me. It ebbed and swayed—at its worst I struggled to breath. Everyone chattered tensely. The only direction you could see was up. The ornamental façade of an ancient building with a large clock on it rose above the heads of the many runners. I realized it was the town hall.

The clock read twenty minutes till eight. The recorded PA voice switched to English. It warned of great bodily harm; if you fall down, stay down. The crowd murmured. The murmurs twisted and lifted into a cheering roar that bellowed up then fell into laughter. Some people staggered drunk; others gave obnoxious advice to an American married couple near me. I argued with the advisers, but what the hell did I know? It was the blind leading the blind. At ten minutes to eight, the police line holding us back broke and the thick mob unraveled and sifted up the street.

I walked a half block and came to a sharp banking turn. A five-tiered wall of cameramen loomed behind the barricades. Photographers working for publications all over the world vie for position here, from as early as 5:00 a.m. This was *La Curva*, the curve, Dead Man's Corner. I remembered seeing the ESPN series on the run in the early 2000s. They'd called it "Hamburger Wall" and described it as the place where the herd crashes every morning. The series described it as one of the most dangerous places to run. I figured I'd start right there.

Bravely, I held my ground at the curve—right in front of the barricades the photographers jockeyed behind. Suddenly a stick-rocket screamed into the sky and burst high above the red-tiled roofs of the city. Wild panic surged up the street. Suddenly I wasn't so brave anymore. I crossed onto the inside of the curve where a bunch of runners stood—a stupid mistake, I'd soon learn why. The American couple materialized and asked me, "Is this a good place to run?" I shrugged.

A second boom rumbled in the sky. Then a wild cheer from the balconies and barricades swung up behind it. A steady stream of runners rounded the curve and flowed past me. Some laughed; others yelled, terrified. A low, deep rumble grew in the distance. The speed and density of runners pouring around the bend grew. Only terror-struck faces flew past now accompanied by a high-pitched scream. The leaden rumble twisted into a sharp hard crackle. The cobblestones and buildings resonated. A large black streak surged through the curve. The crackle exploded. Time froze. The lead bull bucked a runner with its forehead. The man floated on a cushion of air above the bull's snout with his arms flung out. His lips stretched in a wide-mouthed terror-grin. Bulls, steers, and men crashed into the mural of San Fermín next to the photographers' barricade with a thunderous, wooden boom. I gawked rigidly. Most of the herd rose and rumbled past. One bull stayed and dug his horns into the fallen people. The immense sculpted muscularity of his neck and back contorted under his black fur. A white flash swirled in the corner of my periphery. A hard-panging bell flooded my eardrums. I turned. A giant steer barreled directly at me an arm's length away. I dove backward and pressed my hands into its shoulder. The fur stretched taut as a drum. Somehow my legs missed his hooves. The young American couple jogged obliviously ahead of me, hand in hand. The steer plowed through them. Its hooves gobbled them up. Their arms and legs splayed wildly under the hooves. They screamed.

My forward momentum carried me over them. At the last second I leaped and pulled my knees way up to my chest. My feet barely cleared the couple. I stopped and hovered over them. "You OK?" They both writhed on the ground. I reached down to help them when the last bull at the curve bellowed wrathfully and raised his massive black head. His powerful white horns swung up tall. I remembered hearing that a separated bull is deadly dangerous. He broke into a gallop and

I turned and ran as fast as I fucking possibly could. Luckily the final bull rocketed past me on the other side of the street. The thick stampede of people spread to allow him through. Other individuals seemed to force their way in front of him and sprint ahead for several strides before peeling to the side. I kept sprinting forward, at first in terror, but as the crowd slackened I remembered that they released *vaca* (wild cows) into the ring after the run. I sprinted for the arena at the end of the course. As I got to the opening of tunnel into the arena several police officers pushed the immense red double doors closed. A crowd fought to get through the narrowing opening. I pressed into it as well. Then the police pulled out their batons and cracked a few of the revelers in front. I gave up. Another stick-rocket burst above the arena and a joyous cheer washed over the entire city. I cheered and grasped at others nearby. "Did you see that? Did you see that?" They shrugged me off, laughing. I realized that this was bigger than any individual experience, that all of us had shared it together. Then the joy twisted to shrieks again. A wild ramble of shouts and panging bells approached. I had nowhere to go so I climbed up on the barricades just in time. Four steers swept just under my feet. They'd opened the arena doors to let the steers in. I hopped down. The police struggled to shut the heavy doors. Two other runners pushed at the opening. I sprinted and drove my shoulder into the others' backs and we avalanched into the darkened tunnel. The police shut the doors and we ran down the tunnel giggling. Jogged down the dark tunnel and I stepped onto the white sand of the arena for the first time. The brilliant morning light struck me like a warm wave. The entire arena, full to the rafters, gave the hundreds of runners a standing ovation. Then the cheers fell into Spanish songs. Complete strangers embraced on the sand. Others raised their arms like victorious gladiators. I walked around dumbfounded with euphoria among the wild pandemonium.

Then some cops called us to a corral door. I walked over. They motioned for us to kneel. About fifty of us did. I knelt near the back of the shell-shaped group of kneeling men and women. We gave the animal no way to exit the corral except over and through us. It's like Rodeo Poker. We were fucked and we all knew it. Even so, we exchanged smiles and pats on the back.

A red door opened. A cubic black void appeared. Something stirred in the darkness. Fear shot me to my feet, but regret at my cowardice sank me back to my knees beside my new friends. A man in the very front stood and waved the unseen animal forward. Suddenly the vaca's horns emerged from the darkness—corked tips with brown leather straps over them. She galloped and bounded over the first three rows of kneelers. Then she landed hard into the fourth and fifth row. Her hooves dug deep into shoulders and backs. A young guy screamed, twisted, and lunged toward me. The vaca trampled the rest of the way through us. I rose and backpedaled. The vaca bowed her head, slung her horn between a guy's legs, and vaulted him into the air. He flipped sideways and landed on his shoulder. The vaca barreled through the thick crowd and somersaulted another mozo. Hundreds in the ring ran for safety; some leaped the arena walls. I dashed around and tried to stay safe.

As the minutes passed I noticed that some people actually ran at the vaca. I couldn't figure out why, so I got closer to see. They sprinted up and slapped the vaca on the ass. Then they dashed away as the vaca tried to retaliate. I instantly knew I had to do it. I didn't notice the Spanish guys who instantly beat the crap out of anyone who touched the vaca, because doing so is strictly forbidden. Even so, I devised my plan. I'd sprint right at the vaca's ass then slap it as I rushed past. It was a good plan—simple and as safe as possible. I took a deep breath and bolted at the vaca—cutting through the flock of people. As I got close the crowd thinned. I careened close to the vaca when she saw me in her periphery. I reached out to slap her ass and she turned and her hindquarters whipped out of reach. I kept running and exited her wrathful realm. Dejected, I gathered and lined her up again. As I swept past she spun again and I smacked the wind.

I worried they'd take the vaca away before I'd had chance to slap her ass! The realization sank in. I'd have to go in slow, sneak in, or face her outright. I jogged up and slowly stepped to her with my knees bent, on my tiptoes ready to dodge or dash away. She pursued another mozo as I snuck up on her broadside. I approached almost within reach when she saw me. She seethed and whirled around on me.

I jumped backward and smashed into another guy who crept up behind me. We caught each other by the arms and balanced. She twisted on another runner and her big furry dung-spattered ass was beside me. I gathered, leaped in, and smacked her bottom with my brittle palm. She unleashed a high-pitched bellow and whipped around on me. I twisted and dove into a sprint. Another mozo dashed in behind me and clipped me with his shoulder. I flew airborne and fell belly-down. As I descended, I brought both palms up over my head, swung down, and smacked the sand hard. The collision vaulted me back up into full stride. She galloped and seethed at my back as I hauled ass straight to the wall and leaped headfirst. I cleared all the people standing along the outside of the wall. My thighs crashed into their heads and shoulders. Some of them grabbed my legs and I landed hands first on the cold concrete. My shoulder slid out of the socket and I tumbled to the ground surrounded by jolly laughter. My shoulder was an old football injury; it slid back in on its own. The adrenaline coursed through me and stopped any pain. I figured I'd accomplished that one and decided not to get back in. Walked around and out of the arena down the same tunnel I'd come in.

Outside, I walked with a strange purpose. Restless explosive energy pulsed in my palms and shoulders, throbbing right under the skin. Images of the morning's events riffled through my mind: bright visions that ejected roaring shouts and mad laughter as I bobbed and leaped through the Pamplona morning air. An entire giant arena had just urged me through a daring act on the sand where matadors and bulls danced and died. I kept pondering if it were real. If there was really a place in this modern world of sitcoms and McDonald's culture where just about anyone could show up and partake in this epic, wild tradition. I actually pinched myself. The up-close sight of those immense bulls—TV does them no justice. Their heads stand shoulder height; they're incredibly wide; and their necks, backs, and shoulders bulge with enormous, sculpted muscle. They're fantastically fast, agile, and powerful. I wondered if someone had died that morning. No one had, but injuries hospitalized several runners. I didn't know any of this at the time, and later I'd realize I didn't know anything about the experience I'd just survived. In the coming years I would become a tour guide for the run and grow disgusted by people who came to fiesta without any knowledge. Even later I'd realize it was my duty to inform them.

I walked to a café beside one of the large circular intersections that mark the modern section of Pamplona. Inside locals packed the long room. The Spanish smoked cigarettes and cigars as they drank coffee. I found an open space next to a standup counter, stepped up and ordered. A white-haired guy with a camera hung around his neck stood beside me. We started to chat. His name was Ned. He was a photojournalist from London. I told him I was a writer. He asked me if I'd run that morning and I glanced down at my shoes. A dusting of white arena sand clung to the cuffs of my jeans.

Ned asked me eagerly what happened, and over some strong Spanish espresso—I told.

"You must write this!" he urged.

I laughed, then considered it. He told me about the professional runners—a term no serious runner would ever use, but Ned was just learning too. Then he explained about running on the horns, the way the best Spanish runners ran over the centuries. These new concepts shattered my notions of this experience being a once-in-a-lifetime thing. There was a deep tradition on the street of foreign runners who traveled across the world to Spain every year to run. Some became legends.

"I'll shoot it, you write it." Ned smacked me on the back. "We'll get it in somewhere big, you'll see."

At the time I was a completely unpublished writer, aside from my small college journal and a few obscure online sites. I figured, what the hell? We walked to the Plaza de Castillo where runners gathered afterward. There we found thirty or so Americans, English, Scots, and Irish standing around in front of a bar named Txoco. I asked stupid questions. "Are you a professional bull runner?" as I scribbled furiously in my little Moleskin notepad that I had tucked in my back pocket. The guys just laughed in my face and turned away. I didn't know any better. Then a portly Scotsman with white hair and a beard rolled his eyes and answered my questions. I asked about the cows that ran with the bulls and he laughed.

"There's no cows out there on the street, mate."

"I saw cows out there."

"No you didn't, you saw cabestros."

"What's a cabestro?"

"It's a bull with family jewels snipped," he said as I diligently took notes. And with that, I began my slow and painful education in the run. The Scot's name was Graeme Galloway. Galloway was a veteran of more than twenty fiestas, and over the next decade he'd become one of my dearest friends.

Matt Carney became the first American listed as one of the five great runners of a twenty-year span. At the time, he was the only non-Spanish citizen to ever earn that prestigious appointment. The Spanish accepted him as one of them. Before Matt died of cancer in 1987, he made a request that the room he owned, in the heart of town, be left open for any young man who lurked at the edge of the group. Matt asked that his friends bring that young man into the group, and if he had no place to stay that they should give him Matt's room for free.

After my awkward introduction to the serious foreign runners, they pretty much ostracized me as a nut-job kid who thought he was a journalist. It was a pretty accurate assessment actually. Somber, I lurked at the edge of the group after that. I observed them as they drank and ate in the picturesque Plaza de Castillo well into the night. They hung out among the chrome tables and chairs in front of Bar Windsor. I leaned against the stone archways and listened to the British eloquence. I wondered if they were descendants from Hemingway's era. I rehearsed in my mind things I'd say to Hemingway's grandchildren: *Your grandfather's work changed my life.* I wondered if they were writers. Some were. Most descended from James Michener's era. Michener wrote the nonfiction work *Iberia* in the late sixties, which dedicated many pages to San Fermín. Later Michener published *The Drifters*, which fictionally chronicled many of the then contemporary Pamplona characters. Harvey Holt partially embodied Michener's close friend Matt Carney. I knew nothing about Michener's history at fiesta then, as I hovered in the shadows of the stone archways. Lonely, I watched and wondered what these characters from *The Sun Also Rises* were talking about. Mistaking me for a pickpocket casing the group, they ran me off a few times. They never offered me Carney's room, or maybe a guy named Jim did, and I cut him off not wanting any charity. Can't really remember . . .

Slept in my cold stone bed at Hemingway's feet and ran the next morning. I did better and strode alongside the herd the first half of Estafeta, never getting closer than about ten feet. Ned kept insisting that I watch a run. I decided to watch the next morning.

OBSERVATIONS

I milled through the busy morning traffic of runners looking for a place to watch. Finally I ended up at the curve. Two small, unoccupied balconies hung above the barricades where the bulls crashed most mornings. Small, closed wooden windows stood behind the balconies.

I scaled the fencing as the photographers and television crews set up on the scaffolding. First I stood on top of the fencing, reached up and grabbed the steel bars of the closest balcony. Then I pulled myself up and climbed in. It was just big enough for one person to squat in. Some of the people watching clapped. I smiled and waved down to them and tried to get comfortable.

I didn't know at the time, but a very special breed of bulls was set to run that morning. They came from a ranch called Jandilla. The Jandilla weren't so famous yet, but this bloodline began to impress their legacy on Pamplona the year before. The Jandilla were huge and muscular like most bulls that come to Pamplona, but they also possessed astonishing speed and insane ferocity. They inflicted twenty gorings the morning of July 12, 2004. A runner named Julen Madina received eight of those wounds. By then, Julen Madina had established himself as one of the greatest runners of all time; he'd run on the horns of bulls in Pamplona for over thirty years. Running on the horns is the act of leading the animal by running in front of its face and horns. If done successfully the animal accepts you as its guide and follows you up the street. Madina famously ran on the horns of bulls all the way from La Curva to the bullring in one morning. That's over 400 yards with the herd—a superhuman feat. Afterward the media dubbed him one of *Los Divinos*, divine mozos who run with outstanding grace and bravery. If you look over the footage of the past few decades, you'll see him most mornings in Pamplona, wearing white, his round head shaved and small hoop earrings in both ears, running the end of the course, bringing the bulls into the arena.

The most dangerous situation in bull running is something called a *montón*, or a pileup. For runners who run near the arena there is nothing they fear more than a serious montón. When bad pileups occur there are often deaths and injuries numbering in the hundreds. One person falls in the tunnel, several fall on top of him, then an avalanche of bodies collapses to the ground, plugging up the narrow passage of the tunnel. When the herd reaches this plug it attempts to plow through. It pushes into the bodies; goring, breaking bones, and suffocating those unfortunate ones on the bottom. And sometimes mozos die there at the bottom in the darkness, underneath the tremendous weight and pressure.

As the Jandilla approached the arena that morning in 2004 there was a terrible pileup forming in the tunnel. The bulk of the herd navigated around the pile and through the tunnel. The trailing two bulls fell. Trigueño, an enormous pitch-black bull, plucked Julen Madina out of the pile and gored him repeatedly. One serious shot near the spine almost killed him. A brown striped bull named Zarabrando turned backward and gouged at several of the fallen. Years later, Julen himself would tell me what happened that morning in horrific detail.

"I was running with the Jandillas like any other day. I was coming down on Telefónica and there were lots of people. The *encierro* (bull run) was very dirty. People were falling over. They were crossing in front of me. I couldn't see the bulls. I had a bull at my back very close. I was trying to stay under control. I had to keep looking down and measuring the space. I saw that by the left side of the tunnel a very great cork was forming. People were falling over and piling up. I decided to go toward the right side of the tunnel to avoid the problems. I entered on the right side with a bull very close to my back.

"What I could not see was that behind that first pile there was a second pile. I fell over directly on top of that second pile. The bull [behind me] was very aggressive, so as soon as I fell it gored me. It lifted me from my belt and shook me vigorously. I tried to grab my belt buckle to loosen my belt but I could not, so the bull continued hauling me before he dropped me. I landed on top of a group of people and I lay very still, without moving because I knew that there were a lot of people who were going to shout so the bull would raise its face and go away. Or, that is what I hoped. But the bull stayed with me and he kept on goring me. It lasted twenty-two seconds and nobody was able to take the bull away. Aside from the gorings, I remember hearing this noise, a *zzzz zzzz*, like a stabbing sound.

"The bull then took to me from my butt cheek and lifted me and kept me on his horn. Then he dropped me, and I noticed a severe pain. The other thing that called my attention was the bellows of the bull, how it snorted, the energy with which it was attacking me. I could hear the noise that the hooves made in the ground, and the burned scent of the hooves scratching against the ground. I was lying face down and I stayed quiet, quiet, quiet. He gave me a terrible beating. I remained on the ground totally crushed and I remember that then I thought, *I can see the street, so the pile is being broken. What the bull didn't do now, the people will. There is an avalanche of people coming, and they are going to massacre me. They are going to crush me and step on me.*

"So, I dragged myself and I got underneath the wall [an opening low in the tunnel], hoping that the help would arrive soon. I remember that I was falling asleep because of all the blood loss. I was talking to myself a lot. I told myself to breathe slowly, breathe through the nose and your mouth, control the breathing, because I thought if I breathed slowly the blood would flow slowly. With an accelerated heart rate the blood circulates faster and you will bleed to death faster. I thought, *If someday this had to happen, this is the best place, here in Pamplona. They have the best doctors and best resources. They'll help you. Now wait and be calm.* That is when I heard voices and I saw the Red Cross guys. They tore my clothes and made a tourniquet. One of them put his fist in my wound, in my left leg to stop the hemorrhage. They carried me to the horses' patio, and they performed surgery at the nurses' station right inside the arena."

Julen never resented the animal who gored him. Later he said this was a small price to pay for all the joy the bulls gave him. He recovered quickly and was preparing to run on that morning one day shy of a year later, July 11, 2005, as I crouched in the small balcony above the curve.

After about twenty minutes up there a woman in a balcony across the street noticed me and got on the phone. Five minutes later the window opened. An older man with a police officer led me out through a nice apartment and onto the street where I resumed my search. I walked urgently up and down Estafeta Street asking people if I could watch from their balcony. I had no idea that most balconies cost fifty euros for one space; I was waving a ten euro note and begging. The police began to clear Estafeta. The officers closed in on me standing about half a block from La Curva. I caught eyes with an older woman four flights above and begged my heart out. She disappeared from the balcony, and just as the police started to push me up the street she emerged from her doorway and waved me in. She brought me upstairs where I stood behind some children in the balcony and waited. I had a perfect view of La Curva. My gracious hosts offered me wine and food even though I couldn't communicate with them. Their smiles made me feel right at home.

I was grateful Ned had convinced me to watch. This perspective opened a whole new understanding of the course. I saw my folly standing on the inside of the curve. It blinded me to the pack's approach. I watched as many runners foolishly gathered there. Across from them a pocket of runners in colorful shirts gathered. They stoically shook hands and embraced each other. Then guys with green shirts and thin willow canes walked past; their shirts read PASTORES. They were the official Pamplona herdsmen. The pastores stopped and embraced each of this group in the doorway. One of the guys in the doorway was bald and wore spectacles. His green and red sweater was bright and bold. He greeted everyone eagerly and generously. I'd later learn he was an American named Tom Turley. The year before he'd made his bones as a runner on the same morning Trigueño nearly killed Julen Madina in the tunnel.

Back in 2004, the Jandilla hooked and gored several runners along the early part of the course, but when they reached the curve they crashed hard and the herd dismantled. Most of the pack continued up the street. Trigueño and Zarabrando remained. Turley hailed Zarabrando with a shout and ran the brown-striped bovine's horns for a long distance up Estafeta. The act was remarkable and heroic. Turley helped keep the animal moving up the street and stopped Zarabrando from halting and attacking his fellow mozos. Even with all the blood the year before with the Jandilla, there seemed to be nothing special in the air. It was just another morning in Pamplona.

As I stood on the balcony the rocket rose into the sky in the distance and burst. A joyous roar swelled throughout the balconies. About thirty seconds later bodies poured around the corner like a raging rapid. There was a huge swell in density, then a quiet before the final surge. The bulls blistered into view and crashed into the wall. Three tumbled over each other, and when they rose they turned backward the wrong way up the street and went after several runners. One animal disappeared up Mercaderes. Two galloped up Estafeta. The final animal, a jet-black bull with huge, wide shoulders and a bulbous neck named Vaporoso, stood mystified. Tom Turley appeared and called to Vaporoso. Vaporoso charged and Turley ran his horns for thirty yards. Vaporoso gained on Turley. Turley peeled off to the side. Vaporoso surged on, and I noticed a portly man running ahead of Vaporoso. Vaporoso picked him out of a dozen others and accelerated. The man's name was Xabier Salillas. Salillas ran as hard as he could until his legs began to fail him. His strides desperately elongated as Vaporoso closed. Salillas collapsed into a doorway directly under and across the street from my balcony. I gripped the railing and peered over the heads of the children; one little girl whimpered and burst into tears as she witnessed the mayhem. There were easily 100 people within Vaporoso's reach, but he stopped and loomed over Salillas. Then Vaporoso dug his horn into Salillas's gut, lifted him up, and slammed him into the boarded-up shop door. Salillas slipped off the horn and fell to the ground. Vaporoso stabbed the horn in Salillas's thigh and bashed him against the wall. Vaporoso continued to ferociously gore Salillas. His horns ripped through cloth and flesh.

He's killing him. I'd seen people die horrible deaths before, and I was sure now I was witnessing it again. A terrifying helplessness gripped my heart like a massive claw. Time stretched. The horror filled my visual plane as I ached to help. Running down the stairs and into the street didn't even cross my mind. Then a man in a purple-striped shirt appeared behind Vaporoso and grabbed hold of his tail. I'd later know the man as Miguel Angel Perez, one of the great mozos of Estafeta. Perez held tight to Vaporoso, and he stopped attacking Salillas and looked backward to see who gripped his tail. Salillas, to my shock, bloodied with no less than four gaping wounds, took the opportunity to crawl away. Salillas scurried across the street and Vaporoso, with the hundreds of men around him trying to distract him, turned with Salillas and followed him. Perez held tight and Vaporoso dragged him across the way.

Vaporoso twisted to see his adversary gripping his tail. Then he looked up the street to where his brothers had gone and listened to the roars and chaos they inspired. He turned toward them, and as he did, Miguel Angel released his tail, dashed before Vaporoso's snout, and led him up Estafeta and out of sight. I walked back into the room from the balcony and saw the live television as Vaporoso flung a man into the air then continued through the tunnel and into the arena where he encountered one final man who aimlessly ran around on the sand. Vaporoso rammed and flipped him.

I ran down the stairs to see a dozen medics surrounding Salillas and already fastening him to a stretcher. I kept asking, "Is he dead? Is he dead?" No one seemed to know. The ambulance came and I walked off, looking for the men who came to Salillas's aid. I found few answers, and it wasn't until the next day when I saw Salillas on the cover of a local paper in a full-body cast on a hospital gurney giving the cameraman and all of fiesta the thumbs-up that I realized he survived.

Overwhelmed, I spent the rest of my time in Pamplona contemplating what I'd witnessed. Sitting in the Plaza de Castillo sipping San Miguel beer, I played the images over in my mind and something clicked. From my bird's-eye view I realized this was more than just a thrill, a rush, that there was a logic to the madness. That this was an elaborate art, a fiercely loyal brotherhood, a place where grace and heroics melded seamlessly the instant circumstance called for it. It was an honor to witness. I wanted to meet these men and shake their hands and know them and know what it was to be one of them. I felt guilty that I'd done nothing to help Salillas. I wanted to make it up to him and all of those who came to his aid. I ran the remaining days of fiesta. As my bus pulled out of Pamplona, I knew I'd return.

I'd been a Chicago Golden Gloves boxing champion and traveled a good portion of the world, all expenses paid. It'd gotten to a level where if you don't commit completely to training, your opponent will seriously hurt you. All the drinking, drugs, and street fighting were tearing my life apart. They began to take their toll, and I received a couple savage beatings in the ring as a result. Many professional trainers and boxers told me bluntly that I had the potential to be a very successful professional boxer. More importantly, I knew deep down I could. But there was something broken inside of me that I couldn't quite describe, something that I was born with. That genetic flaw, combined with the partying, took boxing from me. It's something I never got over. The run replaced boxing as my obsession, and I threw all my passion and fury into it.

CHAPTER TWO:
POSSE
2006

Got some work in construction with my family's company when I arrived home. Things went well at work, but I ended the day with such physical exhaustion I didn't have the energy to write. Knew if I didn't get away I'd never complete a quality novel. My deepest dream was to become a successful novelist. Irvine insisted I had to write "every fookin' day" for hours if I ever wanted to be a real writer. With the hard labor and my chaotic drinking and partying and the revolving door of women I kept stepping through, there just wasn't any hope for me to write in Chicago. I saved money and figured when I got to three grand I'd drive down to New Orleans and rent an apartment in the Marigny, live simply, and write for hours every day. Then Hurricane Katrina hit. I didn't know what to do. I contemplated my dilemma as I sat in the old Filter Café in Wicker Park, a cool, Chicago artist neighborhood at the time. A girl named Stephanie and I started talking about Mexico. She told me about a little town in Guanajuato called San Miguel de Allende. It was an old Spanish colonial town built on a large hillside, full of artists and writers and expat Americans. An idea struck me. I could go down there without speaking Spanish and still get by, maybe even learn some Spanish along the way. My money would stretch for months.

I landed in Mexico City in November, jumped in a cab, and tried to communicate "bus station" to the cabbie. He drove me to a subway station at the other side of the airport and charged me twenty bucks. I jumped on the subway and found the bus station. I paid thirty bucks for a luxury bus to San Miguel de Allende. The sun set as we slowly swayed through the mountainous region of Guanajuato. In the darkness we rounded a hill and the brightly lit city spilled into view. It splayed up a long sloping hillside glowing deep yellow. Numerous cathedral spires launched up to the sky, a big castle hung to the side. I gawked, and instantly knew I'd found a special place in the world. Rented a room at a cheap hotel and I went out that night, wandering up the cobblestone streets in the unbelievably beautiful ancient pueblo. San Miguel was the town where many believe Jack Kerouac finished *On the Road* and was the place Neal Cassady walked away from when counting rail ties to the nearby town of León when he died of a sudden aneurism. I knew nothing of this then but the town enraptured me. An American dance instructor helped me find a $200 two-bedroom apartment a quarter mile from the main Jardin in the town center, where elderly Americans fed pigeons in the morning light. The scent of incredibly good cheap food enticed me everywhere I went. Beautiful women and artists swarmed down each stone street. Dozens of galleries lined every sloped avenue. The art ranged from experimental to traditional Mexican. I was intending to go into a gallery on the corner when I walked into a smaller one next door. It was dark, and as I entered I realized I'd made a mistake and was about to leave when a cute, little Mexican chick with dark-brown eyes and short hair clicked into view. I tried to apologize in Spanish and explain that I was leaving when she said "Hello" and smiled. I decided to look around. Instantly a bright-orange fireball of an image leaped off the wall at me. She explained the artist was a woman name Serafina. "Nice," I said and looked at another painting. It was of a Spanish fighting bull. I laughed and said, "I run with the bulls in Spain."

The girl scrutinized me and said, "Yeah, right." I laughed and said, "No, it's true, it's true. This past summer." She wouldn't believe me.

I tried to convince her. She explained that she thought bull running was stupid, and she hated bullfighting and protested the bullfights in Mexico City, her hometown.

She told me her name was A-Need. I tried to say it but couldn't. She spelled it for me: E-N-I-D. I still couldn't say it right, but she laughed at the way I tried. We were clearly a perfect match, so I asked her out. She hesitated but said yes.

We went out for drinks that night and I took her home with me to look at the stars from my rooftop, but she wouldn't even give me a kiss. OK, maybe one peck on the cheek. I took her out for dinner the next night and ate the thickest, rarest filet mignon I had ever eaten, and it was only twelve bucks. I bought a bottle of wine from the restaurant, which caused quite a scene, because we didn't exactly look like a couple that could afford it. Then we walked all the way up the hill to the lookout point at the top of the city. About halfway up the hill I grabbed her and pressed her against an old oak door. I kissed her full and hard and felt her give in to me and knew that she was mine or could be mine. We walked up the hill holding hands. We talked and drank on a grassy hillside between some bushes. She wanted to know about America and all the places I'd traveled and I told her everything I'd done and everywhere I'd been and she didn't believe a word of it until I pulled out my passport. That's when she realized my name was William, not Bill. The soft and sweet way she said *William* blew me away. I didn't correct her and she called me William from then on. I brought her home with me and it went well and well into the night.

And that was the start of my time in San Miguel de Allende.

I woke each morning to the calls of roosters. Put on Tom Waits's *Mule Variations* and I cooked four eggs with cheese in butter and tortillas with refried beans. I'd fix myself a thick cup of Nescafé and go up on my open roof and smoke cigarettes and watch the horses and donkeys in the walled-in ranch that bumped up against my apartment. I'd go back down and take a huge dump. Then back to the bedroom to chant. I'm a practicing Nichiren Buddhist and member of Soka Gakkai International-USA. We chant the title of the Lotus Sutra, which translates as Nam (devotion to), myoho (the mystic law), renge (simultaneity of cause and effect), kyo (sutra, the voice or teaching of a Buddha). It's based on the principle that world peace comes through individuals satisfying their desires and finding happiness. *Nam-myoho-renge-kyo, Nam-myoho-renge-kyo, Nam-myoho-renge-kyo . . .* As I chanted, the voices of my characters would begin to speak to one another. I'd chant until I couldn't hold it anymore and rush to the computer to write the dialogue, and then build the scenes around that. The writing fictionalized the many tragedies of my childhood. The catharsis of writing about those things truly healed me deeply. As the book took shape I realized I was writing about my great yet flawed father, about his redemption. My goal was to write 1,000 words each day. I met that goal for forty-something days straight; sometimes I'd surpass it by a bunch. I'd finish writing by three or four in the afternoon and then go and eat. Then no matter how we'd left it the night before, I'd find myself walking toward the gallery to be with Enid. Even if I was so mad at her and didn't want anything to do with her, I walked to her, my white snakeskin cowboy boots clicking on the stone sidewalk, and she'd be there and I'd help her close up shop and take her out for dinner and we'd walk the town and dance and drink and go home and she'd read my writing from that day and I'd listen to her laugh at the jokes in the dialogue and then we'd fuck hard into the night with her screaming so loud that I knew all my neighbors hated me. Enid helped transform my life into a rambling machine.

It went like that for over a month until I got scared of the feeling that snuck up into my heart each time I made that walk to the gallery. A feeling I thought I'd never feel again after the intense loves in my past. She was also afraid of what was happening and confessed that she had a boy back home in Mexico City who she was in love with. He didn't want her, but she felt I should know she still loved him.

That stung but also gave me liberty. I went out the next night without her and met a crazy white lady in a bar called La Cucaracha. She was a raunchy ex-beauty queen from Georgia who'd married a Mexican matador, though he'd passed away leaving her a thirty-five-year-old widow. Everyone in town lusted after her, and she'd had affairs with several rich and powerful men. We made out near the piss-stinking bathroom, and when we came back to the bar, all the roughnecks in the saloon began to threaten my life. We left and went out dancing deep into the night. At about four in the morning, we were walking to her car when she noticed a new designer-clothing store and wanted to window-shop. I was pretty hammered and stopped with her. She was going on and on about how she wanted to buy some dress when I looked back to where we'd come from, and suddenly two surly little Mexicans rounded the corner with hostile gazes. I grinned at 'em, glanced back at her and joked, "I'm gonna get in a fight."

I looked back. They sprinted directly at me. I readied and as the first closed in he reached back to punch me. When he swung I noticed a softball-sized stone in his hand. I ducked at the last second and the stone glanced me behind the ear. I stumbled forward into him, gathered and cracked him with a short right cross. He crumbled to the sidewalk. I went to kick him square in the head to finish him off but I was so drunk I missed. My foot sailed over his head. I slipped on the stones, flew up in the air, and landed flat on my back right beside him. The other one rushed at me as I jumped to my feet. The lady screamed. "What are you doing?" I yelled in her face. "RUN!"

The other one windmilled both his fists at me. The blur of wild motion threw me off. I caught his hand as it swung at me. Something sliced deep into the pad of my palm. Wet electricity splashed inside my fist. It didn't click that he was cutting me. He hopped back and swung his other fist. I grabbed his hand in midair. Something sunk deep into my palm in almost the same spot. He yanked his fist away and what I assume was an ice pick stuck and pulled my hand with it. I unhinged my hand from the pick. His starved, yellow, junkie eyes told me he'd kill me if I let him. He lunged at me desperately and hit me in the ribs. I countered it with a left hook that crashed into the side of his head and wobbled him out into the center of the street. My cowboy plaid shirt hung off me in long ribbons. He'd sliced it to shreds. I ripped what was left of my shirt off. His friend got up and fumbled with the big stone. I lunged at him and he gave ground. The chick screamed at me: "Why are you fighting!" I turned and screamed in her face: "RUN! We're getting mugged, bitch!" *I'm not bleeding much. He didn't get me good.* The one with the box cutter and ice pick stopped staggering. I laughed at them and screamed, "I'm from Chicago, motherfuckers! I will fucking beat you both to fucking death right now!" They backed up. They argued with each other, then the one with the big stone came at me tentatively with the stone cocked and ready. I gave ground to him, waiting for him to swing that thing as the other guy grabbed at the chick's purse. Finally he swung it at me. I dodged it and slammed him facedown into the stone curb. I rained down savage punches through his flailing arms; his head bounced off the curb. A whiny girlish scream poured out of him. I laughed and looked back at the chick. She wouldn't let go of the purse! The guy finally gave up and rushed at me. I stood. Again I backed them down the street, taunting them maniacally. They argued with each other until one of them pulled a three-foot chain out of his pant leg. *Really! How many weapons do you motherfuckers got?!*

I sighed, shook my head, and said, "Let's go, you motherfuckers are gonna have to fuckin' kill me." They glanced at each other, thought better of it, turned and ran away down the dark street.

I inspected my hand. The ice pick caused a puncture wound beside my lifeline. The box cutter left a two-inch slice along the bottom pad. I picked up my plaid cowboy shirt; it dangled in unrecognizable strands but there were only superficial scratches on my chest and stomach. We got the car and came back. I had a pack of Marlboros in my shirt pocket. I looked around and found them on the sidewalk. I laughed insanely and screamed, "You motherfuckers didn't get a fucking thing!" Then I lit a smoke. Back at her place I realized that the guy had stuck me in the ribs with the ice pick. It'd gone in at a lucky angle and didn't hit anything, but it could have easily popped my lung.

My bad karma didn't end there.

Banged that crazy white lady and that led to a two-day drunk where I didn't write a fucking thing. She just kept telling me I should help her write her memoir about marrying a matador. When I finally did get home I sat down to write and spilled a full cup of hot coffee on my keyboard. The screen went blank. It sizzled and smoke lifted off the keys. When it wouldn't turn back on I realized I'd lost 40,000 of the best words I had ever written.

After I stopped screaming at myself, I wondered why all of this was happening. In a moment of clarity I found myself thinking about Enid. I realized I was deeply in love with her. She'd blown wind in my sails, she'd made me laugh like no other girl before her, and let's face it, the sex was incredible. She was a city girl and all her sensibilities matched mine. She was in love with me too, and the power of that love had driven us apart.

I contemplated all of this as I drove around with the crazy lady to different bars; murderous stares targeted me each place we went.

Something kept telling me, *what are you doing with this skank? You love Enid.*

I'd been a coward in the presence of the purest love of my life, and all this darkness was the consequence of my cowardice. So I went to find Enid. We talked for a long while in the back of the gallery. I confessed I loved her and she did the same. A couple weeks later I ran out of money and we said goodbye with a kiss and my promise to return.

Luckily I salvaged my novel off my fried computer. Found work that winter and I came back to Mexico, but now Enid was in Mexico City. She helped me get a cheap apartment in a very dangerous section of La Neza in Mexico City. In the film *Amores Perros*, the assassin lived there.

The first night in La Neza, Enid and I bought a quart of Victoria and climbed way up to the roof of my building. The bright lights of the city spread around us and ascended the mountainsides that surround D.F. like a cloud of pulsing lightning bugs. Enid was more beautiful than ever with her short black hair, dark skin, and big full lips. I marveled at how I'd found this gem of a girl and ended up in this monstrous third world maze as we passed the quart back and forth. Some neighborhood kids began to call up to us and talk shit from down on the street. So I poured some beer down at them and called them "little motherfuckers," playfully. They just giggled and repeated "Motherfuckers! Motherfuckers!" and before you knew it we were exchanging lessons on swearing in our respective languages and swiftly becoming friends.

I wrote every day and hung out with Enid at night. This family that lived down the block from me befriended me. They were six kids from about eight to sixteen years old; a few of the boys were there for the welcoming party swearing lessons. They wanted to learn more English, and after I'd written all day they'd come and knock on my door yelling, "Willians" (they thought that was my name) until I came downstairs. They'd take me to go play soccer or play video games at the arcade; they taught me Spanish and I taught them English. I thought I'd have a check coming from home but it never came, and I was extremely low on money. So I survived mainly on Ramen noodles. When they found out I didn't have money for food they began to trick me into coming to their home to eat dinner. I would refuse to go, but their mother would ask me to come and eat. The generosity of these people was just heartbreaking. I only was ever in their kitchen/dining room but the last day I was there one of the kids brought me into the bedroom to see something. Ignorance made me assume the house was big, but when I stepped into the other room I saw that they all slept in the second room. This just magnified my gratitude; they were so poor and had given me so much. I finished the book, ran out of money, and went home in early February.

Worked, saved, and came to be with Enid that June. Luckily I had money this time and gave the family a letter thanking each and every one of them for all the wonderful fun we'd had. I put a couple hundred bucks in the envelope. Knowing they'd give the money back, I told them not to open it until I left. I'd still go to visit those guys, but they moved away and we lost touch. Afterward I took Enid to a small town on the beach in Veracruz. I asked her to marry me on a little dirt road down the street from the house we'd rented. She said yes. I promised her that I would be a better man and I've striven every day to be that. We made crazy plans for our future. Our dreams filled us with astonishing hope.

BUFFALO

Returned to Pamplona that July. I'd stayed in contact with Graeme Galloway. He offered for me to come and work for him in his travel group, the Pamplona Posse. I said, "It sure as hell'd beat sleeping on the street," and signed on. I walked up to Graeme the afternoon of the sixth of July outside of The Harp bar on St. Nicholas. He staggered drunk from the Chupinazo and didn't recognize me. He kept asking if I was a punter. I didn't know what the fuck he was talking about. Exhausted from the long trip I almost told him "go fuck yourself" and walked off, but eventually they handed me a drink and the job of bringing punters, tourists staying with the Posse, up to their rooms above the bar.

The Posse consisted of several dozen workers from all over the English-speaking world. Australians, Canadians, New Zealanders, Irish, Scots, English, and of course a few Americans; most were in their early twenties. I found an instant kindred spirit with a forty-something American from New Jersey named Gary Masi. Gary was an ex-New Jersey cop. He was big and athletic and a sick fucker. He reminded me of my football buddies. It was Gary's and my job to settle any disputes with punters, assess and fix any damage they caused the several dozen apartments throughout the old section of town, and to kick out any punters who'd overstayed their booking. We played good cop, bad cop, and I was always the bad cop. Each morning after the run we went back to the restaurant above The Harp and ate a free breakfast: either eggs with bacon or *Rabo de Toro*, fighting-bull tail stew, butchered and bought straight from the Plaza de Toros. It's a thick, spicy concoction, wholesome and hearty. Eating Rabo de Toro gave me this sense of completion: the hunt, the kill, and the feast. I ate Rabo de Toro every morning and drank red wine. After that, Gary and I'd take a full bottle of red and drift downstairs and out into the brisk and vibrant fiesta morning with our to-do list—passing the bottle back and forth along the way. The adrenaline of the morning's run still buzzing through us, we tried to top each other with gross-out jokes; Gary always seemed to win. It was a paradisiacal existence. I threatened any cocky Englishman who spoke out of turn with serious bodily harm while Gary explained that it was time for everyone to leave or pay for an extra day. We'd laugh and bust each other's balls along the way.

Was sitting in the plaza one night when Galloway introduced me to an elderly woman named Frosty. She was a frail, white-haired lady in her eighties and a bull runner. Graeme would position her in between two drainpipes along Estafeta behind Bar Windsor where she'd puff on a Marlboro Red as the herd rambled past. Frosty also had a long, storied history at fiesta, where she never lit her own cigarette. I lit a bunch of Frosty's smokes as she told me stories about her decades at fiesta.

"One morning I was there on the street smoking my cigarette when the glorious herd swept past. Suddenly a few moments later a marvelous black bull appeared. He stopped right in front of me. I just froze, thinking, good heavens Frosty, what have you gotten yourself into now? He looked at me just a few feet away and tried to figure out just exactly what I was. Then the great Spanish runner José Antonio appeared. José called to the grand animal and swooped him away up the street. I really love José; he's a dear chap."

José Antonio wasn't just a heroic runner who saves frail, old grandmothers. José also happened to be deaf and mute. His brother suffered from the same disabilities. His brother also had an anger problem, but José was different. He was very kind and friendly. José is one of the greatest communicators I've ever encountered. He'll give all of himself to tell a simple story, using body language and objects and even writing words when needed. He is an incredibly giving friend as well. He runs the curve. To run with bulls is incredibly difficult, but to do it without the use of a fundamental sense like hearing raises the danger to outrageous heights. But the fact that José Antonio stands in the near center of the curve and waits for the animals to hit the wall before running just shows you the type of phenomenal, raw courage that churns in this man's heart.

This time, I did plenty of research on the run in the leadup to Pamplona. I found an interesting article in the *New York Times* by a New York bar owner named Joe Distler. A Spanish newspaper recognized Distler as one of the five greatest runners of a twenty-year period. I'd met Distler briefly the year before and asked him a few questions. He was one of the nicer guys, with his spiked gray hair, big smile, and peppy Brooklyn accent.

45

Distler was a successful businessman when he read about the great American bull runner Matt Carney. At age twenty-two, Distler set out to travel to Pamplona and run with Carney.

"On my first run I ran into the arena way ahead of the herd. The Spanish taunt runners who do this and mockingly call them *valientes* (brave ones). I ran to the wall and jumped it, and when the herd entered the arena, the sight of those incredible bulls scared me so much that I pissed my pants. I was hitchhiking my way out of town when I stopped. I realized if the run had had such a powerful effect on me, that there must be something important back there on the street. I went back and followed Carney the next day. Later Carney became my maestro. The run was different back then. There was only a handful of runners on the street. It was wide open. It wasn't until television and later ESPN came that the thousands of runners poured in from all over the world."

Distler became a legend to the Pamplonicos by running on the horns of bulls for over forty years. He had the grace of a ballet dancer and a magical fluidity and speed to find his way into the pack. That, combined with his raw courage, luck, and fate, allowed him to become just the second American in history to run as the very best Spanish runners do. Matt Carney and Joe Distler are the only two foreigners to ever truly become one of them, one of the greatest runners to ever run an encierro. Distler is also known as the Iron Man of Pamplona because he didn't miss a single run at Pamplona in all that time. A bull gored him in the nineties and dislocated his hip, which doctors eventually replaced. This along with age forced him to find a new way to continue to get close to the animals.

The article outlined an old-fashioned approach to running the curve. Chema Esparza, one of Joe's Spanish maestros, taught it to him. The technique is to stand in a doorway just before the curve along the outer wall of the bend. Then you wait until the herd passes and crashes into the blind turn. Just as this occurs, with split-second timing you dash into a sprint and cut along the inside of the curve. As the animals rise you sprint in front of them and lead them up Estafeta Street.

After experiencing the panic and chaos the year before, I realized I needed a plan. Distler's plan was the cleanest I'd heard yet, and I jumped at the chance to run with Joe and the others at the curve. I hadn't brought any running shoes. I was going to run in my white snakeskin cowboy boots.

Before the third morning of runs I shook Joe's hand and said *suerte* and he replied *igualmente*. But I had no idea what it meant and fixated on it, hoping I hadn't pissed him off. I couldn't see much along Mercaderes as the bulls rushed down the slow slope. Then they rocketed into view like a careening black mountain range. The exiting runner pushed us all against the wall. The bulls and steers slipped and slid on their hooves as they tried to halt and make the turn. As the last animal's hindquarters slid past, several runners surged forward fast and cut hard along the inside of the curve. I followed. The animals slowed and slammed into the wall as I accelerated and breathed in the rank stench of bull dung and adrenaline. They bellowed and cried as the bells banged and the spectators above roared. The final bulls slipped as I closed in on them, three beasts slid in unison, their mountainous backs swelled and contorted as their momentum carried them through the turn. Their hooves skated over the stones. I could have reached out and touched them, but I didn't. Some powerful force sucked me toward them but I feared it. I pulled away as they gathered and accelerated past and up Estafeta.

The rush impacted me so strongly that I thought I'd run beside them for twenty yards, but the photos proved I was only really beside them for a moment then drifted away. Still it was my first outstanding run. I was in the herd's space and it thrilled me. Rushed over to Photo Auma, a shop in Plaza de Castillo, and I bought a bunch of photos. I showed them to anyone willing to stop for a second and look. In the most impressive image of my run the photographer cut my body out of the shot. The only thing that remained in frame directly beside a rising bull was my white snakeskin boot. I was most proud of this image and boastfully shoved it in everyone's face. Once again I became a jester for the serious runners. Even Frosty couldn't help but laugh in my face and pat me on the head. Most people dismissed the photos as not me and spread the word that I was nuts.

I caught wind and got surly and stopped showing my images. Got seriously drunk and I fell into bed at 5:00 a.m. at my place on Estafeta. I didn't wake until the cameraman climbed into the blue box attached to my balcony. I was brutally hungover and stumbled into the bathroom and vomited. Knew I couldn't run like this and was morbid over not being on the street. I watched television and the cameraman on the balcony waved to us, and sure enough, his camera went live. A shot of the street below spread across the television. I felt somewhat better as the excitement flooded all over the street from balcony to balcony. People asked me if I was a runner and I nodded, but I was even more regretful at missing the morning's run. The police released the runners from Town Hall and I watched them round the corner and dash up empty Estafeta Street. Just as the rocket went off, the fog in my mind cleared. *I can still run! I can run down these stairs and out onto the street and run.* I rambled down the stairs and out the door onto the street. A few seconds later, *bam,* the herd hit the wall at the curve, and I ran up Estafeta and didn't get close at all but was so grateful to have run! I barfed on the cobblestones afterward and went back upstairs and slept for a few hours. Later I explained to Gary and Galloway that I'd run and they rolled their eyes and thought I was telling lies again. I finally screamed at them. "If you don't believe me come over with me. I just opened the door and walked out onto Estafeta!" They looked at each other and it finally clicked; of course it was possible. I was right.

The next morning they were there with me, sitting on the sofa, and we slipped out onto the street together without incident. That night Graeme dubbed the apartment "The Alamo" and that name remained for several years. Graeme and Gary wanted me to run Santo Domingo. I agreed, and we didn't use the Alamo that morning and ended up singing the "San Fermín Pedimos," a prayer for protection to the idol of San Fermín, the patron saint of fiesta. They placed the idol in the tall stone wall near the beginning of the course. Hundreds of runners crowded around. It's one of the iconic images of fiesta. They even have a board with the song lyrics written in Spanish and Basque.

I ran Santo Domingo for the first time. It's extremely fast. The rocket bursts and the bulls are already closing in on the police line. I ran the center of the road and was trying to run fast but it was crowded. As I looked back over my shoulder an older man was in my path, moving slowly. I slammed into his back. He fell and I toppled over him and smashed my knee into the asphalt. The herd crackled past. The collision with the ground tore my jeans and scraped my kneecap. I was too pissed off and proud to take care of it. It wasn't until the next morning that the waitresses at the breakfast place sprayed it with peroxide and gave me a bandage. My run made TV for the first time that I knew of. I was there for a few strides even though I'd fallen. It was the first time I'd ever fallen in the run. It wouldn't be the last.

I ran the curve the next day and didn't get very close. There's a scent that remains after a street fight. It's a lime smoldering of adrenaline. There'd been a tussle at the curve that morning; two runners sprinting with the pack got into it, and there was a photo of them punching each other just feet from the horns. As I walked around the curve at about noon that day I caught wind of it. That scent always sparks bright memories in my mind. I started to strategize how to master the curve when the California boys walked up. They worked for the Posse. One was this tall kid with long blond hair and the other was a short squat guy. The tall one had this arrogant pompous attitude that rubbed me the wrong fucking way. They'd been dismissive of my running so I'd invited them out the night before to run with me. They didn't show.

The tall one gave me a snarky smile.

"Where were you guys this morning?" I asked.

"Ah, we decided not to run," he replied.

"So pussied out, huh?"

He laughed in my face and said, "Yeah, whatever."

"I ran the curve this morning. I started right here." I replied nodding to the doorway.

He laughed. "You never ran the curve in your life."

I thought about it and said, "You know what . . . " and popped him in the chin. He flopped on his ass and lay down flat. His boy rushed up and I flinched at him hard and he lunged away so wildly he almost fell down. Then I leaned over the tall blond and grabbed a handful of his hair and smacked him alongside the head. I told him just exactly what kind of a pretty boy California pussy he was. Then his midget short friend came barreling into my back and I fell on top of the tall one. The midget landed on top of me and that drove my bad knee into the stones so hard I thought I might have fractured my kneecap. We all held each other in a strange body lock. The families of Pamplona slowly eased past smiling and talking merrily. Some even laughed at us.

I said, "If we all let go and break clean, it's over."

"You sure?" the midget said.

"Yeah, I'm sure."

We got up and broke clean. I told the pretty boy he was a coward ass pussy, but I said I respected the midget for having his boy's back. Walked back to The Harp and about ten minutes later Galloway came up and scolded all three of us and made us shake hands. We did. I sat down and drank beer with some of the Posse and they asked me about my knee, and I said it was fucked but the beer was helping.

They laughed and about fifteen minutes later there was a ruckus in The Harp. I stood up and saw Owan, the owner of The Harp and the restaurant above, push two short Moroccan guys out and try to close the garage-style sliding door of the packed bar. The Moroccans pushed back in and jammed the garage door. I got up and stood silently beside Owan, who was savagely mad and screaming in their faces. They all spoke Spanish and they didn't like what Owan said. One slapped Owan softly on the cheek. Owan screamed something insanely and stormed back into the bar for what I assumed was a weapon. Figured he was going for a club or knife or gun to fuck these guys up so I screamed in their faces, "GO AWAY!"

They looked at each other mystified and put up their fists and snarled at me. I took a hard step at the hairier one and pushed him with all my might in the chest. He flew airborne and landed hard on the street. His head cracked on the cobblestones and his eyes rolled up in his head. The other went to punch me so I pushed him square in the chest and he flew and cracked his head. His whole body convulsed like something was electrocuting him. I screamed at their unconscious bodies: "GO THE FUCK AWAY!"

The first one started to get to his feet on unsteady legs and staggered across the street. Owan emerged from the bar without a weapon, ran up and snagged him and slammed him against the brick wall across the way. The barback dashed out and tackled the other one as he tried to get up and they both fell at my feet.

"I'LL STOMP YOUR FUCKING HEAD!" I shouted and raised my boot and stomped the Moroccan's head into the cobblestones. There were about 300 people watching and 50 or so women screamed simultaneously in horror. I grabbed the Moroccan by the back of his shirt and his pants, picked him up, and threw him as far as I could down the street away from The Harp. He got to his feet and the other rushed over and they backed slowly down the street with their fists up as Owan, the barback, and I stalked them. Then I noticed a mother obliviously pushing a double-stroller with two toddlers in it toward us, a ways behind the Moroccans.

"STOP!" I screamed. "There's kids here!" The Moroccans somehow understood that, looked back, saw the kids, nodded, and jogged away. A lot of the people in the street clapped at the conclusion of the performance. I didn't pay for a drink for a very long time after that and never paid for another drink at The Harp. And I drank a whole lot. I know what you're thinking: pretty funny that a practicing Buddhist is violent, right? Well, Buddhism was the only thing keeping me from fucking killing somebody.

When Graeme got back about fifteen minutes later, someone told him I was fighting again. He shrugged and walked over to me and said, "I'm gonna have to let you go, Bill."

I shrugged and said, "Can I sit here a while and keep drinking?" Then an uproar of support swelled in my favor and a few seconds later Owan came out of the bar and told Graeme the whole story. Graeme apologized and commended me for what I'd done. He gave me five euros and told me to go buy a cigar for myself. I got up and my knee throbbed and wouldn't straighten for a while. I walked off and bought the cigar and came back limping badly. As I approached The Harp from about a block away Gary stood in the center of the narrow channel of the street, sipping a quart of San Miguel beer. His sangria-drenched shirt clung to his muscly torso. He looked my way and his blue eyes lit up on his stubbled, dark face. When Gary saw me he smiled and I smiled and I knew I'd found a lifelong friend.

Galloway walked out beside Gary and handed me a beer as I limped up.

"This cunt is a proper cowboy," Galloway said to Gary. I just laughed.

"He is," Galloway said. "Really, you are, Bill."

Gary patted me on the back. "And what's his cowboy name?"

"Well, it's gotta be something good. How 'bout Buffalo Bill?"

"Buffalo Bill it is."

"Can we call you that, Bill?"

"I don't give a shit, Graeme; you can call me whatever you want as long as you keep giving me beers."

And from then on in Pamplona I was known as Buffalo Bill.

On the sixth morning the herd soared past me at the curve. I broke into a sprint crossing behind their path. A bald Spanish runner streamed alongside the pack on the inner curve. The black bull nearest him slid. The animal gathered his hooves and found purchase. He opened his frothy mouth and raised his head upward in a slow graceful lunge. One of his long tall horns embedded into the bald runner's thigh. The bull lifted and the man floated up into the air. The horn's upward thrust halted. The mozo unhinged and ascended up another few feet. He floated above the chaotic runners and animals in a long arcing flight, then descended and flopped on his back as the animal and the herd galloped up the street. The mozo screamed and clutched his thigh. The wound plopped dark blood in a gooey smear on the cobblestones. Red Cross medics moved in, and I remembered the sweeper steers and the other runners and I helped form a shoulder-to-shoulder wall to protect the man and the medics from the sweeper steers trampling them. Then we got out of the way of the medics so they could get him off to the hospital.

I finally sobered up enough to realize my knee was completely fucked. It swelled to the size of a Chicago-style softball. If I was walking it was fine but if I tried to sit it wouldn't bend. If I was sitting for a while, when I tried to stand it wouldn't straighten. Galloway convinced me to go to the hospital.

I took the bus to the emergency room. A woman and some children cried and pressed to get into a curtained room. Inside a man screamed on a gurney. The curtain opened. The bald Spanish runner from the curve writhed as the doctors inspected his wound. One of the more painful things involved in a goring wound is the clothing and debris that gets thrust into the hole by the horn. A bull's horn has splinters at the tip. Those splinters break off when they insert into the body. Goring wounds are extremely dangerous. The animals continually sharpen their horns on any hard surface. You can watch them do this from the castle wall above the corral in the night before their runs. The horns are porous and they will dip the tips of their horns in the large piles of dung in the corral. In effect they are turning their horns into poisonous spears. Goring wounds are guaranteed to infect. I was pretty lucky; my knee was just busted. The doctor took an X-ray and said the kneecap wasn't broken, just a severe contusion. An infection also festered in the knee from the filthy street. He prescribed ibuprofen and an antibiotic and I took the bus back to town.

I remember waiting for the fireworks that night with the Posse. They have the best fireworks you will ever see, and they have them every single night of fiesta. We all sat in a big circle in the grassy field in the dark. Lights illuminated the white stone castle walls as thousands of people filled the fields beside them. My injury really impressed Graeme's son Will; he asked for the X-rays. I gave them to him. He was a nice kid. I'd get to watch him grow up over the coming years. Galloway told me I shouldn't run the next morning, but I assured him I would. We drank and watched the fireworks explode above us and were very happy.

The second-to-last run I came up to Top of Estafeta with Galloway and Gary. As the herd approached I ran alongside Galloway. Suddenly he hip-checked me and I fell into a doorway. He glanced at me and nodded. He was just trying to protect me because of my knee, but it infuriated me. I fought through the bodies to get back out into the street and ran alongside the herd pretty close. Didn't tell Galloway it'd made me mad. I just smiled at him at Bar Txoko afterward when he brought me a beer.

The final morning we were in the Alamo waiting for it to start. Galloway and Gary tried and failed to talk me out of running. I assured them if my knee didn't loosen I wouldn't try for it. They asked me where I planned to run and I told them the Curve and they looked at each other and sighed and then we all laughed and told each other *suerte* before we left.

I stood at the curve and waited. I tried to squat to stretch my knee but it wouldn't bend and I doubted I'd be able to run. After the rocket the adrenaline loosened it up a little and I tried really hard to bend my knee. The herd ambled toward us. I decided to try. As they crashed into the wall I ran, but my knee didn't cooperate. It wouldn't bend and I couldn't muster much more than a painful jog. I watched the herd accelerate away. *Goodbye till next year.* Suddenly there's a whirl. I look back and a straggler bull rambles directly for me as I float slowly through the curve. The sudden terror limbers my knee and I sprint deep and hard and painlessly. I veer right as the bull tears up the center of the street. The way the adrenaline limbered my knee shocked me. A while later I found a photo of my flash on the horns. It wasn't much but it was something.

Got on the bus that night and I jumped a flight over to London. Johny Brown invited me to read from my novel on a legendary radio station called Resonance FM. Stayed with Johny for a couple weeks and we rehearsed a great show with live music and even performed to a packed house at the 12 Bar, a classic punk rock venue just across the street from the station. We also did two different hour-long segments on his show *Mining for Gold* on Resonance FM. Johny gave me a book on black magic voodoo and I found a passage on white magic. White magic is good magic that can cause good luck and positive mojo. My novel wasn't anywhere near being ready for publication. I was just starting out on a long journey. But the inspiration and excitement Johny gave me by doing those performances was exactly what I needed. Johny Brown was my white magic voodoo and I'll never forget it.

Made it home a broken bag of bones and I luckily got enough money together to fly down and spend some time with Enid in September. I got back home and was completely run down. That's around the time I began to lose my mind.

CHAPTER THREE:
THE BATTLE OF GYPSY HILL
2008

My grandfather on my mother's side suffered from bipolar disorder. My uncle on that side and his son had it as well. Psychiatrists diagnosed me with a behavior disorder in junior high. I struggled with anger and violence my entire life. But suddenly around the fall of 2006 I started to have trouble falling asleep. I'd lie down and try but hours would pass and I just lay there on my back wide-awake. I'd start to think very rapidly. If something had happened that day, some small slight, I'd fixate on it. Slowly build connections with un-connectable instances. I became very obsessed with my food and felt people were messing with it. My stomach ached and I vomited a lot. It never crossed my mind that doing a lot of drugs and drinking a ton might have been the cause. The less I slept the more these insane rampaging theories blazed through my mind. It got so that I wanted to take revenge on the people who were hurting me. I had no idea that what was hurting me was a psychological disease that I was born with. I was suffering, and I wanted to exact my revenge on others. I had a list of people I would attack. Then I rationalized that if I attacked these people I'd go back to jail, and I refused to ever go back to jail. Everything escalated in my mind until I was planning to kill people. Near perfect strangers: the guy at the Chinese food place, the guy from the burger joint, the server at Starbucks, they'd all worked together to poison me. Then it escalated to my father; my father was poisoning me. My mom was even in on it.

My niece lived with us then, and she cried in the middle of the night because her parents were getting divorced. I somehow turned that into a theory that someone was attacking her in the night, that someone was molesting her. In my mind my father was molesting her, and then I had the righteous authority to kill him for that. As insane as I was, I couldn't bridge the gap between what was happening in my mind and reality. Ignorant people often wonder, how could the parents of the Columbine and Virginia Tech killers not have known? Because insane people hide their insanity. They ask, how could the killers not know they were insane? One of the definitions of insanity is that the person doesn't know they're crazy. It's a mysterious place to be, floating in that deep abyss of madness. Some people get lost there and never snap out of it.

It all came to a head one night with my father. I confronted him in the kitchen about him doing things to my food. He told me to get out and dialed 911. I broke the telephone, then I barricaded myself in my bedroom. A mound of letters from court and crumbled papers littered my dresser as I slammed it against the door. The police officers stomped heavily down the hallway; their Mace and nightsticks clanked and jostled. My reflection in the mirror startled me, dark bags hung under my eyes, my face contorted and flexed in animalistic shapes. I screamed viscerally through the door. "YOU BETTER BE READY MOTHERFUCKERS! I'M GONNA BEAT THE FUCK OUTTA YOU AND TAKE YOUR FUCKING GUN AND KILL YOU WITH IT!" Four or more cops stomped up to the door in a line. Just when they were about to break it down my dad stopped them. He asked them to leave. My dad told them that he didn't need their help anymore, he was sorry for calling them, and that he would handle it. We talked and I calmed down some and I promised to let them get me some help.

The next morning I was on my way to work when I just started driving in the woods around 95th and LaGrange Road in the south suburbs of Chicago. Terrible images and thoughts flashed through my mind. They slashed straight through the core of who I was. The torment was too much. I decided to kill myself. Then something told me *No, no, you have to kill all of them first!* I decided to go on this rampage and kill as many people as I could. Suddenly a potent terror gripped me. I trembled uncontrollably. Then I drove into this forest preserve and called my dad and I asked him if he was hurting my niece. He said, "Oh my god, Bill, you need help. You need to come home now, and we need to get you some help."

He brought me to a psychiatrist. In the car outside he told me that this was a real chance at life. That I needed to tell the psychiatrist everything or she wouldn't be able to help me, and that I might die or do something terrible if I didn't. I told the psychiatrist everything and she advised me to check myself into a psych ward at Hinsdale Hospital immediately. They sedated me straight off. I walked around the ward like a zombie, drooling all over myself for a couple of days. They tried different medications. I was set to go down to Mexico City for Enid's sister's wedding and I didn't want to let her down. I called from the hospital and tried to explain to her that I'd lost my mind and was in the hospital. It was a rough time. I barely made it through. Absolute despair rained down on me as the medicated fog began to clear in my mind. I remember sitting in bed in my room, wanting so badly to die and have all the torment end. Then I began chanting quietly *Nam-myoho-renge-kyo;* it was literally the only thing that kept me breathing. They held me for a little over a week. I decided to lie to the doctors at the end because I knew they wouldn't let me out otherwise. Things in my head were still very bad. They released me, and I went out the next night to a warehouse party. I lurked in the dark room at the edge of the dance floor. Voices leaped out of the darkness and seeped into my mind. Some skinhead attacked this guy and I grabbed the skin by his throat and threw him down. The rest of the people at the party commenced to beat him and drag him out. I went home and flew to Mexico City the next morning. At Enid's sister's wedding I got drunk and somehow convinced myself Enid's friend's boyfriend was hitting on Enid, so I asked him into a side room and beat the shit out of him. They stopped the wedding because of the fight. Enid nearly broke it off with me but somehow it didn't happen. We stayed together, and that winter I got some work in construction on the Modern Wing of the Art Institute of Chicago. It was brutal work in subzero temperatures. The wind rushed from the lake and just about blew you right off the scaffolding. But I saved a ton of money. Columbia College Chicago accepted me into their MFA in Fiction Writing program. Enid came to Chicago to visit that summer on a tourist visa. We realized we could get married and she could stay. And so we did.

Mania and depression are two very dangerous monsters. Every day they try to get me alone, separate me from everything I love and all the light in the world so they can torture and destroy me and urge me to do horrifying things to others and of course in the end to myself. Mania comes in many forms and we've seen it rise in epidemic levels in America. Yet we seem not to want to face it. We'd rather blame guns. What we need to do is simple; help the sick people, discover new ways to engage them, and find them before it's too late. We need to start a nationwide conversation and work on new ways to identify it and capture those who are on the verge of acting out these horrific plots. For many, the difference between them becoming another psychotic killer rampaging through a school or office building or public square is as simple as a pill and some psychiatric counseling, maybe a few weeks in a psych ward, maybe more, but it would be worth it. And for anyone reading this who is involved in that pursuit or just plain gives a shit at all: I will donate my help and insight, anytime.

Because of the timing of our marriage I didn't go to Pamplona for fiesta that year. It was one of the hardest choices I've made. Our love is probably the only thing that could keep me from fiesta. Missing fiesta tormented me. Every day I got home from work and refreshed my YouTube search until that day's run appeared. I watched the videos meticulously. There were several bulls that separated from the herd, called *sueltos*, that year. They all wreaked havoc in Telefónica. This tormented me, especially because most of my friends ran there. If a suelto had gored one of my friends I would have crumbled into a hysterical mess for not being there to try and save them.

One suelto that year named Universal became legendary when he gored seven different runners all by his lonesome. When a bull is in the pack it wants to stay with its brothers and the steers. If it separates, it loses its herding instinct. Directionless, it descends into madness and unleashes its primal fury on anyone it comes across. The mozos instantly try to hail the animal, calm it, and lead it up the street. I wanted very much to run with a suelto and help lead him to the arena. I'd read in Hemingway's *Death in the Afternoon* about a pass in the bullfight called a Veronica. They named it after Saint Veronica who wiped Christ's face when he fell carrying the cross. The matador wipes the face of the bull as he passes. It opened the door to more reading about the metaphor of the ritualized sacrifice, which is *corrida*, crudely translated into English as bullfighting. I realized that if these bulls were to represent Christ then we as runners were there to ease the suffering of the sacrificial beast. We were there to lead him to the arena, the place where he would die. These sueltos, who were lost, sacred beasts, became even more precious to me, and I could feel my destiny melding with theirs.

Enid and I rented a little place in the Pilsen neighborhood on the near southwest side of Chicago, and I began my MFA studies. It was hard to focus in the classes because I was still adjusting to the medication. One of the meds was this experimental stuff that ended up getting pulled from the market because it was giving weird side effects; one little boy started growing breasts while on it. I stopped taking it on my own, and since I couldn't afford to see a doctor I just tried to figure out my disease myself—tweaking my own medication until I found the right mix. Of course I failed a lot in the process and still struggled with severe mania and depression. I kept with the other medication, which was primarily a sleep med, and started to use it only at night. I noticed that my disease was drastically altered by my sleep pattern, and I could end a psychotic manic phase by simply taking an extra pill at night and sleeping hard for ten hours. I'd wake groggy but stable. This is a battle I struggle with to this day. But during that time it was a much harder fight because I was still drinking heavily and doing hard drugs—all of which nullified the effects of my meds.

Looking back, I used the encierro to self-medicate. I spent so much of the year depressed and in anguish over my novel and struggling to overcome the sense of hopelessness and despair that every artist endures—in the beginning especially. The run was something to look forward to. No matter how bad things were in my life, I knew fiesta was around the bend and I'd be able to taste the richest life I'd ever experienced again. *Ya falta menos* is a mantra San Fermín regulars use. It means it's almost time for fiesta. That mantra helped me through my darkest days, weeks, and months. Then after fiesta the epic high I'd return home with would last months and aid me through the first part of the year that I had to wait to run again. And to this day, *Ya falta menos* remains a mantra that helps me cope with my disease.

In the fall of 2007 I came up with an idea to start a Story Slam in Chicago. There were a few happening on the East Coast. I asked my friend Marc Smith, the originator of Poetry Slam at the Green Mill jazz club in Chicago, if I could use the word Slam in the name and he said sure. One night I got a couple friends together to spring the idea on them and see if they wanted to help. We ended up getting in a bloody fight with some off-duty cops. A smartass friend of mine started it, but the two cops pinned him to the jukebox. I stumbled onto it and just reacted and broke a bottle on one of the cop's heads as the guy pulled his gun and nearly shot Enid, my friends, and me in the face. We ended up getting arrested later and I was looking at several felony charges. Enid could have been deported over it because her status was in the documentation process, but miraculously that didn't happen, because the cop got physical first and pulled his gun. And probably because my brother was a Chicago police detective, they released us without pressing charges. Still somehow I thought I didn't have a problem with booze and drugs and kept drinking for almost exactly one more year.

I started the Windy City Story Slam at this crazy, little illegal underground arts space called Q4. There were only seven audience members at the first show. I naively figured that was a good start and pushed harder. The show became wildly successful. Within six months we built a substantial audience. *Time Out Chicago* did a feature on it and then the *Chicago Tribune* did one too. It was exciting because it was a show that presented storytelling as a fun competition. It was new and fresh and just getting started.

FALL DOWN STAY DOWN

July 13, 1995, a twenty-two-year-old American from Glen Ellyn, Illinois named Matthew Peter Tassio showed up to Pamplona and decided to run. He was running at Town Hall and fell in the center of the path. As the herd approached, Tassio struggled to get to his feet. The lead bull gored him in the heart and threw him twenty yards up the path. Tassio bled to death in moments. This is one of the major tragic illustrations for the most important rule in bull running: if you fall down, stay down.

Pamplonico Chema Esparza began running a few years after Joe Distler did. The two were contemporaries and very close friends and running partners.

"It was so empty in the seventies we could choose the bulls we wanted to run with from a hundred yards away."

Esparza was one of the greatest to ever run with bulls. Hollywood producers selected Esparza as a guide for Spike Lee when Lee came to film a Levi's Button Fly commercial. "Spike Lee is a black man, but when he saw the bulls for the first time in the street, I look in his face and his face was white, he was so scared."

When Hollywood came back to Pamplona to film for *City Slickers 2* they chose Esparza for Billy Crystal's body double during the running of the bulls scene.

Esparza had one of the most dramatic experiences in keeping with the most important rule: if you fall down, stay down.

"In 1991 at the curve I made a stupid mistake. It was the most dangerous moment that happened in all my life. At the curve, everything that you expect to happen there, you're going to be wrong, because anything can happen there. Some days the bulls fall down, other days they don't. I ran that morning and suddenly was in the middle of the herd. I had one bull pressing against my left side and another bull pressing against my right side. They were crushing me and there were a couple bulls behind me. I thought, 'Oh my god, this is the end of my life.' So I think I made the correct choice. I laid myself down in the street and the bulls are very honest. They are noble animals, really humble animals, and they jump over things if they can. If they can they avoid anything in their way in the street. If not and they step on you, they can break any part of you, your arms, ribs, anything. I was on the ground afraid. Nothing happened! I fell down. The two bulls behind me jumped over me. I said, 'Wow!' My friends were watching on the balconies and they said, 'Are you OK?' The bulls didn't step on me! Because if a bull steps on you, they break something. If they step on your head, they destroy it like an egg. I'll never forget this moment."

Went back to fiesta that summer, this time with my cousin Dylan. He was engaged to get married and he wanted one last wild excursion with me. We'd gone on plenty of rowdy trips over the years, including a few to New Orleans for Mardi Gras. We boarded the plane and headed over and I tried to explain everything to him on the long flight. Dylan fit right in with the Posse. Everything had changed from the years before; the Posse Headquarters was now set up at 33 Estafeta. Gary brought over his cousin Larry, a big ole cop from North Carolina.

I worried a lot about Dylan. It's one thing to put yourself in danger; it's a whole other thing to guide someone else into a dangerous situation. We'd been in a ton of bloody street fights together, but this was different.

That first morning, Dylan and I decided to run Top of Estafeta with Gary and Galloway. As we walked up the street, an excited grin spread across Dylan's face. My heart pattered fearfully in my chest. Dylan didn't look scared. *My god, did I not tell him how dangerous this is?* I grabbed him by the shoulder.

"Dylan, this is fuckin' serious, man. You gotta be ready. This is gonna be fuckin' crazy man. Focus!"

Dylan's face got stern and I felt bad that I'd darkened his mood but hell, it was my duty.

We all hugged and wished each other *suerte.* I told Dylan to try to stay close to me and run when I ran. Fear gripped his face; it made me glad, because fear will keep you alive on these streets. First-time runners swamped Estafeta—afraid and exuberant. The rocket burst at the edge of town and twisted them all into wild panic. The initial swell pushed us all into the wall hard. The stickiness of fear glued us to the boarded-up storefronts. Wrenched myself free and struggled near the center of the path. I peered down the street as the rushing waves grew in speed and density. The screams exploded and the street quaked violently. As the pack approached I yelled at Dylan.

"Get the fuck out here, man!" Dylan couldn't hear me. I roared again and watched his face wilt in fear and confusion as the tangle swallowed him.

The camera flashes soared along the balcony toward us. I shrugged at him and went.

Ran and fought my way in against fast mozos in the center of the street. Suddenly a bull rushed up near me. I elbowed my way in front of him. His horn bobbed beside me as he galloped. I surged in and could have touched his horn when the animal unleashed a startled bellow. Then he lunged and hooked his head my way. His horn tip hit my side and I floated up—airborne. Wind swirled through my ears. *My god, I'm gored!* Then he whipped his head downward and slammed me to the stones.

I gripped my stomach. *No wetness. No blood.* I felt my belly and found a small hole in my white T-shirt. Someone grabbed me from behind and yanked me to my feet. I stuck my pinky through the hole. *He snagged my shirt, Jesus!* A surge of panic ballooned at my back and I realized there were more coming—the herd was broken and strung out along the course. I ran to the center of the street, and sure enough a bull galloped there. Everything cleared. I dashed near the horns of the animal. A bulky Pamplonico named Juan Pedro Lecuona ran directly on the horns of the animal, leading him perfectly. I slashed beside Juan but not quite perfectly in front of the horn. Ahead, a wall of disintegrating chaos blinded me. A mozo suddenly materialized directly in my path, crumpled on the ground. I leaped trying to clear him and snagged my foot on his back. I flew in the air for a long moment, parallel to the ground, arms and legs stretched like Superman. Looked back, I soared eye-to-eye with the bull. His glossy black eye stared at me afraid and urgent as he snorted. Frothy drool dangled and whipped from his lips. I slammed belly flat on the wet cobblestones.

Another mozo grabbed me and picked me up and I was running again. What seemed like the main herd approached and I tried to slow. As I slowed, a man who was running directly on the horns screamed and pushed my back. I decelerated and he slammed his fist in to my traps. I tripped up and fell again. I lay there flat on my stomach, covered my head, and didn't move.

Then slowly one last animal approached. A police officer in the nearby fencing screamed at me and slammed his nightstick against the wooden barricades. From the ground I looked back and saw the pitch-black suelto creeping up slowly. I stood. The suelto progressed my way. His wide horns almost pointed out sideways. I worked toward the arena—daring to get close, but not to really get close. That'd come later. I entered the tunnel with a bull for the first time. The many runners between us caused a cacophony of terror as the animal's hooves crackled and rambled down the zigzag bricks of tunnel.

Ran into the ring and I jumped the fence as the animal cut onto the sand, swinging his horns viciously. That's when I remembered! *DYLAN! My god, that was the craziest run of my life yet.* Dylan just had an extremely rude introduction to the run. Then he was there beside me and we embraced, grateful that we were both okay.

Dylan's experience that morning is one of those classic first-timer stories.

"So we're standing there on the side of the road just waiting for the rocket to go off, there's this mass quantity of people and I really don't know what to expect, you know? Graeme had it down that after the rocket, we got to wait ninety seconds before we even start running. As soon as the rocket goes off, everybody starts going crazy, people start screaming and running and shit, and I'm wondering if something else is going on. We got ninety seconds before we start running, why is everybody freaking out, ya know? So at this point I knew shit was getting serious, and I swear that ninety seconds felt like a week. I didn't even know where the bulls were, I just wanted to start running. I saw you going out further into the street and you're like, come on! Come on! I'm like, I don't want to get too far out. You were literally right in the middle of the street!

"So we start running at the ninety-second mark. I'm at three-quarters speed running and all of a sudden the ground starts shaking, trembling, and as I'm looking back, it was like the parting of the Red Sea. Then all of a sudden three rows of people come and smash me against the side. I think one bull had run by. I started feeling super vulnerable, so I bullied my way out of there in a panic. When I got out, I was in the lane and I looked back, I saw two bulls coming. I don't think I looked back ever again. I just turned and ran as fast as I could to the next open spot, but there was hardly any open spots except for right on that bend. So as I got to the opening I jumped up on that barricade and turned to look back. My arm kind of swung out when I looked back and the bull passed right under my arm; I could have touched the bull. My heart was beating so hard, it was red-lining at this point!

"So, I wanted to get into the arena and now I'm looking down at the tunnel, then I look back and I see there's a couple more straggler bulls coming, so I basically just jumped down and ran as fast as I could through that tunnel. I'm not sure how close the bulls were because it was too scary to look back at those things, man. I could just feel the ground shaking as they were coming. I run in through the tunnel, and as I run in there, I kind of like, relax for a second and slow down. Suddenly a bull that was already in the ring barrels right back at me. I went into full-blown heart pump again and I turned and Supermanned over the wall. I wasn't taking any chances. I didn't even touch the top of the wall, my shoe flew off and I fell on the ground and laid there for ten seconds, like 'oh my god it was like coming right at me!'

"I find my shoe and look up and you're literally right next to me. You were right there, I was like, thank god! In that moment all I could do was just scream, just scream at the top of my lungs.

"Pure mayhem."

It was the kind of extreme experience that could spook anyone, especially a guy about to get married and start his family life. Dylan didn't run again the rest of fiesta, but he still had a hell of a time. Me on the other hand, that morning only sucked me in deeper. I'd nearly run on the horns, a bull hit me and slammed me on the ground, and all I wanted was more! I ran pretty pathetically for the next few days. The panic sucked me into the walls a couple times. It's quite possible deep down the trauma of the bull hitting me shattered my courage, but in my conscious mind I wanted it bad. I wanted to become a great mozo and now I'd finally found a tiny shred of success. There'd be more to come.

BERSERKER

Fiesta was joyful and exciting as always. A new group of youngsters joined the Posse and tremendous fun lurked around every bend. One night we sat in a little grassy courtyard with a small hill in the center, waiting to eat dinner. Thirty of us lounged on the cool grass talking as they handed out the plates of food. Thousands of fiesta goers milled past on the sidewalks. A group of about twenty Gypsies hung out at the other end of the park. About ten mangy dogs hunkered with them. I chatted and cracked jokes with Dylan at the edge of our group. Two Gypsy girls walked over as the Posse chefs dispersed dinner. The girls smirked innocently, clasped their dirty hands, and begged for something to eat. Galloway told a Posse girl:

"Give 'em a bottle of wine and tell them to fuck off."

The Gypsy girl took the bottle gratefully, then her demeanor suddenly flipped. She swore viciously at Galloway. Then she kicked Gary's cousin in the forearm three times while continuing to berate Galloway. This nice little British guy named Brendan jumped up and ran over to try to quell the argument. As he got close, the girl grabbed the bottle neck and deftly flipped the bottom upward. The round bottom of the wine bottle smacked into Brendan's mouth. The glass drove a tooth all the way through his lip. He screamed and spun toward me. Blood spewed out of his mouth. I got up and Dylan did too. The mob of Gypsies rushed over like a barbarian battle charge. I contemplated punching the girl with the bottle but just couldn't bring myself to hit her.

Then a fat, mowhawked Gypsy dude ran up. I smiled and cracked him in the eye. He went flying and stumbled away. The ugly Gypsy girl smiled at me, very surprised by my response. She walked calmly right to me with the bottle.

I readied and shouted, "Come on, bitch. I will fuck you up!"

She stopped dead in her tracks. It wasn't at all the response she'd expected. I started screaming real crazy. All the Gypsies who were rushing up stopped and reconsidered. They slowly backed away as Dylan and I taunted them. The dogs weren't intimidated though. They threaded through the dustup and lapped up the food on the plates in the grass.

"I'll kill your fucking dogs too, motherfuckers!" I didn't mean it. I like dogs. The Gypsies couldn't understand what the hell I was saying, but the essence of my words hit home. They retreated to their side of the courtyard. I mistook them for peaceniks and screamed "Peace" and flashed the peace sign. They were actually anarchist Gypsies who are very dangerous in Europe and often pull stunts like this where they attack people and steal their food and belongings. Usually the people don't know how to react and get overrun. The police showed up and Gary took me away to cool off. A huge hematoma swelled up on Gary's cousin's forearm, the size and shape of a baseball. The last I saw of those Gypsies was the guy who I'd stuck in the eye. His brow swelled shut and blood streamed down his dirty face. He screamed at us and raised up his shirt and showed us his big hairy belly then turned around and mooned us.

After the Gypsies left I started to lose it again. It was a historic date for the ETA—a night authorities killed one of their leaders. They'd threatened an uprising. Riot police gathered at many intersections. I was sure the Gypsies would want their revenge. I figured instead I'd grab a knife and go find them and cut them the fuck up and make sure they never came back for more. Dylan played along and we both grabbed steak knives out of a Posse apartment and stalked around. The explosions of fireworks and bottles breaking suddenly sounded like concussion grenades as I crept, fiercely eyeballing any Gypsy-looking groups, ready to dive in and shank the first one to make a move.

Dylan could tell I was working myself into an insane frenzy. I convinced myself that every Gypsy I saw was one of them. I was gonna cut somebody nasty, some innocent fucking Gypsy or maybe one of the ones we'd been fighting with. Finally Dylan stopped me and threw his knife in a garbage can.

"I can't do this, Bill." Dylan looked at me. His brown eyes trembled with fear. "I want you to stop; it's going too far."

I snarled into the hundreds of passing joyful faces.

"I love you," Dylan said, and then he turned and walked away.

It startled me. I sighed, standing there alone, gripping the knife in my pocket. *Fuck, I'm going nuts again.* I imagined myself stabbing some fucking innocent person. A sixteen-year-old Gypsy girl sat in a doorway. She just pleasantly enjoyed herself—petting her gnarly dog. I dropped my knife and cooled out. Caught up with Dylan, I apologized, and thanked him for snapping me out of it. I was very grateful he'd lured me back to sanity. We never ran into those Gypsies again.

Cooled it and we went to Plaza de Castillo and chilled with the Posse. Galloway sat drunkenly in the chrome chairs at Bar Windsor. His short gray hair tufted up wildly as a red bandanna circled his forehead like a crown. His big, red circus conductor jacket draped off his pudginess. Its illustrious gold stitching contrasted with his many gnarly brown hide necklaces and bracelets that clung to his dirty skin. Galloway collected characters and the Posse was his grand circus of wild souls. He was the loving conductor of that circus. We told and retold the story of the fight with laughter that spilled into raucous hilarity. A British comedian named Milo McCabe rolled with the Posse that year. He fucking loved what I'd done and did several brilliant imitations of my "Dog Killer" rant. Somewhere in that night they added an appendage to my nickname. In Scotland the kilt-wearing warriors would go into berserk mad trances before battle and scream indecipherable threats at their adversaries. They called them Berserkers, and Galloway dubbed me "Buffalo Bill the Berserker" for the way I screamed at the Gypsies. There was something incredibly easing about laughing at myself, and Galloway always found a way to make me laugh at myself. The reason I'd gone so crazy was because I deeply loved the Posse. They were my family, my special family in a very special place. I'd kill to protect them in a heartbeat. Galloway knew that. Galloway was the father of the Posse, and I was a loyal son to him. As we laughed, the rage and fear that had nearly driven me to stab somebody finally cleansed from me and vanished.

Galloway saw a lot of chaos at fiesta over the years. He was on hand for the historic ETA riots in 1979.

"I'd been persuaded to climb the fountain that people jump off of now. No one jumped off it in those days. I climbed it, and as I was trying to get down I fell off it [twenty feet] onto a broken bottle, fucked my back up, ambulance job. And there's this Australian girl there stroking my head as we're waiting for the ambulance and she's saying 'you're cool, you're hip, we'll meet and fuck later,' at the time I'm thinking my back's fucked, I don't think anything like that will happen. They took us to the hospital and fixed me up. And I signed myself out because I was going to run with the bulls in the morning. It was 2:00 a.m. and I could hardly walk, and so I got back to the campsite and I couldn't lay down so my friends made a hammock out of a tent and they put me in the hammock. The next morning I wake up and want to run with the bulls! I'm shouting at my mates saying 'get me out of this hammock you cunts!' 'cause I couldn't really stand, and I wanted them to carry me to the run. I was seriously addicted to running.

"Anyway that's the day the riots happened and Ramon Rodríguez was accidentally shot with about eight bullets in the arena. It's normal that there are a few protesters at the end of the bullfights. There was always a standoff with police. I'd gone the year before and there was a riot, and I got hit with a rubber bullet. We were just drinking at the bar called the Muscle Bar. It was like the fourth or fifth of July and the riot police just come in the bar and start clubbing people so we had to run out the other exit, and we were running up the road there and the police were there shooting at us with rubber bullets and one hit me in the back. So that was kind of the way things were back then.

"In 1979 it started in the ring. Rodríguez was an activist and there were a lot of theories that he was targeted by authorities. Riots sparked off and they canceled fiesta. The next day I was still hurt but I wanted to go up and get a photograph beside the fountain. So I'm walking up there with my back sort of all bandaged up with these belts and stuff. As I get to the monument this crowd comes running past and the police start round the corner firing submachine guns into the air. I had to just hobble away. I could hardly move. I thought fuck it, I'll take the picture with the fountain some other time."

On the final morning I ran at Top of Estafeta, and as the herd approached, encierro opened up for me. The bulls were very light brown, almost white. I saw them easily and they galloped smooth and slowly. I cut into the herd and up beside a tannish-colored bull. A large branded number twenty-three spread along his side. Ran beside him for several strides, then I couldn't help myself and placed my hand smoothly on his undulating back. At first my hand bounced on him. A nearby pastor shouted at me. But then I strode in his cadence and my hand melded with his gait as I glided beside him. I knew it was illegal to touch because if it's done wrong the animal may peel off from the group and attack. When the pastor saw that I was being respectful, he allowed it. The animal wasn't bothered. The lumpy muscularity of his back stretched and constricted smoothly under the fur. It was my first harmonious contact with an animal on the street. Didn't want to push my luck so I decided to stop. I slowed and dipped off to the side. As I did a chalk-white bull appeared by the fencing, coming straight for me. The long white hairs on his neck sprouted and curled wildly around his placid, noble face. The bull resembled a white buffalo. He fell on his belly eight yards away from me—nothing between us. I stood on the horns of the downed beast, a poignant opening that I wasn't pre-pared to walk through just yet. He began to rise, and I lay down on my belly and rolled under the fencing. I settled there on my back laughing joyously as the majestic beast galloped past. The honor to be so close to the pack, the fear of my destiny, and the pure joy the animals gave me once again strained and constricted in my heart. It was over for the year, and I was safe and so very grateful for the gift of another outlandish fiesta.

CHAPTER FOUR:
CAPUCHINO
2009

G ot home charged up for anything that could help me advance on my dreams. I pushed even harder with the Story Slam and writing. In September Irvine invited me to read at the music venue the Metro in Chicago and introduced me to the club's owner, Joe Shanahan. Metro launched the careers of bands like the Smashing Pumpkins, and Shanahan won a Grammy for his work as an event producer. It was absolutely amazing to grace the stage that so many legendary musicians and writers had. It was an honor I'll never forget. The crowd was excited about my performance, and it was a big success. Later in the month we packed the alternative arts space Q4 with over 300 people for a storytelling event featuring Irvine. We set up a live-feed video projection so that the performance in the capped-out basement would project on the main level, which was also full. Afterward, I wrote Joe Shanahan telling him about it, and he said we had to do a Story Slam at Metro. I wasn't foolish enough to book the very next show at Metro because the venue holds about a thousand people and we didn't have a show that could draw that many. Then I figured we could hold the Windy City Story Slam All City Championships at the Metro in January. I pitched the idea to Joe, and he said the door was open.

Kept pushing hard with the show but the drugs and drinking progressively unraveled my mind. At a Story Slam in November I got drunk on some quality whiskey, then snorted a couple rails of white, and toked on some hydro, all in the minutes before the show started. Held it together for the first part of the event, then I completely lost it. I was ruthlessly harsh with my friends. Finally I got into a crazy screaming match with Enid and then I did something I'll never forgive myself for in the midst of it. I'd finally cracked. I was maniacally insane.

Tried to kill myself several times while I walked home across the entire snowy city. I walked straight into traffic three times but the cars swerved around me. Attempted to goad gangbangers into fights but they for some reason decided not to shoot or beat me to death. I finally got home and realized I was going to lose everything if I kept drinking. I somehow got Enid to come home. She was planning to leave me. And I started on the road to sobriety. Realized I would die a lonely, pathetic death if I didn't. Enid would leave me and I'd probably kill myself. I couldn't survive without her love. Enid's love fortified my entire life.

The first week was incredibly tough. I went down to the SGI Buddhist Center in the South Loop each morning that week and stayed for hours chanting. In Nichiren Buddhism you chant to fulfill your wishes. All I wanted was my life back. I'd break into tears at the thought of what I'd nearly destroyed as I chanted in the almost empty room all day. Life was nearly unbearable, but slowly it calmed.

I booked Metro for the first annual Windy City Story Slam All City Championships that January. Local news outlets did several stories on the show, even Chicago's NPR affiliate WBEZ Chicago Public Radio did a big story. I made friends with a producer named Aurora Aguilar for a show called *848* and kept in touch with her. The All City Championships was a monstrous success; 907 people came through the doors that night. We had several glitches; about half of the storytellers didn't have the chops to stare down nearly a thousand people. I even lost it late in the show and threatened a few rowdy attendees. If I'd've been drinking, I'd have leaped into the crowd throwing blows. There were three fistfights and security threw out about twenty people for a variety of incidents: drugs in the bathroom, fights, drunkenness. It was regular punk rock show stats. Clearly, it wasn't your average literary event. By the end I was spent, but the wild success and controversy catapulted me into the arts spotlight in Chicago as the creator and host of a hot new show. I even got a stalker and some hate mail. My response to it all was to vent violent public threats online, which I was, of course, very willing to back up in reality. I continued to push hard with the show and it rambled on.

As San Fermín approached, I pitched Aurora Aguilar to do a story on the running of the bulls in Pamplona for Chicago Public Radio's *848*. She was hesitant, but I urged her with a raw, enthusiastic pitch and finally she said yes. I planned to strap a microphone to my chest and get sounds from inside the run itself. I had no experience with sound engineering and couldn't back up any of my promises. But sometimes you have to promise the world then make it up on the fly if you're going to take that next step. If it blew up in my face I'd still be where I was as a writer, an unpublished nobody. If it even sort of worked I'd establish myself as an exciting new Chicago journalist.

There were two moments in my sobriety I dreaded more than any others. One was after that first run in Pamplona, and the other was the first time I hung out with Irvine. I'd had some of the best times of my life drunk and rampaging through Chicago and Dublin with Irvine, and I knew that seeing him would be about the hardest time to say no. But I did it, and he didn't mind at all and told me he'd gone months on the wagon before and it was always good for him. He praised me for stopping and wished me luck. Some of my other friends couldn't handle my sobriety. They stopped talking to me and spread rumors that I was still drinking. Quitting something and trying to change your life can show you who your real friends are. I didn't give a damn if people drank around me. The first night of sobriety I went to a bar and hung out with my friends. Figured I better get used to it. And I was wise enough to know that sobriety wasn't for everybody. Some people really enjoyed drinking and it hardly hurt them or their relationships in any way, and they led healthy, productive lives and drank when they felt like it. Alcoholics Anonymous honestly helped me through the first month, but after that I just white-knuckled it the rest of the way.

There is an incredible tension that builds up in you in sobriety. I don't know if it's from the restraint it takes to not drink or the change in your brain chemistry from lack of alcohol, but when you implant that tension into your work incredible things happen. You get addicted to working and your projects flourish. I put tremendous energy into the Story Slam and things really started to happen. I created the first ever city-versus-city Story Slam, Chicago versus Philadelphia, and we performed in front of over 300 people at the Philadelphia Library as part of their city book festival. The crowd went completely nuts, but Chicago lost on some questionable hometown judging.

Enid had always wanted to visit London. She first learned English from a teacher who was from London and had a crush on him. She imagined London as a bright, sunny place, with nice people who were very sweet. I tried to tell her that London was a dark, rainy place and the people were, for the most part, surly, even though Johny and his friends were all great people. They were for the most part the exception to the rule. She didn't believe, it but I didn't care. We booked a weeklong trip to London before San Fermín.

Enid hated London. It rained most of the time and she wasn't impressed with Big Ben. She called it Medium Ben, because it wasn't half as big as she expected. We had a great time with Johny and his girlfriend Inga. Johny even had me perform with The Band of Holy Joy in a legendary arts venue called the Shunt Theatre. It was a quarter mile of dark, brick-arched tunnels that housed theaters, cinemas, music venues, and art galleries. Enid loved it, and it pretty much salvaged the trip. We spent the last few days in a little suburb called Crystal Palace where it was sunny and the people were nice.

Aurora Aguilar realized I had no idea what the fuck I was doing and asked the great WBEZ sound technician to help me. Mary was very diligent in her emails and patiently walked me through several different ideas. Tried the different techniques while I sprinted over the grassy fields in a hilly park near our hotel. Mary settled on the idea of taping the microphone to my chest under my shirt. With the little Radio Shack recorder and microphone I had, it was the best option.

We flew to Spain and I introduced Enid to fiesta. She quickly fell in love with it. There were plenty of wily girls from Australia and England for Enid to get drunk with. She melded right into the Posse.

The night before fiesta began, Galloway woke me from a dead sleep. He said he needed my help. Somebody was being abusive to Owan in the Plaza de Castillo. I jumped out of bed and rushed over with him. The perpetrator was gone, and Owan had calmed.

I sat down at a table at Bar Windsor with three Ernest Hemingways. They were a variety of ages and images, different beard lengths, and fatnesses. The finals of the official Ernest Hemingway look-alike contest had just been decided. There was a quiet guy sitting next to me. His name was John. He was soft-spoken and insightful. It took a while for me to realize that he was Ernest Hemingway's grandson, John Hemingway. I told him his grandfather's work changed my life. He said that was nice to hear. John was also an author. He'd written an acclaimed memoir titled *Strange Tribe* about the relationship between his father and Ernest, and about his own relationship with his father, Gregory. It's a beautifully written book that reveals some interesting insights into Ernest's exploration with sexuality and gender. John's father Gregory was also a cross-dresser. He had a partial sex change before his tragic death in a Florida detention center. John renders quite a profoundly complex picture of his Nobel Laureate grandfather, his father, and bipolar disease. I didn't tell him I suffered from it. Was still hiding it from most people. Regardless, John and I hit it off right away.

On the opening morning of runs, I confessed to Gary that I was planning on wearing a microphone and asked if he would tape it to my chest. I couldn't get it to stick right. Gary laughed at my attempts and showed me how he used to tape wires to undercover police officers' chests. He took a long piece of tape and wrapped it around the small microphone twice in the center of the tape. Then he wrapped the tape completely around my chest. Then he doubled another layer of tape around that. It was completely secure. I couldn't believe my luck. Started recording as we got in the "elevator to hell," as Galloway called it, and rode five stories down to street level. Gary and Galloway made ridiculous jokes about the imaginary homosexual intercourse we'd had the night before and called me "gay boy." All I could do was laugh, thinking of what my producer back in Chicago would think of the tape of the ride down.

Whiffed on my run the first morning but I knew my hardest test lay before me at Bar Txoko. Everyone was drinking and Galloway grinned at me and said, "Fancy a beer, Buffalo?"

"No, Graeme, it's for real. I'm done." I grinned at him.

"Okay, well, will you hold this ice cold beer while I go get another round?"

He handed me the beer. The strong smell of the San Miguel on tap made my adrenaline-dry mouth ache for a sip. The coolness of the plastic cup just heightened my thirst. I knew if I took that sip I'd drink the rest of the day and the entire fiesta and would probably be divorced by the time I headed home. Still, the ache to sip clutched at my mouth and throat. Finally I put the beer down on the stone street and laughed to myself at all the madness that beer had caused my life and all that it threatened to take from me. I whispered "no thanks" and when Galloway came back he gave me a wink. That was the dreaded moment. After not taking that sip I knew I'd made it. Knew there was real hope for sobriety. Enid walked up later and I grabbed her and kissed her hard and long on the mouth and told her I loved her. She just laughed obliviously and asked me how my run was.

On the second day, I slashed through the street and ran with the pack for a strong distance. The bulls were thin and fast. A white sheen gleamed on their black fur as they knifed through the crowded street. I came through the tunnel into the arena with the animals behind me and one in front of me. The explosive roar of the 20,000 people inside the plaza surged up and washed over me. It felt like I was scoring a touchdown in the Super Bowl. I unleashed a loud victory cry and raised my rolled-up newspaper in the air triumphantly before I cut out to the side. Later I found a photo where my paper blocked Juan Pedro Lecuona's face. He was directly behind me running right on the horns of a bull. I was embarrassed for doing that sort of amateurish move, but I also realized there was a whole group of runners around Juan who were running the pack very well in an almost protective formation. I analyzed the way they ran and recognized the faces and shirts from older photos and videos. This was a hard-core group of Spanish runners working together to lead and protect the animals.

I wanted in.

Captured good audio and I uploaded it to my computer, but it was difficult to know if it would work in the story. Aurora gave some more tips and I went out the next day and had a good run, but when I reached in my pocket for my recorder it was gone! I'd fallen and it must have slipped out of my pocket and disappeared. I plummeted into despair and tried not to think about it. I had bigger problems.

The Jandilla were set to run the next morning. Their presence at the corrals under the castle wall always heightened my terror. I tried not to focus on it and spent some time with Enid. We went to the fireworks before sunrise. There was a crazy little Scottish guy named Gus Ritchie and his father staying with the Posse that year as punters. Gus was a snarling, hard-drinking nutter from Glasgow, Scotland. He assured me Glasgow was the knife-fight capital of Europe and that all police officers in his neighborhood knew if they wanted to arrest him, "Wee Gus," as they called him, would go down swinging.

I really didn't give a crap and was trying to get that part of my life behind me as much as possible. My dislike for Gus turned to hatred as I started to get to know his kind father. Mr. Ritchie was the absolute opposite of Gus: a tall, thin, kind man with soft, childlike eyes and a warm heart that poured into any words he spoke. We all sat in the grassy field near the fortress walls watching the orange sunset. Mr. Ritchie's eyes suddenly sparkled with tears and he said, "I've always believed a place like this existed in the world, where people act this beautiful to each other." Tears streamed down his face. "And now I've been there, now I've been there . . . " He was putting words to the exact emotions San Fermín stirred in me. I was about say so when Gus snapped at him to "come off it and quit crying like an old sap." I really wanted to beat the fuck out of Gus then.

Instead, I distanced myself from them and curled up with Enid on the damp, cool grass near the Posse as the night took the sky. I was happy, happy at all Enid and I had overcome and how a couple no one would have ever given a chance at making it had made it. How all the big dreams we made were starting to come true little by little.

As the time for the fireworks approached, the entire field filled with Spaniards. The Africans wandered among the revelers selling all types of flashing-light necklaces and batons like you can get at the circus. Throbbing neon lights speckled the dark crowd and percolated like lightning bugs. Suddenly a commotion erupted and Galloway called out.

"Buffalo! Buffalo!" Genuine fear strained his voice. I rushed over to him. Two Spanish guys jumped up. There was a guy stumbling around near them. One of the Spanish guys hit him with a good shot to the side of his head, and as he fell, the other Spaniard nailed him with an even better punch and the guy collapsed flat on his face behind Galloway. When I got close Galloway grabbed my arm and pulled me to him. Everyone shouted to sit down, and that the police were coming. I crouched next to Galloway, trembling.

"Who is that?! Who is that?!"

The guy tried to get up but was seriously dazed.

"It's some drunk American cunt. I don't know him," Galloway explained. "He was stepping on people in the dark."

I took a deep breath, relieved it wasn't one of us. The Spaniards were pretty tough and good with their hands. I looked over at them. They scowled at me as they sat. A little girl cried in the middle of their family group. The American guy, being stupid, must have stepped on the little girl and got a smack for it. I was thankful I'd been cool enough to not jump in headfirst to save some asshole. Then the drunk American stood up. He was crying and bleeding and smashed.

"You're a couple assholes!" the American screeched at them.

The Spaniards looked up at him, shaking their heads and sneering. I knew at any second they'd really fuck him up. Something in the guy's pathetic stupor made me feel sorry for him. He was an absolute fucking mess. I got up and showed my palms to the Spaniards and talked to the guy.

"Hey man, be cool, okay . . . I'm gonna get you outta here."

I walked up slowly and bear-hugged him. "You're gonna be fine," I whispered.I walked him carefully out of the maze of people sitting in the dark field as the fireworks streamed into the sky and erupted above. The bright bursts lit our way. I walked him to a wooded lot at the edge of the field. He explained he was on military leave, waiting to be deployed to Afghanistan. He was there with his brother. He'd lost him, and he'd been looking for him for a whole day when he stumbled into the Spaniards. I tried to cool him off as he wept furious tears. He was planning to run the next morning. We stood near a tree as the fireworks lit the sky like flares.

"You're a fucking mess, kid. There's no way you can run tomorrow."

"Fuck you! You don't know what the fuck you're talking about!" he screamed, clenching his fists. "You don't understand. You don't understand what it means if I can't find him." He broke into agonized tears.

I took a deep breath. I wanted to stay with him and look out for him but he didn't want any help.

"Look, kid, this is all I can do for you. Go to sleep right here by these trees. You aren't gonna find your brother like this and you can't fucking run like this."

"I'm gonna find him. We're gonna run tomorrow, together." He wiped his tears and blood into a smear across his young face. "Come on, let's get a drink." He started toward the bright carnival across the street.

I just sighed and said "good luck." I walked back to find the Posse as the fireworks ended.

I found them packing up. One of the Posse girls hugged me. "You were the hero again, Buffalo," she said.

I just kept worrying about the kid and wondered what he had ahead of him. Afghanistan and Iraq were still rampaging.

Enid was mad at me. She walked up and crossed her arms over her chest.

"Why do you always have to be the one to do something?"

I shrugged. "I don't know."

I'd let that ruin the sweet time we'd been having and hadn't gotten to watch the fireworks with her. I was sad and tried to make it up to her as we walked back to the plaza.

Nightmares and tremors troubled my sleep. A heavy dark force entered my room. It hovered over me. Its weight pushed on my chest and it whispered urgently. *Don't run tomorrow . . . It's a bad day . . . A very bad day . . .* I tried to rouse myself but it pinned me to the mattress. I woke in bed with Enid. The glass door to our balcony clanked with the breeze as the fiesta night rumbled on below us at Town Hall. I acknowledged the message from wherever the hell it came from, but not running wasn't an option so I got up to the HQ early. Gary and Galloway tried to get me to think happy thoughts on the couch, puppies and kittens like we usually did before the run. I just smiled and was very grateful to be there with them and not alone on the street in the masses of strangers. We entered Estafeta and I fell into the zone, turned my mind off, and felt all of it: the animals waiting at the edge of town, the terror of the first-timers, and the serenity of the Spanish across the way.

Nervous, I stood there on Estafeta, awaiting the ancient rite. I gazed down the narrow, quarter-mile straightaway—a slow decline, then an abrupt turn out of sight. The buildings jettisoned up steep on both sides of the street—like the cliffs of a deep-cut canyon. They shrouded the cobblestones in shadows. Spectators perched thick on the railings of the long balconies strung along both sides. Their cameras dangled lazily from necks and wrists. Red-and-white clad mozos flocked the length of the street. Some there on a half-drunk lark. Others followed directly in the footsteps of dozens of familial generations. This is a tradition tallied in centuries. I prayed quietly as I bounced on my toes, inhaling the brisk mountain air and exhaling faint billows of steam: *Nam-myoho-renge-kyo Nam-myoho . . .*

Hope to find a good line to that mecca just before the tips of a bull's horns swirled through my arms and neck and heart. Murmurs echoed between the many still runners. The boarded-up storefronts made Estafeta Street look like a coastal town braced for an imminent hurricane. The hot-lime scent of adrenaline swirled through the air like rumors and parched my mouth.

The stick-rocket tore into the sky in the distance. It burst high above the town. We waited as an immense, panicked roar swelled. It sent the first wave of would-be runners soaring past us by the hundreds. A portly, stubble-faced Englishman with a sangria-stained shirt swept past. His terrified eyes bulged. All of them sprinted at full gait toward the valientes' embrace in the arena. I waited and knew there would be a second wave and a third. Galloway spouted out the countdown beside me in his visceral Scottish accent. Then it got to fifteen. I let the gushing current of bodies drag me downstream—bounding on my toes. I looked back—hoping for a glimpse of the pack. Then I saw the sparkle of camera flashes approach the near balconies—like two surging swarms of flickering lightning bugs. I turned and ran without looking back.

I bolted into the center of the street. Swiftly, I dipped past runners who cut across my path. The canyon of buildings ended in my periphery. The warm, clear light touched us. The street widened. Double rows of four-plank oak barricades suddenly corralled us at each side. The thunder of the herd rose up behind me and rattled the stone beneath my sneakers. I took the soft bend at Telefónica and glanced over my shoulder to pick them up. The steers trotted out front again—tall, upright, and fast. White fur with brown patches stretched around their giant heads. Their malformed asymmetrical horns warped like dead-wood branches. Bells dangled wildly from their necks and panged like cymbals. I slowed and let them pass. A gap in the crowd opened in the steers' wake. I saw them. The lead bull galloped low and deep. Its wide neck pulsed and flared. His silky jet-black fur stretched taut over the bowling ball-sized knots of sculpted muscle at the shoulders. A silver sheen glimmered across his back. He raised his massive head. His torso stretched. The horns reached out and up like a cleric, arms raised delivering a sermon. He loped down the slowly declining stone slope. Behind him, four of his dark-furred, hulking brothers kept pace hooves clapping over stones. Spaniards in bold-colored shirts speckled in among them. Others in white stood sucked up against the barricades motionless—making way.

I crossed the lead bull's snout to let him approach on the right and at the callejón he was close. We rambled toward the tunnel. The barricades funneled us into a bottleneck of sprinting men and galloping beasts. The rank, acrid stench scorched my nostrils. Adrenaline shot white light through my thighs. I dashed into the tunnel at full-gait, breaking and torquing to get in front of the horn. And for a moment, I was there, in front of the horn. All of us formed into a herd—one force rambling forward. The tunnel cleared. Hooves crackled at my back. The air compressed all around, then wind, a roar, sand beneath my shoes. A rocket exploded above. I dip to the left and they pass into the center of the ring. The crowd loved them. Everyone rose to their feet. A tremble of applause shuddered through the circular stands of the full 20,000-seat arena.

Most of the herd passed into the corrals quickly. A huge boom swelled into the sky outside the arena; it wasn't a stick-rocket. The crowd reacted to something else with torrential roars and gasps. Up in the stands on a huge Jumbotron screen, a heavily muscular brown bull stopped and scanned at Telefónica. Then he tore into a runner in a green shirt—gored him and cartwheeled him into the air. The crowd roared over the arena walls. I realized it was a live shot. *Go out and help bring him in.* It was that simple. Across the ring, several Spaniards in bold, striped shirts made that same decision and tore toward the tunnel in a tight pack like a fleet of fighter jets. I followed.

As I got to the tunnel a black bull refused to enter the corral in my periphery across the ring. His forelegs planted straight hooves deep in the sand. He tossed and thrashed his horns up and through the dobladore's large, pink, luring cape. I remembered a dream, someone speaking to me in a calm familiar voice. *There'll be two left.*

I ran up the tunnel and slowed at the callejón. Something dragged at my chest as I pushed against the current. Then there he was; the brown bull, his silky almost orange fur gleaming metallic in the sunlight. One of the greatest contemporary Spanish runners, David Rodríguez Lopez, engaged him. Rodríguez was clad in all white with two crisp green patches at the chest. He turned the animal over and over. The bull swayed, his massive neck wrapped in rippling muscle as he gouged at the other mozos. Five pastores stood behind him in their green collared shirts. They formed a wall that sealed off the mob of onlookers down the street. I knew this may be my only chance to help bring in a suelto.

I worked my way up slowly along the left-side barricades. He turned and galloped heavily past, scanning. The number 106 was emblazoned into his flesh—it stretched bulbous across his side and dissipated like cloud-letters. Blood smeared on the tips of his sharpened arm-length horns. He paused and I passed him. Suddenly he halted and locked on me. A light-brown ring encircled his black pit of an eye. My heart thumped. He looked like a ghost, just two arm lengths away. My body's motions began to freeze involuntarily—the legs, then the arms, the neck. It swept onto me cold as the touch of death. The hard-oak post pressed against my back. Another runner darted past and waved a red silk scarf before his gaping froth-covered mouth. The bovine turned with this motion, and my body was suddenly mine again. I limbered and went. Jetted around several runners, and I came to face him— side by side with the others. I bent my knees and pointed my right shoulder down toward his snout. Stretched my rolled-up newspaper and I waved it low in his line of sight. He unleashed a wrathful bellow and lunged toward us. His thick horns hooked slightly inward—like they were reaching out to snatch the life from us. I twisted and leaped into a sprint. The runners behind me reacted slower, steadier. I tripped on their feet. Someone shoved my back and I toppled belly-down. With my last bit of balance, I dug my shoe into the stones and dove toward the barricade. I stretched my arms like a base runner sliding headfirst. A cop and another runner, as if they were waiting for me on the other side, each caught me by an arm. They pulled me under and to my feet, and in one swoop I was safe and watching the bull make its final turn into the Plaza de Toros.

Hugged the runner and shook the cop's hand. Then I walked out between the narrow double barricades. A shiny black nightstick abruptly pressed into my chest. Beyond it, the neon-orange suits of the Red Cross rushed in to treat a gored victim in a green shirt. He screamed out and gripped his trembling thigh. Bright red blood splattered the blue-gray stones and soaked into his torn white pants. I stepped back through the barricades into the street as waves of faces by the hundreds flashed past. A freckled-skinned woman with long, sandy-blond hair gusted by rhythmically—her long strands fluttered. They bobbed into a blur. All of them headed into the arena for the vacas. I walked slowly against them. A commotion across the street drew me. Someone yelled hysterically. Walked up to the barricades and looked. The medics worked on a man lying on the ground in a brown striped shirt. Another runner hovered over him and screamed inconsolably. The man on the ground looked like he was just resting peacefully. A nearby cop slammed his nightstick on the barricades near my face. I walked away.

Later we found out a runner died at Telefónica. I ran around to the media center and tried to scrape together the facts. There was a lot of misinformation. Some people said it happened at Town Hall. Some said the dead runner was an American. Then a journalist showed me an image of the goring, and I recognized the runner's shirt from a photo I'd bought from a run earlier that week. I was shoulder to shoulder with him as we ran up the street in Telefónica near the herd. The more I thought about it, it must have been the guy resting peacefully on the other side of Telefónica. He was Spanish, I was sure, and argued with the journalists in the press office and brought the photo to *Diario de Navarra* and told them it was the dead runner. They scanned it, and it appeared in the following morning's paper along with an article of what'd happened. Twenty-seven-year-old Daniel Jimeno Romero was running Telefónica and working his way to the herd when he fell into a large pileup. The pile kept him down for a long time. The brown bull named Capuchino fell at Town Hall, and from then on he was a suelto. Capuchino galloped full speed as he entered Telefónica. He didn't see the soft bend until it was too late. He barreled into it in the exact spot where Jimeno was attempting to pull himself under the bottom barricade. Capuchino slammed into the fence at full gait. His horn entered Jimeno's neck just above his clavicle. It penetrated his thorax in a downward angle—severing the aorta. He bled to death in moments. Jimeno was from the town of Alcala de Henares outside Madrid. He was an avid runner whose family had run for generations.

There is a terrible gravity that falls over fiesta after a death. Galloway, Hemingway, and I went to the corrida that evening. Capuchino came out first with terrible ferocity.

"What a beautiful animal," Hemingway said with a somber awe.

Capuchino barreled into the picador's horse and toppled him to the sand with his first mighty upward thrust, though he was the smallest of his brothers. And later, the sword through his heart, the crescent-shaped shadow of the arena cut across his boulderish back. The light bathed the fur on his face gold. Barbed bandilleros clung into the mound of muscle behind his head. Their green- and yellow-clothed sticks dangled down just above the sand as blood bubbled up around the silver handle of the sword embedded between the shoulders. Large beads of deep red rolled down his neck and forelegs and stained his fur purple. The current grew into glistening rivers that cascaded down to dark globs on the white sand at the sides of his coral-colored hooves. The animal refusing to die. Thousands rose to their feet as El Bravo Capuchino finally knelt: noble, with pride, chin raised in the pose of Taurus. His whole torso heaved, mouth agape, spewing blood. Then he rolled to his side. His legs flung out stiff and trembling—kicking up tufts of white sand. Until the mercy of the dagger sliced his spine and he went off. A switch turned. The crowd erupted. Their roar swirled through the circled stands and lifted up to the white light of the Spanish sky and the heavens beyond.

The next morning, I ran Telefónica but pulled up short and didn't go for it. The fear and magnitude of the run settled on me. Enid was very scared. I knew I was putting a terrible load on her by running. She was thinking of leaving town. It made me deeply question everything. I went up to the castle wall to see the bulls and meditate on just what the hell I was doing. The bulls were *Miura*, known as The Bulls of Death, because they killed many matadors over the centuries. They were especially large, and their horns were incredibly wide, long, and perfectly shaped. One black- and white-speckled one was particularly monstrous and agitated. *Why on earth am I putting my life in such ridiculous danger?* I walked from the ledge, but something deep inside kept me there, and I sat on the sloped stone hill. My heart strained, and I cupped my face in my hands and closed my eyes. *One of these animals could fucking kill you tomorrow. Why am I sitting here?!* I tried to imagine my life without the run. I imagined if I gave up on all the special things in my life that I loved so dearly, my novel, my writing, if I just stopped all the nonsense and got a good job like my mom always said I should. I imagined working in some office downtown writing ads, having kids. I saw myself, old, gray, and broken at forty, my spirit wilted, a cog in the machine, a guy who had a dream and let it go, walking aimlessly and anonymously through downtown rush hour. *FOR WHAT?!* I stepped into my daydream, walked right up and accosted myself. The elder manifestation of myself stared back at me with empty gray eyes, startled like he thought he'd never see me again. *What could be so important to give up? I refuse to motherfucking be you! I'd rather die now, here in a place I love.* He watched me and began to grin, the color returned to his blue eyes and they lit like cobalt flames. *There are only a few things in my life that I truly love, and the encierro is one of them.*

I opened my eyes, and I was there on the sloped stone plane before the castle wall overlooking the bullpen. Children ran around excitedly trying to get a glimpse of the bulls. A father bent and picked up his baby girl so she could see. She squealed in his arms and pointed down excitedly: "Toro! Toro!"

HERO

There are special mozos. It's easy to spot them. They run each morning, usually in the same stretch—their *querencia* (haven). They link with the animals. It's as if the animals find them, seek them out as their guide, and follow them to their destiny.

For that handful of special runners, each has a time when fate calls them to be more than men, more than is possible. They become the calm in the chaos, the anchor of order in the whirlwind. For some it is a hidden moment in a small town where their name is forever entrenched in the street, their image burned into the minds and souls of the villagers. For others it occurs in places like Pamplona where the ignorant eyes of the world fumble upon them, mystified by their actions.

That next morning fate thrust itself onto a mozo named David Rodríguez Lopez and formed him into a dynamo. It wasn't the first time this happened with David Rodríguez, and it wouldn't be the last.

Graeme and Gary convinced me to run down at Santo Domingo, and I tried to do the Butcher's Guild run but failed. The pack hit a man and knocked him unconscious. We formed the wall to protect him and the Red Cross workers from the sweeper steers. Unbeknownst to me, true horror was unfolding in the tunnel into the arena as I stood down at Santo Domingo. A white and black-speckled Miura bull named Ermitaño slipped at La Curva and spun around as an American runner, Rick Musica, loped behind him. Musica stopped, petrified as Ermitaño locked on him and charged. Rick backpedaled as Ermitaño surged, when suddenly José Antonio appeared, and he called to Ermitaño. The bull swung with him and followed José Antonio through the curve and up Estafeta.

Later at Telefónica David Rodríguez engaged Ermitaño and was working him up the way. The man and bull danced in a circular fury. It was like San Fermín possessed David and compelled him to exorcise the hellish fury from Ermitaño, and for a moment David quelled the beast, but Ermitaño escaped David's spell and accelerated toward the tunnel. A forty-four-year-old veteran runner named Pello Torreblanca dashed before Ermitaño's horns. Ermitaño bellowed and lunged in an extraordinary leaping dive. His long muscular legs with the white ankles and hooves extended airborne. In midair, Ermitaño gored Torreblanca in the thigh and flung him upward. Many runners came to Torreblanca's aid. David Rodríguez grabbed hold of Ermitaño's tail. Ermitaño's next move was to insert his horn in the center of Torreblanca's chest and lift him high off his feet and pin him to the inner wall of the tunnel. He looked like a man impaled on a tall spear. Dark blood spewed from Torreblanca's mouth. When Torreblanca finally unhinged from the horn, Ermitaño bellowed savagely. In the chaos the others released their grip on Ermitaño's tail. Rodríguez held tight. Ermitaño dragged Rodríguez to where he undressed Torreblanca and split him open for all the world to see. Rodríguez held that tail by himself. It was Torreblanca's only hope to survive. Finally Ermitaño relinquished his attack and tried to swing back at Rodríguez while other mozos dragged Torreblanca to safety. The animal surged through the tunnel to find his brothers in the pen.

Undoubtedly Rodríguez had nearly single-handedly saved Torreblanca's life. Enid started calling David Rodríguez "my hero." I didn't mind it. It didn't make me jealous because, hell, he was a hero. He might have been my hero too. I began to idolize Rodríguez's running. I didn't know the term just yet, but Rodríguez became my *maestro* from a distance. My teacher and guru, though I'd never spoken a word with him. If one day fate called for it, I deeply wanted to help him stop a bull from attacking a mozo by holding the animal's tail with him.

When I saw the horrific goring of Torreblanca on TV, I was sure that he would die. It appeared that Ermitaño had gored him directly in the heart. I deeply regretted that I hadn't been with the runners at Telefónica. Felt I'd let them down by not being there to at least attempt to help with Ermitaño. Who knows if I'd have been much more help than I was with Capuchino? Regurdless, I realized that it was my duty to run Telefónica. That I owed it to the other runners to be there and contribute to the encierro there.

Torreblanca survived. The horn had miraculously slipped between the ribs and the heart. He made a swift recovery.

The final morning, Graeme gave me his old running shirt: a black and blue-striped long-sleeved rugby jersey with the number nine on it. I was very honored to wear it and would do so for many years to come. He then said he fancied a go at the curve and wanted me to run with him there. I reluctantly agreed. Telefónica was my duty, but the Posse was my family, and it was Galloways first time running the curve in all his decades running. We all headed down to the curve for the final morning.

Milo said he was going to follow me no matter what I did. I said, "Okay, but it's seriously dangerous."

As the rocket went off, Milo stepped up right beside me.

I stood beside Joe Distler. He looked very ready to have a go. We weren't talking much yet, but I was watching him closely. He looked anxious and stood way out in the street. Seeing Distler working himself like that gave me shivers. *My god. A guy in his sixties, a guy who was already proven a legend was taking it to the limit one more time.* The magic of that shocked me. I knew I had to follow him.

I told Milo, "Don't follow me. I don't know what I'm gonna do."

As the herd careened around the bend at Town Hall and surged onto Mercaderes, Joe dashed through the curve. *If I ever want to be like him, I gotta go.* Tom Turley dashed past me as I bounced on my toes. A pair of horns flashed through the chaos on Mercaderes and ran out into the curve. As I was dead center in the curve I glanced back. A thundering lead suelto barreled at me. I ran hard. The animal catapulted two runners into the air. A mozo beside me grabbed hold of my shirt and pulled me toward the bull's horns. I dug in and sprinted hard as the bull gathered and made the bend clean. The grayish-black bull unleashed a visceral, screaming bellow and bounded at us. His massive muscular neck flexed and he flung his head and hook-shaped horns high as his forehooves kicked upward behind me. The man's grip broke. The animal's horns hovered a yard behind my back. Whipped my strides, clean and deliberate. The beast plowed forward. I cut out as he catapulted up the street like a rocket. I folded back in toward the center of the street, trying to run with the rest of the pack, but I was too far out to get a good line. Regardless, San Fermín had blessed me with the most spectacular run of my life. I'd led the lead animal through the curve.

Walked around in a daze. I asked myself out loud, "Did that really just happen?" Enid yelled from the Posse balcony above the curve. She motioned for me to come back. I jogged over. She shouted, "Graeme is hurt!" I saw Galloway on a stretcher surrounded by Red Cross. Fiona bustled around him. She told me to go get Will. Greame wasn't gored but he'd hit his head and went unconscious.

I ran down to the HQ and up to the sixth floor. It was locked. I banged hard on the door and rang the bell over and over. I jetted up to the door at the upper level and smashed my fists into that door. Ran back downstairs yelling but trying not to sound too panicked so I wouldn't freak out Will. Then someone opened the door upstairs and I ran up into Will's room and told him, "Your dad got hurt in the run. He's on his way to the hospital. We gotta go and meet him there. He didn't get gored but he hit his head."

Will just stared at me in a mystified, hungover stupor. I told him to get ready and we'd grab a cab, then walked out of the room. Both Will and his girlfriend just sat there staring blankly at each other. I walked out to let them get dressed and waited for about two minutes. Then his girlfriend said, "Buffalo, are you serious?" I ran back in and said, "Will, your dad is in an ambulance right now going to the hospital. Fiona sent me to get you and take you to the hospital! He's okay, I think he just hit his head but he went unconscious."

Will finally snapped out of it and we rushed to the street and got a cab to the ER.

They were doing tests on Galloway when we found Fiona in a waiting room. She was tough and told Will to buck up, that everything would be fine, but you could tell she wasn't sure. Graeme was running when the pastores hit him with the gate that they swing shut after the last bull passes the curve. He fell backward and hit his head on the stones. Finally they brought us in to see him. We tried to be peppy but he was a little shaken and scared, and it was very hard to see Padre like that. Gary found a way to make him laugh at himself and we all had a laugh and told him we loved him before we left. They released him a few hours later.

The replays on TV showed me in slow motion through the curve leading the bull. More importantly, I'd run directly in the footsteps of the greatest living American runner, Distler, and the greatest recent American runner, Turley. In doing so I had possibly the most spectacular run of an American that year. It was an incredible honor.

A few weeks later *Life* magazine published a photo of me directly on the horns of the bull with the guys behind me flying into the air. That's when I realized the two guys who the bull nailed were the cocky Frenchmen who were on my tour the day before and wouldn't take my advice about not running the curve on their first morning. They both ended up in the hospital.

When I arrived home, Aurora called me into the *848* studio at WBEZ and we worked on the script and rifled through the audio. I put together what I thought was a great script—getting the most out of the audio and reading as a sort of a diary of a serious runner. Aurora liked the audio ideas but wanted to cut and edit the script. She wrote a bunch of edits that went against everything I believed in as a runner. I was ready to just pull the plug on the whole operation when Enid talked me out of it. Spoke with Aurora, and she told me she wasn't married to any of the changes and we found a compromise. Then she wanted to go ahead without using the most thrilling audio of all.

We sat in one of the cubicles at Chicago Public Radio. It was about 5:00 p.m.

"Aurora, listen to this audio. This is the whole story right here!" I urged.

"It just sounds like a bunch of muffled sounds."

"I'll explain it as it happens."

There was the boom of the first rocket.

"That's the rocket."

A heartbeat thumped hard.

"What's that?"

"My heartbeat, I think."

"What?!"

"Yeah, the mic is taped against my heart."

"Wow."

There was the sound of hundreds of people running and yelling like maniacs.

"Okay, that's the panicked first-time runners. Wait, wait, there'll be another wave. Hear it?"

"Yeah," she said, her eyebrows raised.

"Okay, that's Graeme giving the false call . . . " WBEZ staffers milled by as I excitedly explained the sounds. "Okay, now they're close. Hear the bells? Those are the steers. I'm running now."

"Now you hear the hooves? The bulls' hooves! I'm running with the pack now. You hear the funneling sound. We're in the tunnel! Now the roar. We're in the arena! That's 20,000 people cheering!"

I spoke loud and urgently. When I looked up, a group of producers, hosts, and writers from some of the top NPR shows in the country had stopped what they were doing and gathered around us. It was surreal.

"Now do you understand why we have to use it?"

"Yes, yes, it works when you describe it. Why don't we just do that? I can play the audio and you can describe it as it happens, and I'll layer them for the piece."

We did it and it worked. A few months later the story won a Great Lakes Regional Edward Murrow Award, the equivalent to the Pulitzer for radio journalism. It ended up a finalist for the National Edward Murrow Award.

The story led to several other pieces for WBEZ; all were received well. It was a strong beginning in the established broadcast/publishing world.

It solidified something for me that'd stay with me for the rest of my life. If you have a dream, you must go for it, daring everything to make a big splash. If you fail, you have lost nothing, and you can learn from that failure. If you dare nothing, you stand to gain nothing, and you will stagnate. If you dare and succeed, you will gain everything. My dream hadn't come true. I wasn't a world-renowned author or among the greatest contemporary bull runners. What I'd gained was a beginning as a runner and as a writer. And my luck overwhelmed me with hope and gratitude, and I planned to take full advantage of my triumphs to gain even greater ones.

CHAPTER FIVE:
SUELTO
2010

My work with the Story Slam progressed and flourished. I also continued to do audio essays for *848*. Did a piece about my life working as a construction laborer and even ran a job breaking concrete with a small crew. The essay went over well, and we made money on the breaking.

I got into it with my brother John when we were pouring concrete one day. One of the forms wasn't filling up and we argued about how to fix it. John is a big bull of a guy. He picked up a handful of wet concrete out of his bucket and threw it in my face. I scooped up the heavy, wet stuff out of my bucket and whipped some right back in his mug. Was wearing a full harness and I told him to let me get out of it. I was walking away and half out of my harness when he charged at me. I rehooked what I could before he got close, then I hit him with a hard jab and knocked him down. He jumped up and grabbed my harness, and I hit him with a right hook that sent all the gooey concrete on his face shooting off in a big explosion. He grabbed hold of me on unsteady legs then he wrestled me to the ground, and the guys on the crew separated us. I got up took my harness and shirt off and my friend Aldolfo gave me a bottle of apple juice to wash the concrete out of my eyes. Then I ran back at John. I lit him up with some punches. He didn't want any of it so he dove at me to wrestle me again. I got him in a guillotine choke. We tumbled into a basket lift and I busted my ribs against it. He kept trying to raise his head, which let me get the guillotine choke deeper. Then I dug in real hard and bowed his head with the guillotine choke and I felt his body strain to breath. He panicked and said *I quit* and tapped my arm for me to let go. I said, *hell no*, and choked him harder. His legs began to crumble underneath himself as he passed out. I knew I could choke him completely out, and then let go and kick him square in the head and knock him into a coma. But suddenly I thought about my dad. Thought about how all our fighting was hurting him. I released my choke on John and held him up from falling over. Didn't want to hurt him or the job that we'd all tried so hard to make profitable. I just didn't want to fight with my brothers anymore. John left, and I went back to pouring concrete in buckets the rest of the day.

I finished my course work for my master's degree in January and decided to take a monthlong trip with Enid to Oaxca, Mexico, to get a strong second draft on my novel. It went well, and I came home ready to go. We held the second All City Championships with another huge crowd; somewhere around 400 people showed. John Hemingway was the main feature, and I walked out of the Double Door, a cool Chicago music venue, with a thousand bucks in my pocket. Then I concocted the first-ever National Story Slam and held it at the Chicago Tribune Printers Row Lit Festival on the main stage in the Pritzker Auditorium in the Harold Washington Library Center in downtown Chicago. We brought in ten storytellers from ten cities across the country and performed to over 300 people.

Heading into fiesta, I secured a gig with Public Radio International's *The World* to broadcast an excerpt of my old essay with some new audio from that year. I also landed a spot on National Public Radio's *The Story* and talked about my first run with the host, Dick Gordan. It broadcast on the opening morning of fiesta. It received a ton of positive feedback but Gordan cut a very important line and made me look a little foolish. I'd said, "I've been running with the bulls for five years, and even I don't feel that I completely understand it." Then he cut the important next line: "And I know a thousand times more about the run than most people, especially those who've never even been to fiesta."

He knew that there were plenty of PETA members in his listenership and he needed to cater to them. I was fine with it, but it propelled me to want to be a better spokesperson for the run.

When we got to HQ, Graeme sprung an idea on me that made my heart sink. He wanted to film a documentary that year about three serious mozos running the entire course from start to finish. Wherever you ended your run one day, that was the spot you began your run the next. Step by step, each of us would run the entire course. I wanted nothing to do with it, but Graeme was so excited about it I just didn't say anything.

I got in the elevator with Gary. He said, "Friendships can't be one-sided, Bill. You have to give sometimes too." That stung, because it made me face the fact that Graeme had given me so much over the years. Without him I could have never afforded fiesta. All the tremendous memories I'd shared with him, it was almost always Graeme giving to me. I knew I had to do it. I even played it up that I was excited about it, but felt that I was sacrificing incredibly valuable days up at Telefónica.

I walked over to Plaza de Castillo and ran into Wee Gus. He grinned at me and said, "Hi, Buffalo Bill!" Gus coming back really disappointed me. Then I found out Graeme hired him as a Posse worker and I almost vomited. *I gotta to deal with this aggro cunt the whole fiesta?!* Gus saw it on my face and seemed confused by it. I just walked away. Fiesta had gotten off to a bad start.

The first morning we were set to do the suicide run. I took a few strides down then jetted up Santo Domingo as fast and as far as I could. I ended up on TV for a good distance but peeled off early because I wasn't comfortable there. I made it almost all the way up the hill to Town Hall.

The next morning I ran through to Town Hall. I strode beside the pack. A gorgeous photo of me running beside the final bull with the epic golden sunlight cutting across the animal's back surfaced later. We started just before Town Hall on the third morning. I crammed in near the front as the police line broke. Tom Turley walked past chatting with a friend. I shouted, "Tom, *suerte!*" He absentmindedly looked at me and shook my hand firmly. An enormous electric charge surged through his hand and throttled my entire body. A powerful rush coursed inside me. I gasped awestruck as he drifted away. *What the fuck was that?* It was like he'd handed something to me.

At the rocket I dashed off, planning to run the curve, but I passed through the curve early and ran up Estafeta. I struggled for position on the slippery street. A dense pack of runners jostled me. Suddenly the roaring herd crashed into the curve. The deafening ramble of the pack swelled at my back as mozos shoved and elbowed me. They grasped my shirt and wrenched me sideways. Glanced back: a lead steer then a gap before a galloping black bull. Made a quick cut in and ended up directly in front of the surging bull. It closed in on me; its sharpened horn neared my back. I cut out of his path. My sneakers slipped on the damp street. Another mozo caught my elbow and kept me up as the rest of the herd rambled past.

After the herd evaporated I leaned against a storefront. My lungs burned and I swallowed back a mouthful of vomit. The near fall and close brush with the bull rattled me, but I was more frustrated that I still hadn't achieved my goal of a long, sustained run on the horns— something I hadn't yet accomplished in over thirty attempts and five years, and a feat many runners never achieve. As I sat there dejected, a commotion down near the curve edged slowly my way. It sounded like a horrible brawl.

I knew it was a suelto and I knew I'd have a chance to help bring him up the street, and that was my final thought. Slowly, I worked toward him, sifting through the crowd. Put your back to the boarded-up shops and wait as the animal slowly moves the runners past you. The bull spun disorientedly. He slipped and fell then sluggishly climbed to his hooves. The mozos nearest him called to him but he ignored them and walked slowly up the path. My heart leaped as he approached. The massive 675-kilogram, jet-black bovine paused and stared at his reflection in a large, dark window. A red streak ran between his bouldery shoulders down the center of his back all the way to his tail. He peered into the glass, hoping for this mysterious black shadow staring back at him to break off in the direction his brothers had gone and show him the way. His name was *Tramposo* (The Cheater) and he was the largest animal of fiesta that year and one of the biggest ever to run in Pamplona. His horns spread wide and tall and splintered into dozens of needle-thin points at the tips. I stepped past the front line of older experienced Spaniards. Bent at the knees and waved my newspaper low where Tramposo could see it. After a tense moment he gathered and lunged. We all turned and ran, the entire glob of one hundred mozos surged like a thick school of fish evading a predator.

At first, mistrust kept me paranoid that I'd turn and there'd be a guy standing still behind me, and he would trip me up and get me gored. Slowly, the other runners instilled trust in me. The animal's rhythmic charges even gave me confidence and faith. Tramposo and I linked. I didn't have to look back to know. Sensed him readying to charge, and as he did the sound of his breath and hooves and even his rank odor told me how close he was and how fast he approached. It was nothing short of mystical.

We worked Tramposo slowly up the long, gently inclined cobblestone straightaway of Estafeta. Suddenly a runner paced beside me in all white, the top half of his shirt bold green. *It's David Rodríguez!* A nervous shudder rattled through me and I almost jumped in a doorway to hide. David's presence intimidated me more than being a couple of yards from frickin' Tramposo! Miguel Angel Perez, who I'd watched save Xabier Salillas my first year, ran next to David. The three of us progressed in a perfect shell formation before the suelto with David in the center. I fought off the feelings of intimidation as the bull stalled his charge in front of us. Then I swooped in closer, waved my paper below his horn in his visual field, and he charged hard and clean.

My legs began to lock up and ignore my requests to jet away as quickly as I wanted to. I decided to get out rather than become a problem. I jogged ahead and crawled out under the bottom barricade at Top of Estafeta. Slimy grime slathered all over my front. As I stood on the other side, Tramposo, as if he was following my scent, barreled into the same thick oak fence beside me. His horn penetrated the thigh of a man who attempted to climb the fence. The horn passed through the thigh and dug into the oak plank with a bang. Tramposo pulled his horn out and gouged at another mozo. Police and medics immediately pulled the man to safety and laid him at my feet. The young man's eyes rolled up in the back of his head. Foam dribbled from his quivering mouth. He emitted a seething screech through his teeth and his whole body convulsed like he was electrified. Blood gushed and spurted from both holes and soaked his white pants.

A slack-jawed Gypsy with a mullet climbed in through the surging spectators along the outer fence. He raised a little digital camera and took a photo of the man's agony. The Gypsy's irreverence disgusted me so much I reached back to punch a hole through his chest, but caught myself and didn't follow through.

I looked back through the inner barricades to the street. David Rodríguez grabbed hold of Tramposo's tail. Tramposo spun and dragged Rodríguez away. David's feet slid like he was on water skis. A sharp stab of regret plunged into my solar plexus for getting out—like I'd broken some sacred bond. I'd let David down. Went to climb back in to help, but a policeman shoved me and I gave up. I climbed through the outer barricades and wandered the Plaza de Castillo, furious and exhausted, listening for the last rocket that finally sounded at seven minutes and eleven seconds from the first.

I watched the footage later as David Rodríguez and Miguel Angel Perez led Tramposo all the way to the sand of the arena and I knew if I was a better mozo I would have been with them.

After that we started midway up Estafeta and I made it all the way to Telefónica, where I ran okay but was a little disoriented. On the eleventh, I ran well and ended up near Julen Madina as he led a Miura bull on the horns onto the sand of the arena.

That evening we went to see Juan José Padilla fight the Miura in the Plaza de Toros. We sat in the Sol section, the side of the arena exposed to the sun the entire bullfight. Usually the Sol section is a raucous food and sangria fight the entire event. The Peñas communal groups with big marching bands play music, eat, and sing the entire Bullfight. But on this day, sadly, the Peñas protested the bullfight due to political unrest. Gary, Gus, Galloway, and I had the whole Sol section to ourselves. I was already a great admirer of Padilla; he wasn't the elegant, regal matador that the elitist aficionados lusted after. Padilla was barbaric in his style, and to this day the greatest showman I have ever experienced. His raw bravery and athleticism are unparalleled in any sport or art form. Padilla is kinetic; it is clear watching him that he gives you everything and is more than willing to die. Padilla in fact embraces the idea of death in every fantastic move with the animal. He thrilled us as he placed his own *bandilleros,* the barbed sticks used to loosen up the thick neck muscle of the animals, in order to lower the head so the matador can slay the beast on foot with a sword. Then later, as Padilla caped the animal in his normal close and dangerous way, the bull gored him in the leg and tossed him into the air. Padilla's completely limp body danced along the horns for a terrible moment. Then he fell to the sand, unconscious. His team picked him up and carried him to the surgery room with his colorful arms dangling loosely. The horrific image assured me that he might be dying and surely wouldn't return to the ring. A few minutes passed and the other matador prepared to engage the animal and finish him in place of Padilla, when one of Padilla's handlers rushed out of the surgery room and shouted for the other matador to stop. A minute later Padilla walked out in blue jeans, the goring the bull inflicted sewed up somewhere beneath. His fancy matador pants lay irreparably torn somewhere in the surgery room. Padilla limped out and crossed the ring as his team distracted the animal. He sat along the step that lines the wall of the ring, scowling at the bull. Padilla's long pointy sideburns trembled. Then he got up and killed the beast that'd nearly taken his life just moments before. As he walked around the arena holding the bull's bloody sawed-off ear—an award for Padilla's bravery and resilience, I knew he was a very special matador and man, but I couldn't have known what tests lay ahead of him.

On October 7, 2011, a bull gored Padilla in the skull while he tried to place his bandilleros in the animal. The wound was one of the worst in the history of the bullfight. The horn went up through his face and plucked out Padilla's left eye. This would likely have been a career-ending wound for any other matador, but not for Padilla. Wearing an eye patch, Padilla killed his next bull just five months later. By the time he returned to Pamplona, Padilla was the most famous bullfighter in the world. I attended his return and sat in the Sol section as hundreds of pirate flags waved amongst the arena: skull, crossbones, and eye patch. Watching Padilla step onto the sand gave me chills; it was an astonishing honor to witness. It brought tears to my eyes.

I wasn't the only artist who loved what the world calls the bullfight and which Spain calls *la corrida*; Hemingway, Picasso, Goya, and many, many others were avid aficionados of corrida. The most prominent contemporary artist who is deeply enamored with corrida, Mario Vargas Llosa, would win the Nobel Prize for Literature that very same year in 2010. Before his acceptance of the award, a Pamplona regular, Rolf von Essen, would invite Llosa to his Club Taurino in Sweden. Llosa attended Rolf's club before his acceptance speech at the Nobel

Prize awards ceremony. This drew outrageous attention to von Essen's club. Years later my dear friend and maestro, von Essen, would put me in touch with Llosa so I could ask him why so many great artists are so drawn to corrida.

"Hemingway, Picasso, and so many other artists were drawn to corrida because corrida is a great art. It is a very different kind of art, because you are playing with your life, your death, in order to produce beauty. This act not only produces pleasure, but it produces a kind of revelation of what the human condition is, how fragile life is, how close death is, and all this produces art in the case of the corrida. I think it is extremely important to preserve something that for centuries has been one of the richest manifestations of creativity in the human being. What the animal rights activists and anti-taurinos don't understand is that the *Toro Bravo* (Spanish fighting bull) is the most privileged animal in the world. There is no sense that the Toro is tortured; on the contrary, the Toro Bravo is a Toro Bravo, he needs to fight to express himself. People who are enemies of the corrida are also enemies of the Toro Bravo. They should know that the disappearance of the corrida will mean the disappearance of the Toro Bravo. Toro Bravo exist because corrida exists."

Mario Vargas Llosa continues to be one of the foremost expert journalists on bullfighting the world over. For me, the corrida was always about purging emotions. It is like watching a Greek tragedy performed by the greatest actors in the world. I love the Toro Bravo so much, and when a great matador like Padilla evokes the spirit of the animal and slays him cleanly and mercifully I leave the arena with a great agony in my heart, but an agony which also nurtures me and strengthens me and I'm very grateful for corrida's presence in my life.

Wee Gus turned out to be nothing like I'd expected. He was jovial and friendly with everyone in the Posse. He even quelled arguments when they arose. The pure joy and heart that his father exuded somehow found its way through "Wee Gus the Nutter," and I was very relieved to see it. He was laudatory about my running and seemed to genuinely want to become a serious runner. He went on the tour with me a bunch and I gave him plenty of advice. But I was still guarded, because I knew the nutter might surface at any moment and I'd have to whup him and send him packing.

On the thirteenth, I was running along the fencing with Gary behind me and I felt the herd sway wide to where we were. It opened up and I dug to get out in the center of the street so I could sprint. There were five of them, three bulls and two steers. Someone behind me grabbed a fistful of my shirt and wrenched me backward and I'm digging sneakers into the dry gray-green bricks of the callejón, swinging elbows back to break their grip. Suddenly I'm free, coasting in a large bubble of space in front of the animals where the fearful won't tread. The tall Basco with the green plaid shirt appeared beside me. He shouted in Basque ahead of us (I can only assume): "GET THE FUCK OUT OF THE WAY!"

I didn't look back, just coasted. The horrific crackle of hooves zoomed up behind me. The swaying bells panged from the steers' necks. The hundreds of spectators along the fencing and the outer balcony of the arena emanated a searing roar. The camera click-click-click-clicks would tell me it was five, a dark brown bull directly behind me, out front, hooking his wide, white horns inward before the others. His torso swung sideways like a car fishtailing. The black mound of muscle behind his head swelled and contorted. Off-white rings surrounded his eyes and snout. And we led them like that through the tunnel into the arena, the Basque at my side, five beasts at our backs.

It was my first true extended run on the horns with a large pack. The long run with the suelto was just that, a long run with a suelto. This sprint with the herd was what I'd been seeking all these years. To stride with the bulls. To lead the animals for a long distance. It was an amazing moment, a final triumph. The television didn't broadcast my run. No photos of it appeared in the papers, but it didn't bother me because I knew eventually they would pop up. They did in the weeks that followed. An American from Philadelphia named Peter Milligan tagged me in some Facebook photos where he was right beside me. He fell and the herd trampled him without serious injury, but in the moment they trampled him I was gliding on the horns——leading the pack. I also found a photo taken by the great EPA war photographer Jim Hollander. It was an absolute classic, facing into the tunnel from the barricade looking over the bull's horns. There are deep, golden sun rays cutting through the dust kicked up by the run. The brown bull surges toward the Basque and myself as we soar into the tunnel. Seeing that photo brought tears to my eyes. To be a part of such majestic artistry was beyond all my hopes as a runner. But that all came later. Before that, something terrible would happen on the night of the thirteenth.

The tremendous rush of the morning made it hard to sleep during my regular afternoon siesta. That night I tried and failed to find Enid, who'd gone off drinking and dancing with some of the Posse girls. The Jandilla would run the next morning. I was afraid. I was afraid I might die or someone might die like Daniel did the year before. I sat with the Posse way out along the castle wall for a while. A stranger offered me some wine and I nearly drank it. I told Gary I had to leave, and he walked with me to the pens where we stood above and looked down at the Jandilla. They were black with one brown bull, just like the year before. The brown bull was darker than Capuchino, almost red. They're called Colorados. He seemed agitated, and that triggered memories of the year before, the frigid fear as Capuchino looked me in the eye.

We came back to find an incident brewing with some of the Posse. I was losing my mind. I got between one of the girls and a drunk guy who was aggressively moving toward her, and he ended up unconscious in a bloody pool.

Terrified, I left, changed my clothes, and came back to look. I saw an ambulance and completely unraveled. I was sure that he had died and

I was done. They'd send me to prison for manslaughter. I'd probably lose my marriage in the process and never run with the bulls again.

I milled around in utter despair when suddenly Gus materialized. He found me.

"You don't look so good," he said with a grin.

I sighed and gripped my head. He put his arm around my shoulder and took me to a quiet back street. We sat down on a dry spot in a piss-stinking curb. It was a small harbor in the chaos of fiesta.

"Well, mate, the lad's in pretty bad shape."

"Yeah?! Oh fuck! Did he wake up when the ambulance got there?"

"Yeah, yes, he was awake when the medics put him on the stretcher."

A glimmer of hope sparked in my chest.

"Gary told the police everything."

"What! He talked to the police?! Fuck, why would he do that? Why didn't they just leave?!"

"He had to, Bill. If they would have left how would it have looked?"

"Fuck! That motherfucker! Did he tell them who I was? Do they know my name!"

"Aye, aye, now I won't have you talking about Gary like that! He's your mate. He loves ya. He wouldn't do that to you, Buffalo."

"Did he tell the cops my name?! Oh god, I'm gonna have to get out of the country."

"I'm not answering that, Bill. You know the answer to that."

I took a deep breath and sat down. "I'm sorry, Gus. I'm sorry I said that about Gary. You're right, Gus, he wouldn't."

"They said it like it happened. The guy came over and was screaming at the lass and someone, they don't know, got in between and the guy got hurt."

"Thank god."

"I think it's gonna be all right, Bill. You just relax. But the cobblestones really cunted the fucker's head. There was blood everywhere!"

"I know. I almost puked I was so scared for him."

"He's gonna be fine." Gus put his warm hand on my shoulder. "You're gonna be fine too. Let's go find Enid."

We went around looking for her, and every time I sighed in absolute despair imagining the guy on the ground unconscious Gus was there to wrap his arm around my shoulder and reassure me. I couldn't believe it. The nutter I was so disgusted with becoming part of the Posse was my rock, my shoulder to lean on in my dark night. And me the Buddhist, thinking I was past anger and violence, thinking I was better than him. The way it all unfolded had me awestruck. But fiesta does that; once you think you have it all figured out, it blindsides you and flips your world upside down.

Graeme forbade me from running the next morning. He was sure the police would be looking for me. Still, I woke in the morning and went to the street. Terrified, I entered the street at Town Hall. The officers seemed to notice me and I nearly ran from them, though in hindsight it was surely all in my head. I went down to Telefónica very fearful. Saw the Basque runner I'd run with the day before across the way from me and figured this may be the last chance to greet him. I walked across the street and we met eyes and shook hands and I said *suerte* and he nodded as the Basque do. I walked back to my side and we waited for the rocket. Disoriented, I ran early and was all mixed up and ran in through the tunnel with some lead steers. I was a valiente for the first time and saw the bread and vegetables flying through the air. Climbed onto the wall and I straddled it as the herd poured in. There was a suelto on the Jumbotron screen. It was the brown bull, just like I'd expected. I considered going out to help bring him in, then thought better of it. Suddenly Julen Madina hailed the animal and lured him into the mouth of the tunnel. I watched as Madina led the Jandilla suelto past the place in the tunnel where one of the animal's older brothers nearly killed Julen in 2004. The majesty of the moment erupted a scream from my chest.

"MADINA!"

Julen lured the animal into the arena in front of me, and just as he stepped foot on the sand the bull dipped and hit him in the lower spine and he toppled to the ground. The bull continued and the dobladores led him away as several young Spanish runners ran to Julen and picked him up. The crowd showered Madina with cheers, and many came to check on him and congratulate him.

Witnessing the end of the incredible arc of this iconic runner was a tremendous honor. Later that year Julen and his wife had a baby girl. Julen decided to retire to focus his energies on his family.

That morning, Gus had had a miraculous run with the full-charging suelto. He cut across Mercaderes and ran its horns for several yards before cutting out. Gus's eyes bugged out as he told me the story at Txoko. Elation filled my heart for him.

Got nervous when they scanned my passport as I tried to get my boarding pass at the airport in Madrid because of the nasty fight I'd gotten in. But they let me on.

I fell asleep on the flight home. The turbulence must have triggered nightmares. I float above Pamplona in the night. A terrible series of encierros unfold below. Sueltos everywhere. They slam runners to the cobblestones with horrific fury—knocking them unconscious. A brown bull throws a runner, the runner's head cracks the stones and he lies still, eyes closed. A wavy pool of blood expands below his head on the cobblestones. I swoop down to see the man and recognize him. It's the guy I'd hurt in the fight at fiesta. I gawk at him, my heart anxious to help him——worry constricting my throat. Suddenly, the waves in the dark pool of blood calm and my reflection appears in the stilled surface of the black pool. It isn't my face. It's the face of a Toro Bravo—red blood streaks down his horns. I wake soaring over the Atlantic. Enid asleep beside me. My mind raced—the sueltos, *they're like me. I can see my mad rage inside them.* I realized, *that's why they're so precious to me. Because I know them, and in quelling and directing their rage up the street, I was learning to calm and direct my own wrath.* I'd failed horribly that night with the guy I left in the pool of blood. Regret ached in my heart. Tears welled in my eyes. "I'm sorry," I whispered. "I'm so sorry."

I'd come so far and yet there it was with me ready to erupt into destruction. I covered my face with my hands and sighed. *Accept it. It will be there your whole life. You have to be vigilant, dig deep and battle it whenever it comes.* Like with the sueltos, I knew I had to always be there to subdue them and show them the path to their brothers. I had to battle my rage and subdue it or perish.

CHAPTER SIX:
BREAK OUT
2011

When I got home a literary journal associated with Columbia College Chicago named *F Magazine* published an excerpt of my novel. It was a big honor. I also landed a job as staff writer at Criminal Class Press. Then I started blogging about the Chicago boxing scene. Things were really going well with my writing, but the Windy City Story Slam kept slipping back into my life and taking it over. I'd had so much success with the show and gotten so much attention for my efforts with the Slam, but it was not what I wanted to do with my life. I didn't want to be a host and event producer. I didn't want to slave away making these events successful for the literary and budding storytelling community when it felt like most of the performers didn't even appreciate it. In fact, all it had done for me was destroy many of my friendships, make me a target for a lot of jealous hatred, and taken huge chunks of time and energy away from my writing. Still, I couldn't let it die, and I booked the All City Championships for February at Double Door, and it was another big success.

Around then I concocted a powerful pitch for a story on Pamplona. I cyber-stalked Joe Spring, the online head of the national adventure publication *Outside Magazine*. My pitch was to cover San Fermín. Joe accepted straight off and offered me 500 bucks to do it. It was a three-part story. Part one was "The Top Ten Ways to Survive San Fermín," the next part was "The Top Ten Most Dangerous Moments in the Running of the Bulls in the Past Ten Years." The final part was to be an interview that I'd conduct at fiesta. They'd publish it later, after San Fermín. I reached out to Jim Hollander to supply photos. We went to work and headed into fiesta. The two posts went live and received huge attention online: thousands of hits, several dozen comments, and hundreds and hundreds of Facebook likes.

I fell into intense correspondence with Gus that whole year leading up to fiesta. He'd really been there for me when I needed him. He wanted to become a serious runner, and he'd had his run on the horns the year before on Mercaderes, though it was brief. He was an honest and serious student, and I poured all that I'd learned into him. I taught him about a runner who'd stopped coming well before Gus's first fiesta. He was also from Scotland, a phenomenal mozo named Brucie Sinclair. Brucie ran the curve in a fascinating way. He'd stand nearly halfway up Mercaderes in a doorway. He'd wait until the last animal passed him then sprint as hard as he could after the herd. He'd cross behind the herd to get to the inside of the curve. As the herd crashed he would catapult along the inside and swing all the way in front of the animals and onto the horns. Then he'd run them a long way up Estafeta. It was similar to the Distler run but worked in a much more dramatic way. I taught Gus "The Brucie Run" using photos and videos. Gus was reluctant, saying that he didn't know if he could pull it off. I urged him and told him it was possible, anything was possible if he believed, had a plan, and fucking went for it! Over the yearlong correspondence I somehow convinced him. Or maybe I just fanned his flames, but he concocted a plan based off of Brucie's run and was thrilled to get to fiesta!

There'd been some buzz on Facebook about a British bullfighter named Alexander Fiske-Harrison who was coming to fiesta to stay with the Posse that year. He'd written a highly acclaimed book called *Into the Arena*, which chronicled his experience living as a *torero* (bullfighter) in Seville and concluded with him killing a bull in the ring. It fascinated and excited me to meet a real bullfighter. When I arrived the HQ was strangely quiet. A handsome English gentleman with an eloquent accent sat in the front room near the windows. Surprisingly, Alexander was as excited to meet me as I was to meet him. Graeme had talked me up as an excellent runner. We sparked a conversation and quickly bonded over the bulls. We traded stories of our experiences with the animals and he schooled me on the great matadors, and I told of the great Spanish mozos Julen Madina and David Rodríguez and the Americans Joe Distler and Matt Carney. He said he wanted to run with me, and I was glad to have him and guide him. Galloway already was calling him a shortened version of his name: Xander. He enjoyed it. Xander lost his elder brother at a young age in a skiing accident. I could clearly feel his brother's presence as a powerful force watching over Xander.

The opening morning I left a little early and ran in good position. The lead bulls closed in on me as we approached the tunnel. A young Spanish runner was beside me, and as we entered the tunnel he nearly crashed into the wall and yanked me so that I smashed into it. My momentum kept me up and I slid along the smooth, white concrete wall. I pushed off the wall to get my balance. The closest bull nudged my back with its horn and I bounced back to the wall. The bulls swayed into the tunnel beside me and nearly crushed me. Their nostrils slurped air. The nearest bull's huge eye was beside my chest; he looked into me steadily as I got my feet together and ran beside him. Another runner fell in front of me. I tried to jump him but landed flat on my belly and rolled into the open slot that lines the lower tunnel wall. Lay there until I sensed a final suelto approaching the tunnel. I crawled out and walked to the entrance to the tunnel and sure enough there was a suelto, but it was a suelto steer lying at the mouth of the tunnel. Another runner pulled his horn to get him to his feet and we ran into the arena.

When I found Xander at Bar Txoko he seemed pleased as he stood in his red Eton blazer. I asked him how his run was. He smiled and described how he got in beside a bull and ran with this animal, his arm draped over the beast's back. Several excellent photos circulated on the various websites chronicling Xander's fantastic run. And when you looked close, you could see that he was running directly on the horns of the bull in the pack behind him. In his first run of the year, and only his second run ever, he'd accomplished an excellent feat. It made me very happy for him and proud that I'd helped facilitate the moment with my advice. But for the most part this was a fearless man who just went for it.

The second morning I missed the pack. Got back to the HQ and I found everyone pretty upset as they ate their breakfast. Then one of the girls said, "Gus did something this morning."

"Did he get hurt?" The replays of the run flickered across the TV screen. I looked at Padre and he shook his head, baffled. "Here it comes," someone said. The shot switched to a slow-motion video of the curve. The animals slid and slammed into the wall. Out of nowhere Gus rocketed into view in his bright, yellow Partick Thistle jersey. He rode the inside of the curve right alongside the animals and as they regrouped Gus shot across in perfect position, just like Brucie.

I screamed "GUS!" and fell to my knees, gripping my head as Gus dashed onto the horns of the entire pack and led them up Estafeta. Pure joy and exhilaration surged through me. *I can't believe it. He did it. He fulfilled his promise. He completed his quest.* All those Facebook messages, the questions and planning and philosophy and encouragement, the yearlong discourse we'd had—he'd gone out and made it reality.

Everyone was saying he'd taken too many risks. That he'd gone too far and would get hurt. I didn't bother to disagree with them; they could never understand what he'd done. He'd put it all on the line and achieved a majestic moment. I couldn't have been more proud of my sole pupil. Walked out of the room to find him and he bumped right into me. I grabbed him by the shoulders and he started to apologize.

"Gus! You did it, you motherfucker! You did it!" I hugged him hard as his eyes lit up and he laughed. We talked a while. I told absolutely anyone who would sit still for a second what my dear friend and pupil Gus did that morning. I was so damn proud and happy for him. Of course, the guys at Txoko weren't so impressed. His run hurt egos. Gus had done something many of them professed to be experts at but hadn't been able to do for years. Boastful arrogance oozed out of them. They seemed to want to shut the gate in our face and laugh from the other side. The best way to honor something you love is to share it with someone new and celebrate that new love. To share it, not to hold it tight and claim to be the only one who truly understands it and loves it. That's selfishness and arrogance. It was the antithesis of tradition.

A bull nearly gored Xander at Telefónica. He'd pressed his back to the fencing and thrown his hands up at his sides as the bull passed only inches from him. There was a brilliant photo of this, which looked an awful lot like Xander was making a close pass with the bull as a torero. I couldn't believe his magic was so strong that he'd had two spectacular runs back to back, though this second one he was much less in control of.

The next morning I fell without getting very close to the bulls. The crowd knocked me down and ripped my hat off. I didn't find it afterward.

That afternoon I went into a store across from Town Hall called Gutiérrez. A bunch of old-style caps lined the back wall of the shop, but they'd closed off that section. The old man who ran it was tall with white hair. He refused to let me in back even though I showed him my money and asked in my broken Spanish to see the hats. He just sneered at me and folded his arms across his chest. I went and got Enid to translate and he was very rude with her too. Asked her to translate for me but she wouldn't, which told me it was bad. Still, he finally let me in back to see the hats. I found a white-and-blue plaid cap. Didn't like the look of it, but when I touched it an electric current ran through it into my hands, and when I slipped it on and looked at myself in the mirror I suddenly felt a strange completion. I bought it. Later she told me he'd said to her, "Why would you marry an asshole like him?" I was glad she didn't translate because it might have ended very ugly.

The experience with Señor Gutiérrez was like a microcosm of what fiesta had been for me so far that year. It was hard and ugly and painful. My running was complete garbage. It wasn't that I didn't try. I guess it was the way I'd been thrown around in the tunnel the opening morning. Watching the tape I saw that a tall young Spanish runner in a striped sweater grabbed me and yanked me. I'd lost control of myself. It did a number on my mind and I was allowing the chaos to suck me into the bodies along the side of the street as I looked back to pick up the herd. In the run, you're either all in or all out. Trying to exist in a middle ground is a very dangerous and frustrating place to be. I was stuck in the middle. To compound this Gus went out and displayed brilliant Brucie-like runs at the curve the next two days. I began to feel like a spectator instead of a runner. His success was a mirror of my failure, and it brought me such visceral anguish that I considered quitting. I honestly couldn't take the suffering anymore. Was sure Enid would be happy, and I knew walking away would save me any more psychological pain. I told her the night of the tenth.

"What if I quit running? How would you feel about that?"

"Are you serious?! That'd be great!"

"I don't know. I'm thinking about it."

"Well, yeah, sure, if you're asking me, quit, that'd be awesome."

Walked around that night by myself. What a ridiculous image. I was solemn, nearly heartbroken—wandering around the greatest outpouring of joy the world has ever known. Then I told myself, *well, if you're going to quit, you better at least give it one more try.* Concocted a plan based off of Matt Carney's legend, I'd stand square in the center of the street. As the herd approached I'd start a light jog and wait until the animals were right on me to break into a sprint. I wouldn't ever look back, just use my ears and peripheral vision to tell me the animals were there.

Somberness swelled in my heart as I made the walk up Estafeta the next morning. I wondered if this truly was my last run. The old emotions stirred in me: fear, the profound danger and grandeur of that final stroll up the street before hunt begins. The utter beauty of the architecture, the balconies, the narrow channel of blue above, the small, black birds cutting through at different altitudes and trajectories.

The rocket went off and I instituted my plan. I jogged in the center of the street—looking down and watching the stone gutter that ran directly through the center of Estafeta as the chaos jostled me. The fury swirled around me like a cyclone as I concentrated peacefully, chanting in a quiet hum "Nam-myoho-renge-kyo . . . Nam-myoho-renge-kyo . . . Nam-myoho-renge-kyo . . . "

I listened for them, for the deep rumble, felt the stones with my feet for the true vibrations. The light bathed us at Telefónica and the pushing and panic suddenly ceased. I entered the one empty place on the street. Juan Pedro gusted past on my right. Something hard like a broomstick glided across my ribs on the left side of my upper back. *Is that a horn!?* Then it passed over my spine; the stick nudged my upper-right back hard and nearly knocked me down. I surged forward into the runner in front of me and extended my hands into him to keep space. The black bull emerged into my periphery and slammed into runners and the fencing to my right. I cut around the runner in front of me as he bear-crawled trying to stay up. His hip brushed against my outer right thigh. The bull careened forward and burst slightly ahead of me on my side. Dug into a deep sprint. I accelerated in front of the bull's horns. *This is too easy!* I was right. A moment later, three runners collapsed directly ahead of me. Juan Pedro was right on them. He tried to leap them, tripped, and cut away to the barricades.

At full sprint, with the dagger sharp horn of a bull inches from my back, I approached the three descending bodies. *Oh fuck, I'm gonna fall.* At the last possible moment I gathered and leaped. As I did the fallen runner nearest me looked up, saw us coming, and rolled to the side. In midair, I jinked my foot on an inside loop. My outer shin glided along his back. There was another runner lying beyond him. I reached my foot up as high as I could and managed to hurdle the second fallen runner's leg. Finally cleared all of it and planted my foot down on solid stone. Astonished, I sprinted down the center of the path. *How the hell am I still up?!* The move positioned me directly on the horns of the bull. Something stirred in me deeply and this electric numbness shot through my whole body. The animal and I linked. And after all the strife I finally felt at peace in that majestic moment that is emblazoned on the cover of this book. It was like the animal, the encierro, and San Fermín chose me, or finally chose to have mercy on me and open the door.

I took long hard strides. The bull lunged forward and nudged its horn into my back again, but this time he pushed and sprung me forward. I leaped and floated and landed again on my feet at full sprint. My back kick swung up and bumped softly against his snout. I felt I was disgracing him by kicking him in the mouth and slid to the side. Took my rolled paper like I'd watched Juan Pedro do so many times and placed it low before his snout where he could see it and follow it. We ran like that for 40 yards. As we entered the tunnel the young Spaniard in a white striped sweater, who'd yanked me on the opening morning, ran in front of the animal. His sweater read *The Royal Champ* in red letters across the chest. He twisted and placed his paper at the bull's snout as his longish straight hair flopped around. In the tunnel he placed his paper over mine and I switched it to place my paper over his, like we were playing swords. Our papers and destinies crossed. We led the bull through the tunnel united as a pair. A big white scar sat centered on his forehead between his horns from sparring with his brothers. We entered the arena like this. The enormous roar hit us like a tidal wave. I peeled off to the left and the kid ran out onto the sand still on the horns, then cut left dramatically, which delighted the cheering arena.

Ran over and I climbed up on a press box and watched the replay on the Jumbotron screen. On the replay the Spanish kid I'd played swords with was having an incredible run with Juan Pedro. He hurdled a fallen runner. Then he dashed past me when the bull first slid his horn across my back at Telefónica. I jumped up and yelled like a soccer player who'd scored a goal, watching myself gliding on in front of the horns of the bull and running him into the tunnel. A Spanish grandfather and grandson sat in the very front row right beside me. The little boy looked up at me very impressed. The old man nudged him and the boy said, "Tu corres muy bien." I smiled and said, "Gracias." Then I climbed out through the stands.

Ran back to Town Hall, and I found Enid looking down at me from the balcony. She said, "How was it?"

"The best run of my life," I yelled up to her.

A reporter from *Diario de Navarra* stopped me and asked a few questions. Enid came down and helped translate, then we walked toward the HQ and suddenly Señor Gutiérrez bumped into me. He smiled broadly, astonished, then scolded Enid. "Why didn't you tell me! He runs like a gazelle!" I grinned at him and thought, *you probably regret being such a jerk to me, don't you?* But I forgave him. He probably had to deal with asshole tourists who couldn't speak Spanish all fiesta. We shook hands and Enid and I moved on. Pamplona showered me with adoration I'd never experienced in my entire life. Perfect strangers came up to me and shook my hand and patted me on the back. I had no idea what they were saying to me but their smiles told the story. It was quite a humbling day.

Found Gus at Txoko and I grabbed him by the shoulders.

"You taught me about letting go and going for it all the way. Thank you." I hugged him.

Joe Distler came up and pinched my cheek and said, "That's my boy."

It shocked me. Joe had ignored me for years and now suddenly he'd embraced me. It was quite overwhelming——all of it. Joe invited me up to his place for a big lunch. I couldn't believe it. Suddenly the guys who'd shunned me for so long were patting me on the back and giving me the thumbs-up. I wanted the same for Gus. He'd been having a better year than me but they seemed reluctant to let him in. The mighty Hoskins Clan was the one group at Txoko who always seemed to embrace Gus and I. They were a working-class English family who wore the jersey for their local rugby team, The Barbarians. The jerseys had white and black horizontal stripes and they were easy to find, often running with the pack at Telefónica. The patriarch, Tony, was tall and thin with a stubbled face and gray hair. He was an excellent runner as well and presided over the group. The Hoskins were tough, humble, and honest. If you had a good run they came up and congratulated you without any hesitation or resignation. There wasn't an ounce of arrogance in this group. They were men who worked with their hands. They were also students of the encierro and closely observed the great runners like David Rodríguez and the many other legendary Spaniards of our day. I liked them a lot, especially the young son Owain, who was tall and thin and a sensational high school soccer player. Owain had been running these long runs where he'd end up on the horns just as the bulls got to the sand. Then he'd glide across the arena, handing them off to the dobladores. The Hoskinses walked with me over to Foto Mena that day when I found the magnificent photo that adorns the cover of this book. It felt like I was with my dad, brothers, uncles, and cousins and it was a very special time for me.

Distler's place was like an encierro museum. Incredible photos dating back to the sixties covered every wall. Distler was pure magic in his day and ran the horns of bulls for decades. He was Matt Carney's protégé but the very best Spanish runners let him into their circle based on his own merit. Distler earned it and became a legend in his own right. Runners packed the place, and the guys who sometimes used to shun me now treated me nicely. It was cool, but they weren't going to win me over with a couple smiles after years of the cold shoulder. Distler was very gregarious and a big personality, but he made me feel like the star of the show. He asked me what happened. I just told him I tried to run like I heard Joe talk about Carney running. "I just jogged in the center of the street and didn't look back until the bull was there, and then I ran like hell!" This delighted Joe, and I took off after telling the story to get back to work with the Posse.

The next morning I was running along the left-side fence of the calle-jón when I saw an opening and slipped in front of the lead animal. I linked with the rambling beast as we approached the tunnel. Three runners fell ahead. One tried to get up. I told him "stay down." The bull kicked his half-raised body as he flowed over him. Inside the tunnel a tourist stood up, stationary, directly in front of the charging bulls. Hoping to save him from the bull killing him, I gave the tourist a quick shove to the side. His leg swung up and hooked the leg of an excellent Spanish mozo in a yellow soccer shirt. The Spanish runner fell and the goofball tourist bounced across the tunnel, hit the wall, and stayed on his feet. The bull stepped on the Spanish runner's head. I swooped around him through the tunnel and looped back in front of the bull's horns and Juan Pedro and I led the two bulls into the sand shoulder to shoulder.

The TV footage cut out our entrance into the tunnel, but I didn't mind. When I got to Txoko people asked how my run was. I giggled and said, "Another good one." They vindictively snarled at me. I just laughed magnanimously. Jim Hollander had seen it and captured three fantastic photos of my run. He saw how I'd replied and couldn't believe it.

I was just very grateful for the experiences and what the encierro gave me. It was incredibly humbling to go from utter despair to pure glory.

Some of the arrogant guys at Txoko asked, "Okay, how'd you do it?"

I just shrugged and replied, "I've been very lucky to get all these opportunities this year, and I'm glad I've been able to take advantage of a few of 'em."

That night, rumors of a Gypsy curse spread through the town. José Antonio communicated to us that a curse lay in wait for any runner who ran the center of the street. I'm very vulnerable to this type of magic, and it terrified me. That next morning I ran the center of the street when an insanely fierce Colorado from the El Pilar ranch barreled into Telefónica. He was seething rage-fully. There was a clear opening to run his horns, but something told me no and pulled me back. I was very lucky because that bull had nailed several runners that morning, including Juan Pedro Lecuona. The Colorado was waiting for runners to run his horns, and when they did, the bull accelerated into their backs and barreled through them. The animal dramatically nailed a runner in the tunnel and threw him high into the air. I ran beside the later set of bulls but got nothing special. Afterward a TV crew thrust a camera in my face. Seeing the Colorado hit and appear to gore Juan Pedro upset me terribly. I tried to explain that the bull was cursed and ended up sounding like a wack job. Later I ran into Juan Pedro; he was busted up but okay. He wasn't gored. I asked him how he was, and he grinned and said fine.

A new figure was emerging toward the end of the course: The kid in the white-striped *The Royal Champ* sweater who'd yanked me in the callejón on the first morning and who I'd shared that illustrious run with through the tunnel on the eleventh with our rolled papers crossed. I read in the paper that his name was Aitor Aristregui Oloriz. Aitor's face is there on the cover of this book directly in front of me. He was a 21-year-old Basque kid from just outside Pamplona. He'd begun to consistently run excellently with Juan Pedro and they were putting on quite a show.

On the final morning I was very much at ease. I'd had an incredible fiesta and was going to take what I could get. I was running the left side of the callejón when I looked back and saw several steers and no chance to run the bulls behind the steers. Decided to call it a morning, I was so grateful for that year; I wasn't about to get upset or greedy. I just smiled at them as they swept up. *See you next year.* Suddenly a small separation opened between the steers and three bulls behind them. I sprinted directly after the steers' butts and sure enough the bulls separated more and I ran the horns and led the bulls through the callejón with another runner in blue and white stripes across from me. The next day in the paper they wrote: "These three bulls were led by one rolled newspaper." Mine was the only paper in the shot. The photo and caption was an amazing honor. Many people didn't believe I'd had such a good run because it wasn't on television. But I didn't care. When the photo came out, it was pretty funny to see their shocked faces.

After the final run Joe and Jim invited me to the runners' breakfast. Rumors spread that Julen Madina was in town. He walked into the restaurant and everyone clapped. It was amazing to see. He gave a very heartening speech. Then we took a big group photo with several of the greatest Spanish runners of the past half-century. It was a breathtaking honor. I chatted with a tall guy with long gray hair and black sunglasses; his name was Bomber and he'd been running for decades. He was legendary for his running and for a lot of different things that I'd learn about over the years.

I realized it would be great to interview Julen Madina for *Outside* magazine. Asked Joe Distler for his contact info and Joe made it possible for me. I called Julen, and Enid translated a wonderful interview, some of which was used earlier in this book. Things were starting to happen. Joe was opening the door for me to step inside this marvelous world and I was very grateful.

CHAPTER SEVEN

BREAK IN

Got home and a few days later *Chicago Tribune* reporter Bill Hageman called and told me the *Tribune* had selected me as a "Remarkable Person," which was a recurring feature. It was a tremendous honor. I could hardly believe it. They did a full feature story on me. A week later the *Chicago Reader,* a Chicago arts weekly asked me to write an essay for their Back to School issue. Then a few weeks later I went on WGN TV to talk about the running of the bulls, the Windy City Story Slam, and the Chicago Golden Gloves. All the attention amazed me, but I felt like I was letting time slip through my fingers with regard to my novel. So I put everything into finishing it. I slaved over edits and rewrites with the plan to send it to Akashic Books, a fantastic independent publisher in Brooklyn. Also, I landed a job with Fightnews.com, the number one online publication for boxing in the world. My job was to cover Chicago's boxing scene, and I even broke the sad story of Joe Frazier's death worldwide. Bomber was a fan of Smokin Joe's, and chimed in about something I wrote on Facebook. Bomber was a CIA agent and did a bunch of work abroad. He and his wife Goldie traveled the entire world together. Bomber was also a master photographer and shot *National Geographic*-quality landscapes. He and Goldie walked across all the continents. In the process they had joined dozens of indigenous groups. On one of their walks they came across an Australian woman attempting to walk all the continents, but she was well-supported: her family was driving a camper and each night she slept in a bed. Goldie was sleeping on the ground and all she and Bomber had was what they could carry in their packs. Sadly, Goldie died during a surgery. Bomber was at fiesta at Bar Txoko when he received the news. It shattered him; the two were unquestionably soul mates. Bomber also summited Everest and spent a lot of time on the mountain. He had snow blindness, that's why he always wore sunglasses. Bomber knew many of the guys on Everest the year of the tragedy that Jon Krakauer documented in his book *Into Thin Air*. Of course, Bomber was also a masterful mozo in Pamplona. He began to send me black and white photos from the seventies; a few showed Bomber running the horns perfectly wearing his sunglasses. He became one of my maestros. He had this deeply spiritual way of encouraging me. He was like a sorcerer of white magic. People told me Bomber said I was like a warrior. That meant the world to me.

Enid and I went back to Mexico for Christmas for two weeks. I always enjoyed Enid's family; their quirks and bickering amused me. Tried to keep myself removed from the squabbles as much as possible. The language barrier helped with that, but it was also a strain because I was missing out on really talking to them. I wanted to know them more, especially her grandparents, who were, without a doubt, one of the greatest couples I've ever come across. Her grandfather once killed a man in a machete fight to defend his wife's honor.

Two things dominated my mind that winter in Mexico City. One was my rewrite of my novel. The other was an encierro in a small rural town. I was scrolling through encierro photos and videos on Facebook, when a new Facebook friend of mine named Dyango Valasco posted a video. The screen shot was of a monstrous stampede of horses cascading down a large dusty hillside. I clicked "Play." The video opened at a pen out in a forest just at the break of dawn. Hundreds of horsemen milled before the pens. Thousands of people stood near cars that lined a large sandy field. Suddenly, the doors of the pens opened up and a big group of people standing in front of the doors scattered out of the way as a herd of six bulls and six steers blistered out into the mass of horsemen. The entire pack of hundreds of animals vanished into a foggy haze all lit up in the sunrise. Later the video showed the animals moving through woods and fields toward town. Finally the animals crested a hill at the edge of town and galloped down it. The horsemen encircled the bulls and steers; then just at the very edge of town the horsemen peeled off to the sides. The herd of bulls and steers soared into the street lined with barricades and the mozos on foot led them up the path. It was a full encierro with twists and bends and thousands of bull runners. I could not believe my eyes, but sure enough, this was the encierro at Cuéllar.

Dyango Valasco, my new Facebook friend, was a sculptor and runner from Cuéllar. Valasco was a very important sculptor in the Taurine world. He was also extremely proud of the encierro in his town, which was the oldest in all of Spain. In 1215, the encierro in Cuéllar became so popular that even the priests were partaking in it. This spurred the bishop of Cuéllar to petition the Pope in Rome to ban all priests from running with the bulls. The letter is an immaculate work of art and the oldest evidence of an encierro in the Spain.

During my time in Mexico City that winter, my rewrite and Cuéllar's encierro dominated my mind and spirit. I'd sit in Enid's brother's Internet shop and type away on my novel, thoroughly cleaning each sentence of passive phrases and any mistakes. When I needed a break, I'd pull up photos Dyango posted of the bulls running down the hillside into town in Cuéllar. The images of the horses and the enormous dust cloud entranced me. It was what I wanted: a clean desire. I needed to go to Cuéllar. I dreamt of Cuéllar often. It stirred me deeply. I wondered why. Why was I so obsessed with these animals, and what drew me to run with them? I obviously wasn't alone in this desire. Millions of people from around the world voyaged to Spain to experience the tradition. It clearly wasn't just a Spanish tradition; it must be a human tradition.

Red meat from the bovine shaped man's destiny more than that of any other animal. The hunting of enormous and dangerous bovine took a lot of systematic cooperation and coordination. That cooperation brought humans together and created societies beyond familial bands. Evidence of one such form of cooperative hunting is found in North America in what's called a buffalo jump. Horses didn't arrive in the Americas until the Spanish conquistadors brought them in the 1500s. Native Americans hunted buffalo in North America for 6,000 years on foot. The most famous buffalo jump is the Head-Smashed-In Buffalo Jump in Alberta, Canada. The American Museum of Natural History excavated the site in 1938; it became a World Heritage Site in 1981. The Blackfoot tribe's expert "Buffalo Runners" corralled buffalo into drive lanes lined by hundreds of cairns, which funneled the herd toward the cliff. Cairns are very similar to the barricades which funnel the pack in Pamplona to the killing grounds in the arena.

This idea of cairns and stampede hunting fascinated me. It seemed to me like this was the oldest core of what we were doing during the encierro in Pamplona. I reached out to fifty-five-year-old Stan Knowlton, a full-blooded member of the Piikani Nation, which is part of the Black Foot Confederacy. Stan is also Head of Interpretation at Head-Smashed-In Buffalo Jump Park. First thing I wanted to know was what a cairn is.

"Cairns are part of a drive lane system that would extend ten miles long that led from the gathering basin to the buffalo jump. They were one to two miles wide at gathering basin and they funneled down to fifty feet wide at the jump. Each cairn was comprised of about thirty piled-up stones with tree branches spreading between each cairn. There's about ten miles of rock forming our cairns here. As you drove the animals, they compressed. It was like loading a spring. If you tried to drive 75 to 300 animals toward the buffalo jump without cairns, they'd just disperse and run away. Plus you wanted them compressed into as tight a group as possible when they reach maximum velocity.

In some places there were as many as six different lanes leading to the buffalo jump.

"Mainly they hunted cows and calves after the rut in autumn because they made for better food and clothing. The males separate from the females after the rut. The herds they hunted were led by dominant females.

"The buffalo runners themselves would let the herds go into the drive lanes. Then the runners would break into two groups. The ones in back would dress as wolves in wolf's fur and mimic wolf behavior and noises. The runners in front would dress as calves wearing buffalo calf fur and start to run through the channels toward the buffalo jump while crying like scared calves. The runners in back would keep the animals moving forward slowly. Once the stampede was initiated the dominant cow would run and move in front of the runners dressed as calves in a protective formation. The runners in back would chase closely, driving the stampede. The cairns would keep the lead cow from cutting to the sides. Buffalo have very bad peripheral depth perception so the cairns would look like impassable walls and blend in with the horizon. The cliff itself is deceptive too; it looks like it simply rolls downhill. The animals don't see the huge drop; it was fifty to seventy feet deep. It's only half that depth today. The buffaloes' legs would break and they'd be completely immobile; the ones who survived the fall were easy to kill, and they processed the animals nearby and used every part of the animal—for food, tools, clothing, and tents.

"A successful hunt could bring in 9,000 pounds of meat. It fed the entire nation, roughly 30,000 people, for the winter. It was their winter survival rations. All the food also provided them with leisure time, which fostered a lot of spiritual and artistic expression."Buffalo jumps are more about the management of the animals; there is less correlation between hunting and this act. There was a very rich connection between the land, the people, and the buffalo.

"A local group from Browning have done two reenactments without buffalo, just people in costumes. My running days are far behind me, but if there was ever a chance to do it again, there are plenty of people who would do it.

"I would like to see somebody actually do a hunt. I would like to see somebody use the cliff up here, and to take the animals and do it so that we can actually record it and see exactly how it happened. In living history right now, no one has actually witnessed a buffalo jump.

"This is how we hunted prairie bison. We also hunted woodland buffalo; we'd run the buffalo into traps made of trees.

"We would also drive buffalo down these steep hills and they would crash into the mud and bog at the bottom, and you could see how they used the rivers and creeks and the canyons."

This conversation with Stan was revelatory for me. Many intellectuals claimed the deepest origins of man and bull rituals were the Minoan Crete Bull Dancers, which date back to 3300 BC. This ritualized and highly coordinated buffalo running, jumping, and killing had evidence dating back to at least 6000 BC in the Americas. How long similar forms took place in Europe and the rest of the prehistoric world is highly debated in the field of archaeology. I reached out to renowned paleoanthropologist Henry Bunn of the University of Wisconsin in search of more evidence of drive hunting that reaches deeper into the dawn of humanity.

"Let me start by pointing out several classic sites of animal drives both from Europe and Africa. There is a site in France called Le Solutré where there are the remains of an estimated 100,000 dead horses at the bottom of a steep mountainside with stone tools and butchery damage. There are also many reindeer and aurochs, the ancestors of Toro Bravo, present at the site. It is a deeply stratified site that dates back to 55,000 years ago and was used for roughly 25,000 years. The classic interpretation was that hunters were somehow convincing fairly intelligent horses to go way up this long mountainside, and then running them off the cliff like in the Head-Smashed-In Buffalo Jump. Experts on horse behavior have since doubted this theory. It could have easily been drives and ambush hunting in the lower elevations, the rivers and canals flowing off the mountainside.

"There is a site in South Africa called Klasies River Mouth dating back over 100,000 years ago. It's on the southern cape of Africa and it contains almost one hundred dead eland at the base of a cliff. Eland are roughly 1,800-pound antelopes. The lead anthropologist on Klasies argued that because of their herd-loving docile nature, hunters could have driven eland off the cliffs there."There is a site in central Spain, about a hundred kilometers from Pamplona, dating roughly 300,000 years back. There are two sites—one is called Torrabla, the other Ambrona—that are several kilometers apart and both involve marshy deposits where not only bone is preserved but wood is present, and some of the wood is burned and in that deposit there are the remains of several dozen elephants. There are other animals present but the ingredients are there; there's stone tools, there's burned wood, and there's dead elephants. So archaeologists connected the dots, suggesting Homo sapiens were using fire to stampede herds of elephants into the marsh.

"The oldest site for driving is the site I have spent most of my years researching, is the site at Olduvai Gorge. It dates back to 1.3 million years ago and involves Homo erectus. It is a site called BK, which is a marshy part of a river channel chock-full of stone tools, and there are the remains of 24 giant buffalo. Louis Leakey, my mentor, and the one who led research on Olduvai interpreted the evidence from BK as Homo erectus driving the buffalo into the swamp, in this case with spears. Then once they were stuck in the mud they couldn't escape and Homo erectus killed them with spears."

The significance of this form of cooperative drive hunting, especially at Head-Smashed-In Buffalo Jump and Le Solutré, was clearly the formation of the original societies and what spawned leisure time for humans to create art and spirituality—the absolute foundation of humanity.

"Years later one of my critics would ask a poignant question: "Why is the running of the bulls such a deep trigger for so many people?" The answer is because running with bovine and large game herds is something our ancestors have been doing for over a million years, since the dawn of human existence.

In Mexico City that New Year's, when it was time to write my twelve wishes, I wrote eleven times asking that my novel be accepted for publication. The twelfth wish was that I would make it to Cuéllar. As the wish list smoldered on the small concrete porch of the apartment, I realized that I'd left out a lot of things, and I accepted that. This magic worked very strong on me. I knew that I would have to sacrifice some of the magic for my two deep wishes to come true. I acknowledged my fate, though I planned to find a way to outsmart it. I came home charged up and ready for my new year.

Then in January I landed the cover story for *Newcity,* another arts weekly in Chicago. The story focused on female boxing promoter who was being preyed upon by the corrupt Illinois Boxing Commission. Landed an even more lucrative gig with *Outside Online*; this time they paid me $1,000, and that covered my ticket for Pamplona. Then the big one came. I got a gig with the *Chicago* T*ribune's Printers Row Journal,* the paper's literary supplement, to write an essay on Ernest Hemingway and James Michener's rivalry and history at fiesta. I interviewed Joe Distler, John Hemingway, and Alexander Fiske-Harrison for the piece. It came out the first Sunday of fiesta.

An American mozo named Dennis Clancey was working on a documentary called *Chasing Red* and selected me as a main character. He even pasted my mug running on the horns as the working cover. He flew in with his cameraman Brandon the weekend of the All City Championships that spring and filmed me at home.

About a month before fiesta, Akashic Books sent news they'd denied my novel for publication on a three-two split in their editorial board. It was hard to swallow. My heart was set on publishing with them. Figured I'd just get through the summer and try something else in the fall. Enid couldn't make it to fiesta for work reasons, so I headed out alone.

John Hemingway brought his son Michael to fiesta that year. Michael was a skinny, pubescent high school kid. He was friendly and extremely excited about San Fermín. I was so excited to be part of the fourth generation of Hemingways to partake in fiesta. During Chupinazo Michael was up in a Posse balcony and he took some fantastic stills of the raucous crowd. Michael was a budding photographer and showed me the photos during breakfast. I asked him if I could include them in my blog for Outside Magazine. As much as they were a document of the 2012 opening ceremony, they were also a chance to look through the eyes of a Hemingway during his very first experience with fiesta, something I'm sure Ernest was looking down on with a smile. It was also a chance to nudge a young artist in the right direction toward following his passion, and I was very glad to have the opportunity to do it. So Michael Hemingway's first photography publication was with *Outside* Magazine. Michael would go on to become an excellent encierro photographer in the years to come. He'd even come down to Telefónica sometimes to shoot my stretch hoping to catch a shot of me.

On the opening morning, I ran Telefónica. Whiffed on the main pack but then a brown straggler bull appeared. The mozos on my left collapsed in a big tangled bunch. I leaped over them in front of the bull's face and led him into the mouth of the tunnel. People dropped like flies throughout the tunnel. I dodged through them, losing my connection with the animal. I finally fell as I got to the sand of the arena. None of this made television and I couldn't find any quality photos, but communing with the bull made me glad, even in all that chaos. As usual, Juan Pedro ran beautifully for 200 yards, leading the pack through the last quarter of the course. It was twice as good as any run I'd ever had, and it was just an average one for Juan Pedro.

Some mozos have a special relationship with the animals. Juan Pedro Lecuona lived in Pamplona most of his life. Both of his parents were deaf, and that made things difficult financially for the family. As a child, Juan would go a ranch north of Pamplona where he worked and lived. At ten years old he would take a pastor's cane and go into the part of the ranch where they kept the stud bull. He'd use the stick to get the bull's attention. "That's how I started learning and understanding the reactions of bulls," he said.

At the age of sixteen, Lecuona was short and stoutly built and terrible at sports.

"I just sucked. I gave it everything I had but I just sucked in every sport, and football especially."

Lecuona ran the encierro Txiki, a run just for kids where they use vaca instead of bulls, but his first full encierro was remarkable.

"I went in with a Miura on my first run into the arena in 1989. The memory of that first run comes very slowly, like a photogram, every single moment. The Miura comes up running and it hits the fence and I start to run. I remember I was trying to run fast but I felt like I wasn't getting anywhere. The feeling was I want to run more but I just can't. In the callejón, the bulls were passing next to me and the bull was right beside me. Back then you didn't have as many pictures. There weren't as many photographers. A photographer named Javier Monero came to me and showed a photo of me running with the herd in the callejón. Back then it would cost six euros for a photo, and I couldn't afford that because I was from a humble family. Years later he gave me the photo. I have it in my home."

A lot of things changed for Lecuona in the next few years. He grew six inches, got thin and fast, and began running encierros phenomenally.

His running became legendary just four years in on July 11, 1993. There was a terrible montón at Telefónica.

"I remember that I was running full speed and the pack was running close behind me when suddenly I see a montón. My intention was to throw myself to the side, but when I got to it I just jumped and got caught in the montón and I couldn't get up. There was so much pressure keeping me in the pile. Suddenly, the first thing I see is a bull next to me named Partidos Reciete, so I think, 'fuck I'm stuck, I can't do anything.' The bull was plowing slowly through the montón, and as he went past I grabbed the bull by the horn and the bull pulled me out of the montón. So when the bull comes out he sees he is carrying some extra weight that's not his, he just looks straight at me. I touch his slobbery mouth with my hand, get my footing, and I manage to run and lead this bull all the way inside the bullring."

Because of Lecuona's experience on ranches and his excellent running, Pamplona appointed him as Mulillero, a person in charge of dragging the dead bulls after the corrida out of the bullring using a team of horses.

In 2010 Lecuona was leading a pack of Miura bulls when one gored him high in the inner thigh. The horn went up and through and popped out the front of his thigh. Juan immediately stood and looked the animal in the eye. He held the wound closed, and when he told a medic he was gored they didn't believe him. Then he removed his hand and a long stream of blood shot out.

Juan Pedro is a man of his word. He'd promised a TV reporter friend of his that he would do a segment on the encierro at Falces, which takes place a month after San Fermín. It is easily the craziest run and the most brutal on the body. They run the vaca down a steep mountainside. Almost every single runner falls on the course. Juan kept his word and ran the bottom section excellently. He fell dramatically on his belly at the very bottom with the pack of vaca hooking for him.

But probably his most magical moment was on July 13, 2003.

"There was an opening in the crowd, I see one toro of the Miura and this bull was running very, very fast like light-speed! So like the mentality of the runner, I knew I was getting in. So the bull was so fast that the people weren't expecting him because he was a suelto and was hitting people the whole course. So the bull was splitting through the runners and people were falling down. I ran in front of the bull when a group of about eight people fell directly in front of us. I stepped through them, avoiding a back, a leg, an arm. I was making it through one step after the other, after the other. I kept finding my places to step through the bodies to the street. The bull was avoiding stepping on the people too, like me, but at some point the bull caught up to me and pushed into my back. I finally tripped on one of the fallen people. In that moment, I reached back and put my hand on the bull's forehead and we both fell. I kept my hand on the head and we both were kneeling, and suddenly the bull stands up and with the same force that I brought the bull down with, the bull brought me up and made me stand up because my hand never left the bull's head. We'd been in contact the entire fall and now we were standing again.

"So I tapped the bull on the head with my paper. I just start running and led that bull all the way into the plaza."

For good reason, Pamplona often picks Juan for promotional material for the run: huge banners and illustrations and even keychains. In a lot of ways he is the iconic Pamplona runner. Though if someone compliments him on his running, he immediately humbles himself, saying, "But look how fat I am!"

In my mind then, Juan Pedro symbolized the epitome of excellence in the encierro. He was consistent; he was brilliant. Then, I was still thinking of the encierro as a competition, and that TV footage and photos in the newspaper were a way to score your runs. I wanted to run like Juan Pedro, and I thought that meant I had to battle the other mozos for the best run; that it was one big competition, and in the end if I wanted to win and be great, I had to somehow beat Juan Pedro.

It's amazing how wrong I was. Juan Pedro would begin to explain this to me over the years, but first he showed me.

The second day I took off much later than usual and ran the horns of the lead bull at Top of Estafeta. There was a surge of runners closing in on my left. Suddenly Juan Pedro was beside me.

We ran stride for stride on the horns of the lead black bull. The crowd swelled on my left. I tripped on their feet. Just when I was about to fall, Juan Pedro reached his arm out, hooked my elbow, and caught me. The move shocked me. I looked at him and he nodded. We ran on like that for several strides. Then another runner on my left in blue and white stripes yelled "JUANPE!" (Juan's nickname) as he struggled through the current of bodies. JuanPe sighed and reached across my chest and they clasped arms and JuanPe pulled him through the chaos. As they pulled, their arms inadvertently pushed against my chest and dragged me backward toward the bull's horn, which neared my spine. I panicked and swung my arms down to break their grasp on each other in order to run faster. They tried to hold tight but I finally broke free. The other runner angrily yelled at me. The animal noticed the chaos and veered around us.

I tried to understand what just happened when the rest of the herd appeared and I started to position to run them. As the pack approached I had a nice line and wanted to cut in front of a steer to run the horns of a bull that galloped snug against the fencing. I crossed the steer's face and he suddenly bellowed, accelerated, and pushed his forehead into my back. It felt soft; I thought it was another runner pushing me and I leaned into it to keep from falling. Then the steer gathered its leverage and leaped hard into my back and I was airborne. I went from running to flying. I slammed flat. My face, knees, arms, and chest cracked the stones simultaneously, then a microsecond later my testicles smacked the pavement. I've never felt pain like that. The herd passed over me without stepping on me. I crawled under the barricades and the medics went to work. Blood oozed from all over. I walked back to Bar Txoko and told the embarrassing tale to everyone's amusement.

Later I went to Foto Mena and found several shots of the interaction with JuanPe. I contemplated them closely. The more I thought about what had happened I realized Juan had saved me and had been attempting to save the other runner, who I later found out was named José Manuel. I'd helped push some bonehead tourists to safety over the years but I'd never considered helping another serious runner in a situation like that. Juan's generosity and grace over those few strides blew my mind and understanding of the encierro. I felt really bad about breaking JuanPe's grasp on José Manuel. I recognized José's blue and white striped shirt. We'd run on the horns together several times near shoulder to shoulder. He'd yelled at me after I broke their grasp and I really wanted to make it up to him. José was an excellent runner in his own right.

Ran into Bomber that afternoon outside Windsor. He laughed his ass off about my crushed nuts story but when he saw the photo of JuanPe catching my arm he took it in his hands. "This is one historic photo!" He guffawed. "To be helped by Juan Pedro Lecuona, a great maestro of Pamplona!" Then he looked to the bright sky hovering over the plaza and shouted, "Viva San Fermín!"

Bomber had a way of giving me chills when he talked. Probably should have told him then but I didn't.

The next morning I ran the horns of gorgeous, red colorado bull. A big pack of bulls and steers galloped behind us when a tall guy with long hair ended up right in front of me. I pushed gently at his back but he didn't budge. He was about to crush me between him and the bull behind me. I said to myself, *damn, you're a brave motherfucker*, and cut out to the side. But then he finally looked back and saw the bull, screamed like a little girl, and dived out of the way. The two bulls behind me nearly hit me and a Spanish mozo pulled me into the fencing trying to save me. I bounced back off the fence and ran beside those two bulls all the way through the tunnel into the arena.

I was frustrated and figured I should have pushed that big asshole right out of the way and I would have had a great long run on the horns. But I just said, what the hell; at least no one got hurt.The next morning I ran in great position entering the tunnel. I was on the horns of a brown bull when a guy behind me grabbed hold of my shirt and yanked with all his might. I lost balance backward and tangled with the other runners. Fell down on my butt. The bull's hooves crackled incredibly close. I raised my hand like to defend a punch and the bull's horn swung low within three inches of my eye and banged into my wrist and was gone. Somehow they didn't step on me.

Shock completely blacked out my memory until later when Peter Milligan told me what happened and said there were pictures up of it. Not running the horns for the first time that year really depressed me until I saw the pictures. It heartened me to know I was on the horns and slightly terrified me that the bull had almost taken my left eye in the process.

The next morning was the Fuente Ymbro. I'd had two of my best runs with this herd. I liked them because their horns bent in a nice upward hook at the tips, which allowed them to push things out of their way instead of goring everything they touched.

I ran well and found myself beside Juan Pedro again. Felt the herd on us and was on the horns of a bull when the mozo in front of me toppled over another runner. The runner on the ground, instead of lying flat so other runners and the herd could easily step over him, rolled on his back and thrust his knees up into the air. I tried to hurdle him and tripped over him. The main herd passed and I clawed my way to my feet when another two bulls surged up. A couple guys grabbed me and pulled and pushed me for no gain for anyone. It just made for some really ugly pictures.

A *Jobonero* (soap-colored bull) trotted heavily past and nearly sliced my stomach open as I sucked my gut in along the fencing. His sculpted body looked as if it had been cut from a giant hunk of ivory. The Jobonero lumbered on slowly, and I knew I could catch up to him. I ran my ass off, inadvertently bumping Peter Milligan into the fencing. I sprinted up beside the bull's horns, leaped and grabbed hold of the nearest horn, hurdled it and positioned myself in front of him. The white Jobonero trotted godly like Zeus on his way to abduct Europa. I linked with this powerful beast and ran his horns for fifteen yards when a runner in front of me began to slow. I pushed the fuck out of him and screamed "GO!" He was a little guy and fell flat. He looked back and kicked his legs up and tripped me so I fell on my face. The white bull trotted past me like nothing could disrupt him from his mythical destiny. I rolled under the barricades and my own personal Red Cross guy worked on me. Hollander happened to be right there and caught a few nice shots of me running on the horns of the bull. Then he took some photos of me laughing as the Red Cross cleaned up my already busted-up elbows, knees, and face. He said, "Caption: crazy, stupid American journalist hurt again in the run." I cracked up. A female medic appeared and talked to me in English. She helped me interview my Red Cross guy and I finally got my medic interview for my *Outside* blog. His name was Jesús Muniain; he was a big, strong, bald guy. He'd been there on all the recent bloody days and I was very thankful to get the story.

I was happy again that I'd had a nice run on the horns, and that made five days in a row on the horns: my own personal record. I missed making it on television again and missed the papers. It just wasn't in my magic to be out there like that with all the attention that year. I was trying to deal with that as Gus and Dennis received a ton of fanfare.

It was difficult in a way to be happy with what I'd accomplished that far into fiesta. Nearly everything I'd done was anonymous, unknown, and unproven. The only thing it rested on was my word and the few people who'd seen pictures or witnessed it on the street. People looked at me as if I were telling lies and rolled their eyes at my stories. I even began to doubt the truth of some of my experiences that I hadn't seen proof of in photos. It was a complex strain of emotions. Then on the sixth day of runs I was in great position to run a big pack, but I got greedy and wanted to peel off and run a later pack. As I peeled away I crossed in front of the Basque runner in the plaid shirt and he rightfully pushed me and I fell. I looked back, waited for an opening, and got up near the barricades. Suddenly Gary appeared beside me and screamed in my face. Didn't know what he was saying when I picked up two bulls approaching us. I readied to run. As I did I noticed Juan Pedro Lecuona running the horns and David Rodríguez running beside a bull. There was a perfect opening for me to run with them. I started in and Gary reached out and snagged my shirt and yanked hard. I tried to pull through it and fell. I'd dragged Gary out into the street with me and he peddled backward as the bulls nearly gored him and luckily flowed over me without stepping on me.

I crawled to the fencing and Jesús, my Red Cross guy, grabbed me by my pants and nearly ripped my pants off, pulling me under the barricades. Jesús scolded me on the other side and walked away angrily. The runners stepped on me a lot and I kind of blacked out. I completely forgot what had happened; all I knew was I hadn't run on the horns. As I walked back toward Bar Txoko I saw my tag-along video guy from the documentary and he asked me what happened.

"Nothing much, I missed and fell." I stepped into a bar to watch the replay and saw Dennis have a spectacular run down Mercaderes, and then the bulls he was running nearly gored him and he got off but then cut behind them and sprinted through the curve and back onto their horns again. It was a spectacular run, the best of an American that year. All of it really sunk me into depression. When I got to Txoko, Gary walked up to me like he was going to say something, but I had no idea what he was talking about. I tell first-time runners and beginners never to get up, but I am an experienced runner and I get up just like all experienced runners do because I know when it's safe to. I really don't know what was going through Gary's head and I didn't even realize that it happened until two days later when Enid told me that Gary pulled me down in the photos.

I really lost it. I fell into a deep depression. I didn't know why this was happening, after I'd worked so hard and prepared so vigorously for this year. It was disheartening. I somehow could hear people talking and laughing about me. About the year I'd had, about my falls, and about all of it. I began again to question why I was voluntarily doing all this to myself, in fact why was I paying money, putting strain on my marriage, risking my life, hurting myself physically. *For what? So people could laugh at me?* I hung my Gohonzon, a Buddhist mandala, and started chanting. I chanted long into the night until I fell asleep. Then I'd wake and chant more and then sleep and wake and chant.

Somewhere in the night I realized I was jealous of Dennis. Of the spectacular year he was having. Then I struggled with how selfish and petty it was to feel that way. *I should be happy for Dennis.* I'd always wanted for there to be a new strong generation of American runners, of foreign runners who could be ambassadors for the run throughout the world, who could speak the truth of what this culture was about. Dennis was creating a high-quality film that could be seen by millions who didn't know the first thing about this culture. He could help put a positive, factual, and accurate image in people's minds before the animal-rights advocates tried to destroy their opinions. Not only that, but he'd reached out to include me in this project. *What an honor! What a chance to be part of something special! Something that could truly give back to Spain and this culture.* Realized also that I had accomplished things this year. I knew deep down that it was real, even though I hadn't gotten the TV or photographic attention I'd gotten the year before. If the petty little twerps down at Txoko couldn't see that and dismissed me as having a failure of a year, what did I care? Why would I put any value on their opinions? Many had never had half the runs I'd already had and never would. They didn't have a tenth of the passion and love for the run as I have and they never would. Dennis did. And that didn't make him my rival. It made him my brother.

Finally I woke and went to the street and up to the HQ. I realized that I'd contributed to some of the falls. When the guy grabbed me at the opening of the tunnel I could have fought harder, let him rip the shirt right off my back and kept running the horns, but I let him pull me down and it nearly killed me. The failures were coming from me, from something deep inside me.

The video guy came up to the HQ, and as I was warming up he was filming. I was alone. Told him and the film that I had found something inside myself that was keeping me from running my best, that even though I'd run so aggressively I'd found that deep down there was something broken. That I was afraid. That I was letting myself drift out of the center of the street. That I took last night, and I think I found it and found a way to repair it and that I hoped it was fixed and that we would see what happens that morning.

On the elevator ride, Gus and I shook hands. I didn't shake with Gary because it wouldn't be on camera anyway. Gary was visibly hurt; I laughed it off, but he didn't. I hugged Gus and wished him luck. We took to the street and Gary walked off ahead of me. The cameraman walked with me and I caught up with Gary and put my arm around him and we walked all the way up Estafeta together like that, with each other's arms around our shoulders. He said something about not being in the film, and I said, "I don't give a damn about the film, Gary, this is our time together, brother."

When we got to Telefónica the police made the cameraman exit, and I was walking around looking up at the blue sky in the narrow channel between the buildings. I asked myself, *why are you doing this?* And three birds soared high across the channel. *Because you love this place.* The answer hummed straight from my heart. Joy overwhelmed me and I shook as many hands as I could: JuanPe, the runner in yellow who I'd inadvertently tripped up the year before, everyone. All of them. I chanted gratefully and joyfully, for everything: fiesta, the encierro, the bulls, the other runners, Dennis, Gus, Gary. Suddenly a voice came to me and said, "You're going to run the horns today."

I shook it off and kept chanting, "Nam-myoho-renge-kyo . . . Nam-myoho-renge-kyo . . . Nam-myoho-renge-kyo . . . " It came again. It was like someone grabbed me by the shoulders and told me, "You are going to run the horns today." I just smiled as the bulls approached. I watched the cameraman on the balcony across the way, and when he turned with the first animal, I ran.

As the bulls approached that morning, I held the center of Estafeta as it gave way to Telefónica. Suddenly, I knew I would have the horns. I glance back and there he is—a lead suelto cutting through the runners. He is black, lean, and fast. A strand of muck spreads across his snout. A channel opens to me. I dash into a sprint, then José Manuel rockets beside me in his blue and white striped shirt. José recognizes me, yells angrily, and shoves my hip. I sway wide and then swing back beside him. Runners cascade like dominoes on either side of the avenue— the pocket preserved by their evacuation. José nudges again and I nudge back; our arms lock, fighting for balance. We sprint shoulder to shoulder directly on either horn—even the cadence of our steps in perfect sync. Thirty yards like this, then another runner cuts in on José. He fights him off. I remember Juan grabbing my arm and José's arm to help keep the herd together, and how I'd disrupted that sacred moment. I reach out and catch José's elbow to steady him. He looks at me appalled, mystified. We enter the tunnel on the horns. José peels off to the left, grabs my wrist for me to follow as the suelto accelerates. *No, José, I'm taking this one to the end.* I accelerate through the tunnel— the bull's snout centered close at my back. We link and become one beast, one force soaring onward. A wall of tourists slowly disintegrates before us. Three fall on the right. One cuts in front of us and stomps my foot as he goes. My rhythm breaks and I teeter to the left. I try to right my balance and momentum. The roar of the arena—brilliant white—envelopes me. I know that there's no hope. I twist in midair and look back. His gorgeous face enters the light behind me—his head up and white horns high. His oily black fur glows. I could touch his damp snout. The bright spectacle of the arena explodes in his eyes. I descend. Falling in an encapsulated moment—my face kisses the warm sand like a pilgrim kissing the holy land. Its embrace is soft and warm. He passes over me and on to the dobladores' pink capes—a majestic rocket of black ferocity.

I don't mind when my run isn't aired on television. If I came to Pamplona to be on TV—I'd despise myself. I had the honor to run with the animal and with the great runner José Manuel and even got to help him in a moment of peril. Couldn't have been more honored with the opportunity. I don't care that the people of Pamplona don't stop to congratulate me. Instead, I want to congratulate them for keeping their beautiful culture intact.

Walking up Estafeta I see Dennis high above on one of the balconies where the crew was filming. I yelled up, "How was your run?"

"Good, how about yours?"

"The best of the year," I replied. We smiled, happy for one another like brothers should be.

When I see José Manuel again the next morning, I walk up to him. He stands in a doorway watching the sky, his face in blissful prayer. Many birds soar high above Telefónica. I reach out my hand and he takes it. We embrace. He looks me in the eyes and pats my face, thanking me. Joy fills my heart and I walk around and shake hands with every single Spaniard and Basque runner near me. All the ones who I've always been afraid to shake hands with, they take my hand without reservation and look me in the eyes and squeeze my shoulder. Then other, younger Spanish runners begin to come up to shake my hand. And I know something has changed forever, something much more important than a slow-motion replay on a television. Tremendous pride swells in my heart at what Dennis and Gus have been doing. Their excellence in and respect for the tradition only magnifying the good foreigners and paying homage to the ones who came before us. Then I can see what I've always wanted unfolding before me—a potent and powerful new generation of foreign mozos. A generation that hopefully one day can stand shoulder to shoulder with the great generations of the past—the generations of Carney, and Distler, and Bomber, and Ibarra, and Sinclair, and Turley, and so many others.

When the run began on the final morning, I started but the others yanked me and something said, *get out, get out of the way.* I let them pull me to the fencing and was okay when the herd passed, and I realized I'd run for Enid and I'd run safe for her and I realized that I should always save one run for my wife, one run where I didn't go all the way, where I was just there on the street to enjoy it and not to run risking life and limb.

I was happy and not discouraged by not running the horns. Didn't care about that anymore. I only cared that I'd gotten to be with my brothers on the street. I'd gotten to be just one of many mozos creating an encierro.

Another bright spot was this seventeen-year-old Canadian kid named Ben. He'd run every day of the fiesta. He was really into it. On the final morning he'd decided he was going to stand in the center of the street and wait until he saw a bull, then run. He did it, and as the bull approached he ran its horns for fifteen yards and then screamed in the slow-motion footage and peeled off to the side. It was such a raw and brilliant moment. He really impressed me, and I was happy for him. I pulled him aside later that day and told him, "You could be the future of the foreign tradition in Pamplona."

He just smiled shyly. "I'm really proud of you," I told him and patted him on the back.

That night we headed down to *Pobre de Mi*, the closing candlelit ceremony. The champion Peña band plays on the stage before the Town

Hall as thousands of revelers crowd into the square with candles. The band plays music; "El Rey" is a popular one, then as it gets close to midnight the music sways back and forth between the deeply sad song that sings "poor me poor me San Fermín is over" to a happy song of counting down the months until next San Fermín. As we sang happily and gloomily, I realized the encierro wasn't about me. I was only one very small and unimportant piece of it.

It's like the buffalo runners of the Blackfoot tribe. I was one of the runners; I had a duty to contribute to the encierro. And to contribute to the encierro, I had to cooperate and coordinate with the other mozos, follow leadership and give leadership at the right times.

I looked out into the sea of sad singing faces and recognized several runners: Steve Ibarra, Juan Pedro Lecuona, runners whose names I didn't know, men from all over the world, young and old. I glanced at Ben who sang behind me with the Posse; his eyes were all watery. *These mozos are your brothers.* That's when I realized what mozo means. It doesn't just mean young men or bull runners; mozo means servant. We are servants to the encierro and servants to the bulls. That's why San Fermín always rewards the humble. We are servants and nothing more.

We had to work together for there to be success on the streets, and success was as simple as completing the ritual hunt, the encierro, in as safe and direct a way as possible. And when it was successful, there was reason for great gratitude and celebration and taking part in the feast, just like with the Blackfoot tribe and the Sulutreans, this was an ancient and fundamental human tradition. As the closing fireworks tore into the sky beside the immaculate façade of Town Hall, I ached very deeply for next year, closed my eyes, and whispered, *Ya falta menos*

CHAPTER EIGHT:
QUEST

When I got home I was very broken up and hurt. I couldn't do as much as normal on the construction site, and I stopped competing with the other workers to be the best, and to have the power. So I just put in my day's work like any other. The encierro was teaching me about cooperation and about being part of society.

I started getting along with my brother Dave better; I tried to quell arguments instead of instigate them. Realized that I was extremely lucky to be working at all in the terrible economy. That my father had worked so hard just to give us jobs. I became much more grateful for everything I had.

Enid and I were all set to go to the Edinburgh Festival, the largest arts festival in the world, to compete in a city-versus-city Story Slam against Edinburgh. Irvine set me up with his friend, the enigmatic underground icon Kevin Williamson. We were all very excited. I pitched the *Printers Row Journal* to cover the event. I hadn't lost hope of going to Cuéllar, and if I landed a story I said I would go. When we got to Gus's house outside Glasgow I checked my email, and sure enough the *Chicago Tribune* Travel Section said yes to a story on Cuéllar's run. Then Xander said he would put in some money to have me at Cuéllar for his story for the *Financial Times* of London. So I changed my flight. I wanted our time in Scotland to be about Enid and did everything I could to make sure she had a good time. We stayed with Gus a few nights and went to a nice city garden in Glasgow and walked around, then to a breathtaking mountain cemetery and climbed it for hours. It was incredible. Padre and Fiona showed up in the camper van and asked what we wanted to do. I told him Enid wants to see a real castle. Padre said "sorted," and the next day he took Will, Rachel, Enid, and me on a few-hour ride to see a castle. At one point we stopped at a lake and fed the geese and swans and even had to run a few suelto-swans up the parking lot using bread to lure them. Then we went to the coast and walked along the shore, just talking and having a wonderful time. We went to this great castle. They cooked some haggis in the camper and we chilled out on lawn chairs. It was the best.

The Story Slam sold out, but we decided we'd still sneak in a bunch of the Posse who'd come from all over Europe to see us. We were lucky enough to go to Milo McCabe's solo show in the hours before our event. I'd remembered one night walking around fiesta with him, just bantering, and suddenly something snuck up on me and whispered, *he's a comical genius.* I tried to shake it off but I finally accepted it. When I saw Milo's poster, there were several rave reviews. I kind of thought for a second it was a joke because they were over the top. Then I saw that the *London Times* called his show "Genius." I couldn't believe it. Is that real? I asked Graeme. He just shrugged.

The show was incredible. It was autobiographical but fictionalized. The story explored his father's rise and fall as a comedian. It had real pathos and was incredibly funny as well, but on an intellectual level it was true genius. All I could say was, "Milo, it's amazing, congratulations."

Afterward Xander showed up to cover the Story Slam for the *Spectator*, a London-based magazine. We showed up with twenty people and no tickets to a sold-out event at Summer Hall. Padre took over immediately and ordered the workers around and got a dozen beanbags put on the floor of this incredible dissection room in the veterinary hospital; they'd converted the campus into the largest private arts venue in all of Europe. Padre expressed that he had always dreamed of performing at the Edinburgh Festival. When I told him I didn't know if one team member would show up, Padre said that he would fill in. I replied that he might just have to. I rocked the house with a story about beating the hell out of my brother when he was still a heroin addict before he beat his addiction and made a family for himself. I worked it around so the end is this image of my brother with his young son looking up at him with so much pride. Felt the crowd lean in when I got to that last line. Enid said a few girls were crying. I beat the local star, Jenni Fagan, who is an internationally acclaimed Scottish author and had brought out a lot of the crowd. Padre stepped in and told a story in a head-to-head heat against Irvine Welsh. Padre of course lost, as Irvine wowed even me, and I have very high expectations of Irvine performing live.

Chicago lost 3-2, but if you subtract Irvine from the scoring we won 2-1, but subtract Irvine from the equation and the event doesn't fucking happen. Afterward everyone was pretty blissful. Jenni Fagan's agent asked me about my story. I told him about my novel and he expressed interest in reading it and gave me his card.

I was very grateful to have the chance to help make one of Padre's dreams come true; after all he'd helped make a countless number of mine come true over the years. It was a love fest that night at a local bar and then we all jumped on the bus and went back to our places in Glasgow.

Enid left the next day. I headed down to London on an eight-hour bus ride. I met up with Xander near his apartment in London. That's when the media frenzy began.

On my first day there, the *Spectator* article hit and Xander established me as an internationally acclaimed storyteller. He also raved about the show. We decided to fly to Almeria, a small city on the Mediterranean, to spend their small fiesta with Joe Distler and Rolf Van Essen. Xander arranged that an unmarked cab would pick us up at his door before sunrise. He said the goal is to sleep on all forms of transportation. We slept on the cab that zoomed us to the airport. We were flying EasyJet; there was an enormous line and we were most definitely going to miss our flight until Xander just stepped up to the front with his royal posture and explained in his posh eloquence that we needed to be checked now. We cut in front of about 500 people and just barely made the flight. We slept on the plane. We arrived in Almeria just after sunrise and slept in the cab to the small hotel. We crashed out and made it to the local taurine bar for drinks that night. It was nice to see Joe outside of Pamplona. It was still hard to get the time with him because everyone wanted to talk with Joe in the packed little bar. The next morning a full spread appeared of Xander in *ABC*, Spain's top national newspaper. Several huge photos of Xander appeared in it. Ana, John Hemingway's then girlfriend, wrote the review and conducted the interview. It was a pretty surreal thing to walk around with a copy of the paper from that very day, with the article about the guy you were traveling with. We watched a bullfight with Joe, and then Xander brought me down to the floor level where I could hear the animal breathe. A guy sitting near us didn't believe that Xander was a bullfighter. I showed him the article and he guffawed.

Later we went to see flamenco in this massive square full to capacity. I ended up sitting beside Joe. We spent hours talking. Joe was drinking wine and telling me some of the greatest stories I've ever heard about bull running and just life in general. He was a great fan of Roberto Duran. Duran even visited his apartment in New York. Joe's restaurant was a haven for A-list Hollywood actors and directors. He was friends with Robert De Niro and Martin Scorsese and they hung around his bar in Tribeca while they filmed *Taxi Driver*. As he told the stories, I felt these explosions of electricity bursting off of him and hallucinated Joe as a twenty-something kid wearing his white panama hat. Ready to scrap at the drop of that hat and running horns like pure magic. Joe told me, "If you continue on this path and continue to improve as a runner, you are going to face a lot of terrible and strange things, trials.

People who you think are your friends will become your harshest critics and detractors. But if you continue to follow your heart and run in the tradition, Spain will open its arms to you. But it will not be easy, my boy; people you love will turn their backs on you. The strangest things will come at you from all kinds of directions you never expected."

It startled me the way Joe was talking. I felt like he was telling me my future, and he might have been.

The honor of that moment astonished me, listening to these breathtaking women sing flamenco in a town hall filled with thousands of Spaniards and maybe just two Americans, Joe Distler and me. I'll never forget that night and will cherish it as long as I live.

The next day Joe and Rolf took Xander and me out for lunch. It was a great feast in a beautiful taurine restaurant with stained glass windows and beautiful toro bravo mounts. Somewhere along the way it occurred to me that I was hanging out with millionaires. I work with my hands and average about $25,000 a year in total income and was just eking above the poverty line. They never made me feel out of place though. I always delve into a listening mind-set when I'm with maestros, and I tried to absorb as much of the greatness and prosperity as I could. Rolf was a leading aficionado of the corrida. But he wasn't snobbish like some aficionados I'd met; he was genuine and friendly and fanned the flames of my interest in the art.

We tried to take the train to Seville but missed it and had to wait until the next morning. We arrived at Seville; the beauty of that city astonished me. This was the Spain I'd heard about and read about. It was the old Spain where every bar had bull mounts. You couldn't walk very far without bumping into a torero. Xander took me to a fantastic tiny bar just down the street from the Plaza de Toros. Several guys played guitars and sang traditional songs. It was a speakeasy bar but the police wouldn't dare to shut it down because it was an institution in the taurine world. The owner had been a torero in his youth and was a devout aficionado. They sang *jotas* as we sat on little handmade stools and drank. The songs were full of heart and passion and I knew instantly that I'd found one of those special places in the world where true magic happens.

Xander took me on a fantastic tour of Seville. It was magnificent. Well, it should be: a British publisher had recently contracted with Xander to write a guidebook of Seville. Xander was probably the foremost expert on the town in the English-speaking world. He'd lived there for a long stretch while writing his memoir and studying bullfighting. It was on this tour that Xander introduced me to *jamón ibérico*. It's these little, razor-thin slices of cured ham. It costs fifteen euros for a small plate, maybe eight pieces. When they touch your tongue they nearly melt. They shocked me so much we had to buy another plate. The pigs live in large pens with oak trees inside, eating only the acorns that drop from the trees. This makes for a distinct perfected flavor. Hunks of ham hang from the ceiling of the bars. The hams start at a whopping $800 and go up from there.

We then met Nicolas Haro, Xander's photographer, who'd done the pictures for *Into the Arena*. Haro had been married to a member of the royal family of Spain, and the *Financial Times* contracted him to take photos for the piece. And he might shoot the photos for my *Chicago Tribune* piece if I was lucky.

Nicolas drove us halfway to Cuéllar and I finished the drive. Pulling into Cuéllar was surreal; there was no traffic. It was an empty little farm town that looked exactly like the rural United States. We drove around the epic white castle and then into the center of town, where it was much busier. I recognized the gray metal fencing of the encierro. We checked into the Hotel San Francisco, a cozy family-owned hotel with a big bar and restaurant. I felt instantly at home. Then we walked the course. It was completely different from the way things looked on television; the encierro course was almost all uphill. Near the hotel there was a long, steep hill, then a curve and straightaway. We walked all the way down to the enormous hill at the edge of town. Then Xander and I climbed it. He took the dirt path and I went straight up the hillside. Looking down over the entire town with the castle on top I realized my quest was complete. *I'm here. I'm in Cuéllar!*

We attended their rowdy but purely local opening ceremony. The Peñas parade through the square, the mayor gives a speech from the balcony of town hall and the teenagers have a mash pit of a sangria fight. We went back to our rooms and had dinner, then I remembered I needed to call Dyango, the runner and sculptor who invited me to Cuéllar. I passed the phone to Xander to translate. Dyango said they were hanging out in the square across the street from the hotel. Figured I probably smelled like a bear and jumped in the shower while Xander and Nicolas walked over. That's when I realized I didn't even know what Dyango looked like. In this modern day of Facebook and all, I only had one photo of him running bulls. There was no way to tell how old the photo was. I went outside and heard a yell and looked and saw a small group playing drums and horns. I crossed the street and found Xander and Nicolas drinking in the park. I sat with them. They said they didn't see anyone. I had no idea what colors or the name of Dyango's *Peña* (communal party group) was. I saw a surly-looking guy walking around. It of course was Dyango, mad because he thought I was taking my sweet time coming out of the hotel, but I had no way to recognize him. And me with my glasses on probably didn't look much like myself in my encierro photos. I can come across as a little bit of a pipsqueak with my glasses on.

I walked around and asked people if they knew Dyango. After about a half hour I ran inside and pulled up Facebook and scrolled through various photos of Dyango and his friends, looking for the colors of his Peña. I found them to be purple and yellow. I ran around until I found a kid wearing a similar-colored shirt and asked if he knew Dyango. He shrugged and turned away, then I looked behind me and saw a family with the colors of Dyango's Peña on. I asked a woman there, and she said that she was Dyango's wife. A few moments later Dyango walked up. Dyango had long, thinning black hair and serious eyes. He wore his purple and yellow Peña colors and looked like an athletic artist. He was a little bitter; he must have been standing across the street for an hour waiting for me to come out.

Dyango then gave us a very stern talk about how to run bulls in Cuéllar. He said that the animals are different in Cuéllar than in Sanse or Pamplona. That once Julen Madina came to Cuéllar and tried to run so close, and he didn't have a good time and he never came back. The sternness he warned me with sort of dejected me and made me feel that I'd done something wrong. I planned to heed Dyango's warning and give the animals space and only run the horns for a short distance. There was another hugely muscular guy with Dyango; he kept giving me dismissive looks. I guess my pipsqueak look wasn't impressing him. I wasn't worried about it though. Knew my running would stand for itself.

The next morning before sunrise Dyango picked us up in his minivan in front of Hotel San Francisco.

As we drove through the outskirts of town, the horsemen trotting alongside the road swiftly outnumbered any modern vehicle. We eased past a staging area where no less than eighty Spanish stallions shivered and neighed, billowing steam in the morning dark. Then a five-kilometer highway ride. Dyango parked along a riverbank facing the exit as cars, horsemen, and walkers oozed into the forest. We came to a clearing in front of the corral, a large concrete structure with two tall steel doors. Both cars and people lined the clearing's edges as morning dew and a low-hung fog clung to the grassy and sandy meadow. Horsemen slowly filtered into the clearing from all directions. A father on a tall black stallion with its mane braided into immaculate knots trotted past us. His two sons on equally beautiful steeds trailed after; the elder thin and stoic in the midst of his obvious fear, the younger a portly preteen yawning in the rising sun. We stood on a small hill under a short, thorny tree where two days later a suelto would gore an old man nine times and his young girlfriend once.

An old man sat at the edge of the hill wearing a cap and puffing sternly on a thin cigar. A walking stick lay across his lap. He possessed the serenity of a man who'd done this exact ritual for decades. We waited, and the tension built. A frightened, whitish gray horse in the midst of the hundreds neighed bitterly, then reared up on its hindquarters as his horseman expertly rode him down and quelled him. At seven, the pen doors swung open and banged into the concrete walls. The herd rocketed through a mass of scattering mozos into the galloping herd of horsemen. A lead suelto soared ahead, angrily swinging his horns. The stampede tore into the pine forest and disappeared into a thick, pink-orange dusty haze.

We jogged to the car and drove three kilometers up the road. Hundreds of cars parked along the edge of a cornfield; that was when I began to understand what a taurine culture is. People from all over the Segovia region drive here just to see the herd gallop past, encircled by the beautiful horses. We jogged to a hillside where many families sat waiting in the bright clean sunlight. The herd never emerged from the pine forest. Murmurs and rumors spread through the crowd. Dyango said we had to go. We stood, and a small boy no older than eight rose and cupped his hand to shade the sun. He looked at me and said, "Los toros se pierden" (the bulls are lost) with a deep aching concern.

We drove to the course near Hotel San Francisco. Suddenly Gus materialized. He'd driven over from Sanse with his friend. Gus's arrival thrilled me. I tried to give him the advice Dyango gave me the day before about not running too close to these bulls but he dismissed it. I shrugged. He was his own man and could handle himself out there. Larry Belcher showed up with his wife, Anna. Larry was a veteran bull runner and former rodeo champion; he lived in the neighboring city of Valladolid and wanted to hang out with us and run the encierro.

The herd usually arrived by nine-thirty, and at ten there was nothing. It turns out the bulls set to run that morning were the cheap set due to a lack of funding. These bulls never interacted with horses before. Four-by-four motorcycles did the work of horses on the ranch they came from. They would not let the horsemen guide them. In fact, they attacked the horses in the pine forest; two noble Spanish stallions gave their lives that morning. The authorities tranquilized five of the six bulls. The sixth disappeared and roamed the Segovia countryside for nine days before a farmer shot and killed him twenty kilometers outside of town.

During Cuéllar's opening ceremony the day before, the mayor made a long speech. He explained why he bought cheap bulls who had never seen horses before. The city had cut back on the funds for the festival. Yet there was an outcry when the mayor proposed to cut one run from the five-day festival; these cheap bulls were his compromise. Now on the opening morning it spiraled into a bloody mess.

As we waited, rumors swelled. Xander caught a nap alongside a boarded-up storefront. Word came the town had decided to release replacement bulls. Dyango vanished. I'd later find out he and several dozen other runners stormed off to the mayor's home. The city called in riot police to quell the altercation when the mob attempted to enter the house to have a conversation with him.

All this left the mozos on the street seriously depleted. There was Xander, Angus Ritchie, Larry Belcher, and myself to give the street team a little boost.

We waited. The first animal soared into view at the bottom of the hill. He ferociously galloped then dropped his head and charged a mozo, then disappeared behind a bend. That old rush spurted in my stomach as Gus and I bumped shoulders and wished each other *suerte*. Four steers swept past and we knew all the rest of the animals down the street were bulls. I waited at the top of the hill and gave ground a little as the barrel-chested suelto surged up the slope, his head high and searching. Gus lingered and I waited with him. The suelto stopped near Gus. Gus got in his space and the animal surged and hooked at him, and was about to gore him when I dashed in the bull's face and he swung his attention to me. I ran as fast as I could and then cut out, but the bull followed me to the fencing. I leaped to the fence and the bull swung and nearly gored me, but Larry called to him and lured him off me and up the street.

Ran up and I passed the bull again as he swung for another runner. I ran for a long distance on his horns with good space between us. Then he was off me and after another runner. I helped work this animal up the street and at the long straightaway before the arena I could see the suelto near me, and another further back down the street, then I looked further down near the bend beside the old cathedral and there was a third suelto. They were spaced out by about fifty yards. Mozos encircled each of the animals, hailing and turning them. I couldn't imagine a more wild and dangerous situation, but I'd only been in Cuéllar for less than a day.

Winded, I decided to wait and check on Gus. Gus was running the suelto very close and fearlessly. I was completely spent and trying to assist him and the other serious mozos of Cuéllar. We worked that bull all the way to the tunnel. Fell into the zone again and I started to lead the suelto myself. As we entered the callejón, all the other runners stepped back and it was just Gus and me on either horn. Gus stood to his side with his red pañuelo in his hand and I was directly in front of the suelto using my white cap to lead the animal into the ring. Weeks later, a fantastic photo of this emerged on the Internet. As we ran in, the earlier bull was still in the ring so we had to dodge it. We worked the animals and tried to help lure them into the pens. All hell was breaking loose. Gus made some fancy circular passes but no one had much luck in getting the bulls to enter the pens.

Later we went back out on the street. The final suelto stood stubbornly in the center of the sunny street. His chest stretched absurdly wide and muscular as he took whooping breaths. His entire body convulsed and it seemed he would pass out at any moment. Everyone stepped back, then Gus decided to step forward. I told Gus, "Don't, man, I think he's going to have a heart attack and die." Gus went anyway and I set up to assist in case the bull got him.

Gus lured the animal with his pañuelo. The bull surged at him and lunged with his horn. Gus leaped at the last moment. The horn hit his thigh and flung him into the air. Then the bull barreled through him and galloped down the street. I rushed over and Gus popped up. Everyone was sure the bull gored him. They ran over and looked at his pants, which weren't ripped. Then more came back and I was behind Gus when he said, "I'm fine," and yanked his pants down and mooned about 2,000 people on the street to much laughter and cheering. I had an up-close view of his ginger-haired ass. It wasn't pretty.

Finally the fantastic morning ended with the final bull entering the corral. Gus took off for Sanse and the rest of us walked around and I tried to express to everyone the incredible moment I'd shared with Gus in the callejón, but they didn't understand or couldn't see it, or I was just completely manic and not making sense. It was a strange morning. The moment with Gus was poetic because I'd taught him to run from his first step on the street. I gave him everything I knew, especially encouragement, and he'd shown me the way to break through my own boundaries. Minus his near goring, Gus had outdone me by running so close for such a long distance with the sueltos and it brought me nothing but pride. We would likely never run together in Pamplona because of the distance between the curve and Telefónica. This was it, our chance to run together, and we'd done it in near perfection on the horns of a suelto in Cuéllar. It felt like the absolute apex of our friendship and running brotherhood.

The second morning Xander and I ran well and I ran the horns of a bull at the bend after Hotel San Francisco. I experienced an interesting moment with a later suelto near the tunnel. He wouldn't charge for anyone. I swayed my newspaper very low in the animal's view. He picked up on it and I watched his eyes dart back and forth as he followed it slowly, and it felt like I finally broke through with these bulls and communed. They were very different animals. The bull spooked me in the tunnel and cut out through the set of red bars that entered into an arena bar. The animal followed me to the bars and looked at me on the other side of them. Sunlight flooded into the tunnel through the arena and splattered across his sculpted face. He looked at me like he wanted to follow me past the bars. I imagined he must have wished for that, and how much he would wish for that if he knew his fate. Then he turned and ran into the sand of the arena, where he would die that afternoon. Felt I'd failed that animal, that my cowardice had caused him to be lost. That he'd chosen me to follow and I let him down.

Later Enid and I were on a video chat and she was threatening divorce, saying that I was out having fun while she was having a terrible time with her new job. It was a nightmare. I was again contemplating if I'd done the right thing, if I should be home with my wife now when she needs me, and just what the hell was I doing in Spain again?

Thoughts of Enid tormented me, and that night when they replayed on TV the run they somehow cut my best moment out. And the stories I'd told fell flat, which stung my feelings even more. My sleep was very troubled, then finally after hours of rolling, I fell into a strong sleep.

I woke startled. Something came to me and said *it's begun.* I jumped out of bed and wished I was at the pens but I wasn't. We had lost touch with Dyango in the midst of fiesta.

Dressed and I got out on the street early. Nerves bubbled in my stomach. Decided I'd run down at the bottom of the hill that morning. The call it El Embudo (the funnel) it's where the stampede of horsemen and the herd meet the narrow street. That was truly the sight I'd been waiting for, for so long.

I stood down at the drain of the funnel, gripping my rolled newspaper. A few dozen runners gathered there. Hundreds of spectators lined the fencing that climbed the hillside. Nicolas stationed on an adjacent fence that looked up to the hill. Xander and I stood at the bottom the hill, limbering nervously. The hill slowly sloped upward; a road traced along one side with a steep embankment. Most people watched from the fencing that lined the embankment. The rest of the hill was a wide dusty harvested cornfield. Across from the embankment and high on the hill, thirty pine trees stood in a grid. As I gazed up the hill, someone rushed up behind me and grabbed me in a rough bear hug. I spun around angrily. It was Gus! He'd come back again! I called him a motherfucker and hugged him. We devised a plan to wait at the bottom of the hill and see who ran first. I knew the crowd would clear out and there'd be a chance to really wait it out and run the horns on our first step. Gus was up for it and we waited.

The first horse emerged slowly over the hill. Then more horses flowed over the crest until hundreds trotted down the hillside. There were clearly two packs of cattle already. The first set contained two bulls and four hard-charging steers out front. Figured it didn't matter; if I had to run steers, I'd run steers. We waited, and the wonderful stampede rushed toward us. The hellacious rumble rattled the dirt beneath us. The other mozos ran. Gus and I stayed. Gus stepped first but he stepped sideways to run the bull that straggled to the side of the pack and I decided to run the main pack. They galloped incredibly fast, much faster than I had anticipated. I ran twenty yards down the hard gravel road. They closed in on me and I veered right to let them pass. As I did, I looked over my shoulder and the last bull peeled off the herd and charged at Gus. Gus tried to escape to the fencing. Gus and the bull disappeared behind a cinder-block wall and I was sure he gored Gus. I stopped and readied to run back to help him, and then the bull appeared again and I ran his horns for about ten strides with good distance between him and me. Then I cut to the side and over the fencing. I climbed back in and ran with the second pack.

Gus was fine; he just had a scare. I ran back for the final suelto. The massive black bull battered the fencing. He heaved his monstrous head upward. His thick horns dug into the metal posts and nearly broke them. Gus stepped into his space. I wanted him to give the animal more room and closed in to help in case it went wrong again. Then Gus backed off and got out.

Hailed the bull and he charged me. I took the bull around the bend and a good ways up the first street. I decided to exit and dove through the vertical slot in the metal barricades. A young Cuéllar runner hailed him and lured him up the way. The mozo dashed up after and I thanked him. We gathered. Gus wanted to exit the course and run around and try to get back in in front of the suelto. I agreed and we took off. Gus left me in the dust. Xander was close behind him. At first I tried to keep up but then realized, *I have to go at my own pace. I have to find my own stride and not try to follow anyone else's. Gus is in fantastic shape and I'm not. If I spend myself running up that hill, I'll be of no help to the encierro.* They beat me to Hotel San Francisco by a block. When I got there I was fine and ready to sprint. Gus and Xander got in and I climbed into the street. Then for some reason Gus got out. It surprised me, but figured there was a good reason, so I didn't urge him on. I waited at the top of the hill and when the suelto came I stood in the center of the bend. The suelto approached slowly. Using my newspaper, I wiggled it slowly and his eye caught it and watched it sway back and forth. Then he readied and charged hard at me. He was too close to the fence and after a few strides his right horn slammed into a rung. But he was fired up and rushed up the street with us again. I helped turn him a dozen times, then was taking a breather when I noticed Xander.

"I'm winded. I can't catch my breath," Xander said.

I told him go up the street and wait.

"You don't want to be in the middle ground and all worn out," I said. "It's dangerous and you're not helping. Go catch your breath and rest. Then you can really help later near the tunnel."

He listened. I stayed and helped turn the bull a few times; the adrenaline coursed through me. My confidence grew the closer we got to the arena. I jogged to the final bend and turned him there. Then I settled in as we approached the tunnel. I always feel most at home near the tunnels. Slowly, I led him. He was reluctant to enter the tunnel. I glanced over my shoulder to see if the arena was packed with bulls again. It looked clear and that gave me more confidence. Xander was directly behind me and that made me happy. Used my slow waggle with the newspaper to get the bull to step into the tunnel. He saw it but was pretending to let the others distract him. Slobber dangled from his mouth in long translucent strings. I knew he wanted that waggling low thing. He was going to come for it any second. His nostrils angrily slurped air. He stepped toward me and I knew he was with me—locked on to my paper—that he was coming, and I hopped and he charged and I sprinted with the animal at my back. As Xander entered the sand he reached up and grabbed the beginning of the arena wall and used it to torque himself in a hard left turn. I followed the exact same move and torqued myself to the left and the animal surged in the arena into the roars of the packed plaza. I jumped out and Xander was there and we embraced and were very happy we were both OK.

We walked back and quickly found Gus and Steve. We drank beers just before the callejón. As Gus and Xander went in to get the second round an old man called Gus a *torero malo* and Gus tried to explain that he was very experienced. Xander was extremely frustrated with Gus. After Gus and Steve left, Xander and I were walking back to the Hotel San Francisco and Xander was berating Gus's insane and sometimes stupid bravery.

"But Gus is the best foreign bull runner," I said.

Xander angrily told me, "That's not true, Bill. You are."

We ran the fourth morning. I let the bulls go and only contributed a little and a bull hit Xander on the fencing but he escaped unharmed. We went to the town of Valladolid to have *Lecheze* (unweaned roasted lamb) at a famous restaurant with Larry and Anna. Part of me was dejected that I hadn't run well, but then I realized that I'd run for Enid again and that I ran safe and just enjoyed the street and seeing the animals. That made me content.

I was getting ready to leave and decided to have one last meal at Restaurante San Francisco; one of the managers of the hotel/restaurant was a friendly woman named Ana who spoke English. She said I was early for lunch but sat me down anyway. I had the place to myself. I planned to have the lamb when she asked me if I'd tried the Rabo de Toro.

"No, I didn't even know you had it here!"

"It is the best Rabo de Toro you will ever eat."

I laughed and said, "Rabo de Toro, por favor . . . "

Was excited because I hadn't been able to find good Rabo de Toro in a few years, since the Posse parted ways with the restaurant above The Harp. Ana brought me a steaming plate of five separated hunks of bull vertebrae in a pool of thick red wine sauce with a small pile of french fries on the side. I used my fork to tap the hunk of beef that surrounded the vertebrae and it crumbled off the bone. I picked up the dark, almost purple meat and placed it in in my mouth. Something exploded in my mind. The moment was absolutely sentient. The texture, taste, and intense high the meat gave me confirmed for me that this was the best meal of my entire life. I love sushi in part because of the way it gives me a mental clarity and high during and after eating it. I'd never had that sort of experience with beef until that moment as I sat alone in the empty Restaurante San Francisco.

Meat was fundamental to the evolution of the human brain. Primates do hunt and eat meat but it makes up a small percentage of their diet. Humans consume a much larger amount of meat. Meat is what fueled the growth of the human brain.

I first came across Henry Bunn's work on the earliest evidence of Homo erectus actively hunting meat in an article authored by Rob McKie, science editor for *The Guardian* titled "Humans hunted for meat 2 million years ago," which appeared September 23, 2012. The piece focused Bunn's discovery of evidence of early humans selectively hunting red meat. As I spoke with Bunn, he expanded on what he said in the article and addressed some new evidence.

"The oldest new evidence we have of *homonins*, ancient humans, eating meat is 2.6 million years old, which coincides with the evolution of the first of our genus Homo, which is defined by having larger brains. This backs up an important theory called the Extensive Tissue Hypothesis, where as humans ate more meat, their gut shrunk and their brains grew.

"It's a small sample of evidence, which you could hold in the palm of your hand, but it shows that our ancestors realized that there was this major nutrient-dense resource meat, that was available to them and they realized how to access it through the use of stone-cutting tools. Because of the limited amount of evidence, it is frankly impossible to use this handful of bones and say how the animal died and that homonins killed it or not.

"But at Olduvai Gorge in particular, there is evidence which stands out above everything else that has about 250 bones with cut marks. All of that is on fairly large animals, gazelle and wildebeest-type animals, and that's the point at about 1.8 million years ago where we really see the evidence spike, where de-fleshing the particularly meaty portions of limb bones is a pretty good indication that early Homo erectus had first access to the animal, and how do you get the animal first? You hunt it and kill it yourself. Some scientists argued that Homo erectus was scavenging from lion kills. I looked at the evidence of mortality patterns of lion prey; my argument was that if the animals at Olduvai were scavenged from lion kills then the mortality patterns would match; they didn't match. In fact they were very different. The patterns didn't match any other predator."

The Guardian article also illustrates a shift in ideology in academia in the 1980s, which shunned the idea of brain evolution being linked to meat eating. The opposing idea was that cooperation in early humans evolved our brains. It's one of those moments when leftist politics interferes with and hinders progressive thought. The fact that meat consumption grew the human brain is a very uncomfortable fact for a vegan to swallow.

Bunn's mention of the Extensive Tissue Hypothesis, ETH, led me to more research on the topic. I found one of the foremost thinkers on human evolution: paleoanthropologist Leslie Aiello. Aiello's seminal theory ETH, is that eating meat led to smaller stomachs and bigger brains. In 2008, Aiello gave a speech at Cambridge University outlining the theory she coauthored; portions of the speech were compiled by Corydon Ireland and published in the *Harvard Gazette.*

"One point five million years ago Homo erectus began to eat more meat: a compact, high-energy source of calories that does not require a large intestinal system.

"Encephalization, the evolution of a larger brain, is the third stage of evolution that led humans to civilization. That growing brain size presented a metabolic problem. A gram of brain tissue takes 20 times more energy to grow than a gram of tissue from the kidney, heart or liver. Gut tissue is metabolically expensive too, so as brains grew, gut sizes shrank. Meat eating made it possible for humans to evolve a larger brain size.

"Homo erectus ate a much larger percentage of meat in their diet in comparison to the two percent chimpanzees eat."

Essentially what Aiello is arguing is that one of the fundamental differences between humans and our nearest primate relative the chimpanzee is the amount of meat we eat. Beef is the second-most-consumed red meat on the planet. The consumption of beef is fundamental to who we are as human beings.

The next day I boarded a train for Sanse, arrived and booked a cheap hostel. Sanse is much more urban than any other place I'd been in Spain. It's an industrial suburb of Madrid. As I strolled through the dark, graffiti-covered buildings my city instinct told me I might get mugged. I couldn't find anyone, but found the dark red barricades of the course. New blacktop paved one straightaway known as Calle Real. Fancy lights strung in displays of mozos hung high above the street. It was a beautiful city with pretty girls and a lively fiesta. The next morning I ran into Gus near the curve and I decided to run the long straightaway. Sanse is like a machine; it's clean, precise, incredibly fast, and competitive. The runners are fierce and the very best. David Rodríguez milled around and then suddenly José Manuel appeared and greeted me in his white gear holding his willow cane! *He's a Pastor in Sanse!* I didn't even recognize him at first!

Ran the center of Calle Real as the herd approached. Then about thirty yards behind me a bull peeled off and gored a runner and tossed several others; they all flipped high into the air. That horror shook me up and knowing that the herd was broken but still galloping disoriented me and I completely missed and felt very foolish.

Afterward I spent the morning with Gus and an American runner in his fifties named Steve Ibarra. Steve is half Mexican with dark skin and slicked-back black hair. He showed me around and to his Peña and gave me a pañuelo. Steve couldn't walk very far without running into friends. He introduced me to everybody. Steve was from the north side of Chicago too, and he had this way about him like he was in a Godfather film. He'd kiss you on your ear like a mobster. There was a lot of pageantry, but deep down, Steve was just a great guy and happy I was there and wanted to show me the best time. I was really starting to like him. We sat down at a bar called Farro and I asked Steve how he ended up such a beloved regular in Sanse.

"I heard about the run here in Sanse through the veteran runners Joe Distler, Tom Turley, and Noel Chandler. They'd been here many years before and I always wanted to come here. I remember talking to Tom Turley before I first came here in 2002.

"He ended the conversation with, 'Esteban fast as hell, fast as hell, it's not like Pamplona, it's fast as hell,' then he called me up two seconds later after we hung up and said 'Remember this, fast as hell, fast as hell.' He did that four times so I had that etched in my mind.

"My running partner Junior and I picked up a trip to Madrid. We both were working American Airlines, working a flight as flight attendants and we landed at 9:00 a.m., and the encierro is at 8:00 a.m. and we leave the next morning at 11:15 so we had just enough time to catch one run. When we got to Madrid we went to our layover hotel, dropped off our bags, came out here to Sanse. We didn't know a soul. The first place we went is a bar called Monte's at La Curva of Las Postas and Calle Real, and we're sitting in there and having drinks. I looked across the bar and said, 'Junior, those guys look like runners.' They were these really fit guys in their early twenties. They're having drinks and they're kind of eyeing us up because at that time in 2002 they had seen foreigners here but every few years, maybe one, maybe two, and they had never seen us before. So they're kind of sizing us up. At Monte's the bathroom was upstairs. I went up to the bathroom and I came down and one of these young fit guys and Junior were holding each other's shirts like they were going to punch each other. I say 'Junior! Junior, what are you doing?' and he said 'This guy is saying, 'You're in Spain, speak Spanish,'' and I'm trying to explain to him I'm doing my best.

"In any case, we separated them and these guys would have killed us. First of all they were twenty years younger than us, they were stronger than us, and this is their hometown, we were outnumbered. So we went to the end of the bar, had some more drinks, walked around town, didn't know a soul, came back to Monte's. The bartender said 'todo bien,' which means everything's cool. And I thought we'll have a nice breakfast there tomorrow, put on our uniforms, and go home and have this heroic story. We went around, partied until about 6:00 p.m., then we went to the Peña Taurina. They said it opened at five o'clock so we went in for a drink. Well, who's working the door, the same runner who'd grabbed Junior by the shirt. He saw us two and he said 'Fuera, Fuera Americanos' (you're not welcome).

"So we walked out with our tail between our legs, had another couple of drinks. We headed back to our hotel in Madrid. At that point I said,

'Junior, let's not be discouraged about tomorrow. I know how these young kids think. We can't prove anything to 'em other than how we run tomorrow. We'll show 'em how we do; if we can hold our own out there, that's how we earn their respect; nothing more, nothing less, it's very simple.'

"We got up at 4:30 in the morning, got out of the hotel at five, took a taxi straight here, had our coffees warmed up. As it turns out, me and one of the young guys who we'd had the problem with at the bar the day before—him and I, we're fighting it out for the lead bull on Calle Real around La Curva and elbows were flying—not purposely, it's just the encierro. He ended up falling down, I ran right onto the bull's horns, and as I did I accidentally stepped on this Spanish runner's head. I ended up running twenty good yards up the street. The whole time I felt horrible about stepping on the guy's head. We end up going back to Monte's, kind of celebrating, having a little bite. And the same guys we had the problem with are in back, and I look and see one of them, his face is all busted up. It's the guy I stepped on. And they're playing the run in slow motion and sure enough they play the part where the guy falls and I step right on his head in slow motion. They're all pointing at me from the back and talking and saying, 'That's the guy right there!' They're pointing our direction and we basically shit our pants. I said 'Oh no, we gotta work this morning and this is what's going on?' They recognize it's me. Just when I'm sure they're going to jump up and kill us, instead all of 'em, they start clapping in unison and chanting 'Norte-Americanos, Norte-Americanos, Norte-Americanos . . . ' They all came over, handed Junior and me beers, and said 'muy bien.' The guy who grabbed Junior by the shirt introduced himself as Oliver, and him and Junior shook on it. I apologized to the guy I stepped on. His name was Juan Pablo, and he said 'Esteban, no apologies necessary, this is the encierro.' Now thirteen years later these are some of my best friends, and I am not only the first international member of the Peña, I'm the first American in the Peña, which was an impossibility before that. I'm now in the family, and I love those guys and they love me but it was a rocky start.

"The very next year went kind of like the year before. I was on a layover but this year I wasn't with Junior. I was by myself. I came out to run and everybody greeted me, embraced me, and I got out there and I ran on Calle Real and I saw the bulls taking the turn, however I missed the one bull. That bull hugged the inside of the curve and was on the right. The rest of the pack was on the left side of me and I thought they were all on the left. I felt the pace quicken. I looked back and there he was, coming at me. I flicked my newspaper but he was already locked in. The horn went through, one trajectory, he was probably just trying to get me out of the way. He threw me. I flew up maybe eight feet in the air.

"I flipped in midair and cracked another runner who was behind me with the top of my foot in the forehead and I broke two toes in my right foot. My foot opened up a big gash in the gentleman's head. The rest of the pack was still coming, and I misjudged the ground and my whole body weight and my head hit the ground. I broke my left hand. Then I covered up. The whole pack ran over me and nothing touched me. I got up and my first thought was 'oh this flight's gonna hurt today!' My back was sore. I didn't realize I'd been gored at that time, but I could barely walk. I was trying to get underneath the barricades and this couple pulled me back in the street and pointed at my leg. My pants were ripped all the way down to my shoe. They were working on the guy that I hit with my foot; when they saw my wound, they pushed him to the side, put me on a stretcher, cut my clothes off, put a towel over my butt. They took me to the infirmary. I had seven doctors looking at the wound. They had me on these, like, gynecological stirrups. There was this big light; they're looking at the wound. They gave me seven shots around the wound. That hurt; that was really painful. It numbed me out and the doctor put on a rubber glove and was pulling out pieces of the horn and showing me the pieces of the horn and I was like 'Oh boy, I guess I'm not going to work today.'

"Before they got me in the ambulance, Miguel Angel Castander helped me call my work friend and tell him what happened. In the ambulance they let this journalist in with me and she asked 'Do you have a comment for the Spanish newspaper?'

"I thought about what Matt Carney said when he got gored in 1977— you look up at the sky, you relax your solar plexus, you think about what you're gonna say, and you ask yourself, 'Is this the way it is?' and you answer your own question, 'Yes, it is.' "So I took a deep breath thought about it. I didn't want to say something ridiculous so I said 'Yes, I do have one comment. Being an American, I'm very proud to have been gored by a Spanish fighting bull.'

"Went to the hospital, the kid whose head I hit with my foot just happened to be next to me in the waiting area. I apologized to him and he said 'Esteban, it's the encierro, no problemos.'

"So I'm in the hospital about the fourth day listening to my headphones. I'm on a morphine drip as well as an antibiotic drip. They're taking good care of me. All of a sudden I feel somebody hit my foot, and it was all the pastores from Sanse standing in their pastor uniforms with sticks, and I started to cry and it meant the world to me. It was a very special time in my life although a very difficult time.

"I was in the hospital for twelve days, and now I come back here to Sanse every year. I enjoy the toros but I enjoy my friends even more. I'm part of the family here and I feel very proud of that."

That night I couldn't sleep at all. I was planning on running Calle Estafeta down the long hill going into the arena. I'd heard about montóns in Sanse and saw footage of a terrible one a few years before. The fear of montóns always tormented me. I loved running the last stretch of the course, but the thought that I'd end up at the bottom of one of those piles, suffocated dead, woke me in cold sweat many nights.

Before the run I stood in the packed space. Two evil-looking girls along the barricades taunted me and said "muerte, muerte . . . " I was very nervous. When the crowd broke I moved down to the top of the hill. As the herd approached I ran. I was very disoriented and suddenly the lead animal was beside me and I tried to accelerate but my legs were shot, and he passed me and I followed him into the tunnel. As I entered the tunnel a swarming pile of humanity grew at the mouth of the arena. The pileup blocked the entire passage and swelled to waist-high. I knew if I stopped I'd make the problem worse. Figured my only chance was to try to leap the pile. As I got close, I jumped and dug my shoe into the pile and leaped as high and as far forward as I could. I landed on top of the pile and slid down it onto my head softly with my hat still on. Crawled out and I scrambled to my feet. I couldn't believe it. *How did I make it over?!*

The mountain of faces and arms and legs grew as people strained to escape. The rest of the herd crashed into the pile and struggled to trample through it. The horror of that image froze me in fear. A catastrophe unfolded before me and I felt helpless until several brave runners ran back to the pile and pried people free. I dove in to help. As I got closer the pile began to unravel; many mozos climbed to their feet. I filed through the escaping runners and saw one guy struggling to get up and grabbed him by his buttocks and yanked him out and pushed him to safety.

I got to the core of the pile and crouched over it. A half dozen hands reached out to me. Horrified faces gawked at me—eyes urging and pleading for help. I reached my hand into the pile, not wanting to have to pick one, hoping one of the hands would grab mine and I would pull them out. Suddenly all the faces turned to my right, all the hands fell limply down. A large black bull plowed through the pile and swung our way. It stepped toward us ragefully. I reached my hand deeper into the pile. No one took it. The bull gathered, dropped its massive black head, and hooked into us. I dashed to the side and the animal drove its horns into the pile. He lifted and his horns plucked several runners out by their abdomens and pinned them high against the bullring wall. A dark red faced pastor named Miguel Angel Castander gripped the bull's tail. He whipped the bull with his cane and the animal swung out of the pile and spun for me. Miguel's eyes fiercely spotted me, and he screamed at me in his deep, visceral Spanish. I dashed away to the wall. He twisted the animal around and the bull trotted into the center of the ring. The rest of the animals finally cleared the pile. I ran back in to help and all I found was shoes, dozens of running shoes scattered atop the sand.

The pile cleared as quickly as it had formed. Then it was over. Stone-cold shock hung on me afterward. White as a ghost, I climbed out through the stands. The medics loaded the ambulances with the fifty or more seriously injured people. Saw Gus walking toward the arena and I screamed his name. Someone yelled to me from a stretcher that medics loaded into an ambulance. I looked and didn't recognize him and thought he was yelling to someone else. Later I realized it was José Manuel. José Manuel was trying to help clear the pileup with the other pastores when a straggler steer barreled through the tunnel and plowed into José's back with his blunted horn. The collision broke several of José's ribs and caused serious internal bleeding. He spent over a month in the hospital.

It was one of many serious incidents with steers injuring people that year. We started calling it "The Year of the Steer." After I was already home, Gus was running the horns of a bull at the curve in Sanse when the steer in front of him slowed down and Gus put his hand out and his hand sunk straight into the steer's anus——all the way to the forearm. It was the end of the year of the steer. And we felt finally, hopefully, that Gus's disgusting and accidental violation of the animal broke the bad mojo surrounding steers.

After I got home, Bomber wrote me about the pileup. He'd seen it on television and saw what I'd done. I asked him about the pastor and he told me, "That is a legend. I only know him as, Angel. He is a master."

Later Bomber told me about his experiences with montóns. He sent me a photo of an enormous montón in Pamplona. It was ten feet high.

The herd is still climbing it, and there is Bomber leading a bull into the sand. "I was able to climb over it and lead the first bull into the ring. We had three montóns in the seventies. I was in the other two, ninety-nine gored, one killed by suffocation. Now you can imagine being buried alive with bulls goring everything in their way? Stuck in there a long time, helpless . . . You heard 'fuck' in all languages. Plus they closed the big doors to the arena. It was dark, man, and we were trapped! A montón for me is the most frightening thing about running bulls. At the end, I just remember walking to the place the montón was and seeing a huge pile of tennis shoes. Then the next day it was about having the balls to take the lead bull through the callejón! Bill, there are older runners who have experienced some heavy days on the streets and they are very humble. That's why it takes years to be recognized, accepted, and respected as a good mozo. I'm still learning, it has been an amazing journey for me. Running the bulls is sacred!!!"

Bomber was preparing for a move. Xander and I wanted to visit him during our trip but he told us just to go run bulls. We didn't know Bomber was headed on the big journey to go see his beloved Goldie. I wish I'd known in time so I could tell him what he meant to me. What a powerful guru he was and that I loved him and was grateful for all he'd done for me. But it was too late when I finally got word brain cancer had a grip on him and there was no way to reach him.

Was getting ready to send my novel out to Jenni Fagan's agent when on a whim I sent it to Jacob Knabb, a friend of mine who was the acquisitions guy and an editor for Curbside Splendor, an excellent small press in Chicago. He almost immediately wrote back saying that Curbside was interested. Jenni's agent didn't get back to me. Within a week, Jacob wrote back and said:

"We want to publish it."

I signed the contract at the Bobby Hitz fight just as an exciting prospect named Jimmy Murphy got into the ring for his epic pro debut.

I landed a gig as the special boxing contributor for the *Chicago Tribune*'s commuter daily *RedEye*. Things were good when my friend Fred Burkhart, a photographer and artist, was near death from cancer and I got the chance to do a big interview with him for the cover of the Chicago arts weekly *Newcity*. Later I considered writing a book about him from interviews. Curbside wanted to do it, but when I went over to Fred's place with Jacob and told Fred my idea, Fred looked at me disgusted and said, "Why would you want to write my book for me?"

I completely snapped out of it and on the ride home Jacob told me I needed to start work on my second book, my memoir on the run. I got home, started on what you're reading right now. I blasted out 40,000 words in a month or so and things began to shape up with it.

Sadly around then we found out Bomber was terribly ill. He died a few weeks later and I was deeply saddened by his passing, though I knew his spirit was still very much alive and with us.

Curbside assigned my novel to an editor named Leonard Vance. I figured he was a white guy but he walked up and was black! His family was from the Robert Taylor homes, the most violent project in Chicago in the nineties, but he mostly lived out in the west suburbs. He told me what he thought of my novel, *The Old Neighborhood*. The things he said were things you dream of as a writer, that just about everything in the subtext of your opus has reached out and touched a perfect stranger. The complexity of the racial aspects of the book didn't offend him, and that was a big reassurance. We got to work and he was very driven and we tore through pages.

CHAPTER NINE:
SLEEPERS
2013

My company got a big job under Interstate 90/94 near North and Ashland in the city. I rode to work every day with my brother Dave. It was a sticky situation because I'd had a lot of problems with Dave over the years. We'd even gotten into a nasty fistfight on a job site several years before, around the time I lost my mind. We'd been getting along better, and as the work started I could see that he was amped up to turn a big profit on it. Our responsibility was to build shoring towers and jack up individual concrete beams so the other crew could work on the piers. It was insanely dangerous but we kept at it. Dave figured out a way to move the shoring fully assembled with a big forklift and cut the work in half. Things were going really good. I was in charge of laying down the stone and mats with the Bobcat, and Dave ran the forklift to move the shoring; the rest of the crew assembled and jacked the beams. We made tremendous profits pretty quickly.

Enid and I took off for Spain. We'd lost the HQ and had to use another apartment to enter the course. It was on Estafeta too and faced out away from the street. The balcony had a beautiful view of Pamplona, the main cathedral, and the Pyrenees.

Ben and Jerry the young Canadian runners, returned to Pamplona and I was damn glad to see both. Ben was fired up to get serious about the run. I wasn't reluctant to push him anymore because he was going for it already on his own. There was no stopping him, and what he needed was a maestro. I could see that he had the potential to be the next great foreign runner. He was crazy brave and super quick and athletic; he'd even bulked up and gained twenty pounds of muscle to handle the crowd better. I figured his best bet was to stick with Estafeta and maybe mimic David Ubeda, who was somewhat similar in size and mobility.

The opening morning I ended up on the horns of a lead brown bull as we entered the tunnel. Joséchu was in front of me and I put my hand against his back to keep distance between us. When we entered the arena I ran out beside the bull. The roaring crowd suddenly turned from jubilance to worry. I looked back to see what was happening behind us but saw nothing. Then I cut off to the left and the terrified roar grew. I looked back again and a big black bull barreled directly toward me. I fell forward and he pushed against my back with his snout. His face felt soft like a pillow and I lay flat on the sand. The two bulls nearly converged hooking for me but trotted on, lured by the dobladores. I scrambled to my feet and Aitor dashed up and grabbed my arm and helped me away. It embarrassed me, but I was glad I was fine and grateful for Aitor's generosity. Later a Posse girl showed me some video of it. It was damn funny. The next day a photo of the incident appeared in one of the papers. The caption read: "This mozo won't soon forget the smell of this bull."

I decided to wear white the second morning of runs. It was the first time I'd worn all white and it excited me. Joe and Bomber and Julen always mentioned that in Pamplona you should wear white to honor San Fermín. I was doing it for Joe and Bomber, the older runners, and for Pamplona. I even got some red suspenders to add some flair and style. It opened up for me and I ran on the horns of one bull and beside another through the tunnel.

Ben was having fantastic runs up Estafeta and Owain Hoskins had some nice long ones at Telefónica and the tunnel. I tried to pump them up and keep them excited and maybe tweak them here and there to help them develop their full potential. They were clearly the future, and it was my duty to embrace them and pass along what I knew. Distler often told me stories about the way Matt Carney fanned his flames. As the years progressed Distler tried several different strategies to run, but Carney maintained his method of jogging up the center of Estafeta, and when he'd pass Distler waiting in a doorway he'd smile and shout, "Center of the street, kid!" I loved that story and that guidance because it was so simple yet so direct and true. If you ran the center of the street you'd have a good run. And if you ran the center of the street in life you'd have a fulfilling and exceptional life. So I began to tell Owain and Ben that every morning when I saw them on the course. "Center of the street, kid." They'd just smile sheepishly and say *I'll try,* and they sure did.

I missed on the tenth. I was bitter and angry when the chaos began sifting my way and I knew that the encierro wasn't over. I waited about twenty yards from the tunnel. Put my back to the fencing and let the bull close in on me as the Spanish hailed him. Then he was close and David Rodríguez was beside me, and suddenly the animal charged hard at a runner in a yellow shirt directly in front of me. The runner collapsed into the barricades. The bull gathered, lowered his head, and thrust his horns up and gored him in the armpits simultaneously. David Rodríguez grabbed the bull's tail. The gored runner tumbled away. The animal dragged David around as he swung for other runners. Miguel Angel Castander was moving in to help when the bull swung toward him and pinned him against the barricades with a few other mozos. Angel had nowhere to go. The bull closed in on him, dragging David Rodríguez with him. I rushed in and grabbed the tail of the animal with David Rodríguez. I didn't yank, just squeezed and held tight and the animal stalled for a moment. Angel cut away and the other runners escaped. Rodríguez whacked my wrist, telling me to let go. I did. The bull dragged him and twisted and whipped around and Rodríguez exited. We tried to hail the bull and he charged hard and ended up passing me. Then he twisted in a circle and Joséchu, another runner, and I scooted past his snout trying to turn him. He wouldn't come. I stood beside his hindquarters and slapped my paper into my palm with a loud crack. Another runner hailed him, and he came but then stalled at the opening of the tunnel. I got in front in the very center of the mouth of the tunnel and dipped my paper low; he saw it but wouldn't come. Then, the others got close on either side and he finally charged. We ran the tunnel in a near perfect form, four of us shoulder to shoulder in a partial circle, shell formation. As we entered the arena I veered right and half a dozen runners collapsed into the sand like it was quicksand. There was only me with the animal closing in behind. Luckily another Bryan Hoskins hailed him and the bull tore into the ring, sending hundreds scampering for cover. It turned out there was a severe goring at the middle of Estafeta. Gus was there and tried to hail the bull in a very dramatic way but it wouldn't come. There were several Spanish who ran the suelto heroically for nearly half the course, especially the one in the yellow sweater who was with him until nearly the end.

The more I marveled at the way the great Spanish ran, the more I realized I could never be like them. That I was far from what they were. But it was a great privilege to assist them when I could. To hold the tail with Rodríguez was such an honor and to have even partially repaid Angel for saving me in the pileup at Sanse was quite fulfilling, but I still felt I'd made a mistake and wanted to apologize to Rodríguez for holding the tail when it seemed he didn't want any help. Stopped David Ubeda and asked him what I'd done wrong. Ubeda said, "When a bull isn't in the process of goring someone there should only be one person holding the tail because they can control it better. If there are two it makes it more difficult."

"Thanks, David. I'll apologize to him," I replied.

When I'd rushed in to help it was because I was sure in that instant the bull would gore Angel or the one beside Angel but still I felt remorse for it. But I honestly wanted to learn and understand the rules—so I could be of more help, so I could be a better mozo.

The night of the 12th I was very distraught and fought with Enid over something petty and stormed off. It was the Fuente Ymbros turn to run. I usually was very happy when they ran because I had great luck with them and almost all of my best runs were with them. But something dark descended on me. Omens leaped out of every shadow. I laid in bed, sick and awake, waiting for Enid to come home. She did and wouldn't talk to me and I tried to apologize for yelling at her and told her I loved her but she just fell asleep, mad. I tried to fall asleep and tossed and turned. In a half dream something swooped into my room from the cracked open window that overlooked Mercaderes. It pulled and yanked at me in bed then Bomber's voice urgently warned me. "Don't run Telefónica tomorrow!" I struggled viciously with the force gripping me and angrily muttered, "Well, that's not a fucking option!" Then he vanished, I assume to tell the others. I sat up in bed. Beads of sweat dribbled off my face. The cool night air blew in and I got up and closed the window.

I woke Enid and told her that I needed her to tell me she loved me because I think I might die tomorrow and I need her to say it. She did and I finally slept lightly and woke very sick with nerves.

When I got to the entry apartment I was very happy to see my brothers and sat on the balcony sipping coffee. The morning light poured over the Pyrenees and struck the red-tiled roofs. The raw beauty washed away the darkness as I reminisced about my time in the street with the Fuente Ymbro. As we walked down the street Owain appeared and I patted him on the back and said, "Center of the street, kid," and he smiled and said, "I'll try my best," but he looked as nervous as I'd felt throughout the night and I wondered if Bomber paid him a visit too.

Left early from Telefónica like usual. I strode cleanly in the center of the street. It was fairly empty. I looked back and Aitor led a fast-galloping suelto. The bull's snout seemed to touch Aitor's backside; the horns seemed to grow out of Aitor's hips. Aitor strode in his long gait. Man and beast soared in perfect sync. Aitor's white-striped hoodie fluttered as I found their pace and approached shoulder to shoulder with him.

As I cruised beside Aitor a woman trips in front of him and he crashes into her back. Aitor starts to fall, miraculously keeping afoot as he bends way forward, his head below his hips. The bull accelerates. His sharp horns bob inches from Aitor's back. I surge in and offer my arm for Aitor to steady himself with. He takes it for a moment while he stumbles in long strides. Then he lets go. He knows there's no hope. He will fall. In that moment I swing my paper up over his head and behind his back and swat the bull's horns to attract him away from goring Aitor. Aitor drops to the stones as the bull shifts his focus onto me. I run in front of his horns. We merge into one speeding force and enter the tunnel.

As I step into the tunnel there are people everywhere running very slowly. I try to cut around them. A small pileup of five people trips me. I try to leap it and fall flat on my belly. The bull ambles on. I immediately crawl to the opening that lines the bottom of the tunnel and slip inside. The room is large, dark, and empty.

Screams volley in from the tunnel and a powerful roar of horror explodes into the dark room. Dozens of runners fly in through the low opening. I reach down and pull them in. Aitor's striped sleeve appears and I yank him through and to his feet.

"Estas bien, Aitor?!" He scrambles away and out of the room. The inflow of bodies stops but the dread continues. I get down on my belly to look out. A regal white bull sits at the opening of the tunnel in quiet meditation. I look the other direction to the entrance into the ring. A horrific mountain of people jams the path into the arena. It smells like bull and terror. Everyone is standing; the pile is over six feet tall with the huge pack of gigantic bovines stacked on top directly in the middle. Mozos nearest the animals twist to face them, trying to climb away from the dozens of curved white horns that stick out of the writhing pile like terrible thorns. Then the white bull climbs to his hooves. The mozos scramble in the tunnel. The white bull gets up and trots into the pile and just barrels his head into his brothers' backs. The montón moans deeply as a wave squeezes through it. Decide I should go out and try to help if I can. I crawl back out into the tunnel and finally clearly see the hundred or so white and red clad people crushed in the opening to the arena. The image is so terrible, agony clutches my heart and I want to cry and scream in rage all at once. The white bull turns and I panic and nearly jump out through the slot on the other side of the tunnel, but he doesn't attack. None of them do. They were afraid and the fear mysteriously calms them instead of igniting them to rage. I'm very grateful for Fuente Ymbro's serenity; it's nothing short of merciful.

Then something gives way and the blockage breaks. The bulls vanish. I help Joséchu nearly close the red metal doors then follow him in. Regretfully, I step over the fallen bodies. Then I'm onto the sand of the ring. I look for the bulls but they disappeared. I go back to the unraveling pile and pull people out until they've all scrambled away. Underneath the montón I find a scattered pile of tennis shoes and five unconscious men lying over each other. Their limbs tangled like a pile of twigs. The sleepers' bodies are horrifically flattened and some are sunk in the sand. Their faces are swollen like big red tomatoes and are slowly turning purple. Their mouths are agape but none of them seem to be breathing. The herd materializes and circles the ring dumbfounded.

I'm afraid. I'm afraid that the sleepers will die if I don't do something, that the bulls will return and finish them off. I grab the worst-looking one by the arm and drag him away. He is young and skinny and blue. His eyes are swollen shut. His head swells terribly like someone has bludgeoned it with a baseball bat. His mouth slurps at the air but nothing goes in. His chest won't expand. Others appear and we pick him up and try to give him to a *Guardia Civil* (volunteer police) over the wall. The officer only yells at us and waves his baton in our faces. We put the sleeper down on the white sand. I look at him and know he's very bad. His face is bluish purple and he is clearly dying.

A mozo with a colorful shirt yells and picks him up. I grab him by the arm and shoulder and help carry him and we cross the ring with him. The boy dangles limp in our hands. He is not breathing and has no pulse. A Red Cross medic appears and I scream "Donde?!" in his face and the medic points and leads us. We run with him, crossing the ring. An erratic electricity exudes from the dying. It ejects sparks out into my hands and numbs them. The life inside him felt like hot electric plasma. It kept disappearing then it suddenly surges into his back and arm where I hold him. Then it vanishes again like the life inside him is running scared trying to escape. The sparks make my hands and arms throb and exhaustion grips my entire body. I nearly collapse as we approach another tunnel. With the last of my strength we carry him through a door up a flight of stairs into a room full of medics and police. A stretcher flings out of a doorway at the top and we put him down unconscious and purple with his mouth urging for air. As I turn to leave they carry two more in behind him—both unconscious and looking very grave. A pale young man gored under his arm walks in—his shirt torn, wet, and red. His eyes are wide open and strangely placid.

More Guardia Civil appear. They push all of us away, including the gored young man. I yell "Cornada!" and point at the bloody mess. And I think he got in before the one in the colorful shirt puts his arm around me and leads me away. I try to make sense of it all as I climb out of the ring trembling.

As I got outside I realized I had to find Enid! She'd just watched all of this on television. I ran down to our place and rang the call buzzer. They shouted she was looking for me at the arena. Then I sprinted down to Bar Txoko and they said she was just there and I rounded the corner and there she was holding her stomach and very pale. I took her in my arms as she cried and we held each other in a doorway for a long time. She trembled and sobbed in my arms. Then she finally calmed; tears streamed down her wet face. I kissed her on the forehead. Then she leaned away, reeled back, and smacked me hard across the face.

"Why do you do this stupid shit!" she yelled.

I just hugged her and said, "I don't know."

There was a pause then finally we broke into laughter. She still doesn't understand why I do this. I kept hugging her as one by one my friends appeared safe and healthy. I remembered why I run; because if something bad were to happen and I wasn't there to try and help, I'd never forgive myself. My friends all hugged us until there was a big group of us just hugging and holding each other and we were all very grateful that everyone we knew was okay.

Then someone told me they'd screwed up with the doors of the arena and I sat with my head in my hands and wondered if the young man was dead. I wondered how the encierro could possibly survive a scandal like that, a death caused by the officials making a stupid mistake.

Later the news came that one of the crushed runners was in a coma. The doctors gave him no chance of ever waking up, and they were waiting for the parents to arrive so they could pull the plug.

When I finally saw the footage of the run I saw Aitor's fall and my attempt to help him. Then after I fell suddenly Owain was on the horns in the tunnel. He led the bull swiftly and suddenly he saw the terrible pileup. He glanced back and the bull was very close and fast. Then he made a decision. At full stride he leaped way up over the heads of the mozos stuck in the pile. The bull attempted to leap after him but crashed snout first into the montón. His horn swung up along Owain's leg but didn't pierce it. Owain crawled slowly over the pile. Then after he got himself together Owain went back to the pile and pulled runners free.

As I watched the footage of the run, I realized that it was partially caused by a man in charge of one of the doors into the ring. He'd opened it to let some of the Guardia Civil in so they could line the ring walls and batter anyone who misbehaved. There was a huge swell of valientes. As the door opened the valientes pried the gate ajar and that set the stage for the terrible pileup. I remembered trying to hand the Guardia Civil the boy's limp body and the officer waving his baton in my face. I recalled wanting to punch him square in the jaw, and I wished I had.

Then I saw a video of another Guardia Civil carrying one of the sleepers by himself and I stopped blaming them.

Because the video on TV focused on the Australian who they handed to the Guardia Civil, a lot of the guys at Txoko said I was lying about what I'd done in the arena. They would ask me what happened and then they'd correct me and tell me that that didn't happen, that they'd seen it on the television and it was an Australian who was hurt. Even guys who I loved tried to correct me. I screamed the truth at them.

"There were five of them lying there not breathing! I saw it with my own fucking eyes!"

I hated the very critical foreign contingent more than ever; even members of the Posse didn't believe me. It was a horrible feeling but more than anything I just worried about the young man I'd helped carry. I was sure that he was the one in the coma because he was the worst off. Every time I closed my eyes I saw his pummeled narrow face, eyes closed, mouth agape. I couldn't believe he'd survived to make it to life support: *my god, he was dying in my hands.* I looked into my friend's eyes as we sat there at Bar Windsor. *You don't believe me.* I got up and left because if I had stayed at Bar Windsor any longer I would have lashed out violently on my critics.

Tried to sleep but I kept waking in the night. My hands throbbed the same way they'd throbbed as I helped carry the boy. Bomber returned to my room that night. He swooped in and hovered near the ceiling and yelled "You had an experience!!!" His love and pride in me swirled around the room but I couldn't handle it and pushed him out of my mind and tried desperately to sleep but found absolutely no rest.

Tears finally came somewhere in the morning. They roused me and beaded up in my eyes. *I can't fucking handle this shit anymore; if that boy dies, if he dies, I won't, I just can't, he can't.* The tears never fell though; my eyes just swallowed them.

The next morning I got the papers at Carmelo's shop. Photos of the boy I helped carry were on the covers of the papers and the San

Fermín section of *Diario de Navarra*. His name was Jon Jeronimo Mendoza, a nineteen-year-old from Vitoria, Spain. Sadly, I was correct and he was the one in the coma. There were photos of other runners and me carrying him across the arena to the surgery room, photos that would spread across the globe. The vindication that my memory was accurate was quickly sunken by the very grave condition Mendoza was in. The papers said he was completely suffocated and his lungs had collapsed, and if he hadn't gotten oxygen at the exact moment he had, he would have been completely brain-dead. If we hadn't gotten him into the surgery room first, he would have died. The window for his survival was mere seconds though now in the coma, they didn't give him much of a chance at survival.

A terrible agony took over my heart. I sat out on the balcony watching the black birds cutting through the bright blue sky above the red-tiled roofs with the green Pyrenees hovering in the background. Tears welled in my eyes and I started to pray, to concentrate and focus all my life force to somehow talk directly to him.

Kid, you gotta wake up . . . You can't die . . . You gotta live . . .

As we waited for the run at Telefónica it was remarkably empty. Many runners came up and greeted me with somber handshakes and hugs. There was a piece on television that morning about an excellent Spanish runner who looked at the bodies of the sleepers and just crumbled and grabbed his head and yelled horribly. He saw me on the street and looked at me in the eyes, startled. I ran terribly, and afterward there were many people apologizing for the things they said to me and the way they dismissed my story, but I didn't care. I only cared about Jon Jeronimo Mendoza and I braced for the announcement and everyone, the entire fiesta, all of Pamplona braced for the announcement that he was dead, that he was gone and they'd pulled the plug.

That night before the closing ceremony the word quickly spread and Mathew Clayfield, an Australian journalist friend of mine, came up and looked me in the eyes.

He put his hand on my shoulder. "He survived, Bill. The boy. The boy you carried. He woke up."

The joy flooded through me and I gripped my heart it was so big and painful and I hugged him and was so happy I just marveled at it. *He made it. He's alive. My god, he's alive.*

We went to Greece afterward. I was a mess, just couldn't sleep. The numb buzz coursed through me at night and nightmares tormented me, of the animals, of all sorts of things. I worked through it and wrote an essay about it all for *ChicagoSide Sports*, an online publication, and Enid and I finally had some fun on a little island riding around on a 4x4 and checking out the cozy beaches.

Got home and poured myself deeper into the construction work. It became clear that we would make fifty percent profit on our portion of the job if we kept up what we were doing. That would equate roughly to $750,000 profit. It would be the largest profit the company had ever made. The rest of the job was reasonably profitable as well, and my father was looking at an enormous amount of money for his cut. It was great because I really wanted to finally repay my dad for all the grief I'd caused him. I'd gotten into several fistfights on job sites and hurt his career in the process. He was always trying to keep the family together, and I was one of the elements who kept driving it apart. We clicked very tightly on the job; our crew had incredible fun. The danger wasn't lost on us, and several times we had accidents that could have easily killed one of us. That bond kept us even closer; it was just like on the street with bulls. The more cooperation and danger in the encierro, the closer I became to the others. The other runners began to be my brothers instead of just fellow runners. The same with the guys on the site. One who was my actual brother; we'd finally mended our past and become close friends on top of it.

Steve Ibarra promised to get me a half-priced ticket flying standby so I could go to Sanse and Cuéllar. He came through with it at the last second. I was very grateful to fly first class for the first time in my life. Dennis decided to come to Cuéllar to get footage of me running and receiving my award and sculpture. *Eh Toro,* a Spanish cultural organization based near Cuéllar chose to award Xander, Nicolas, and me with the Encierro Divulgation award. Dennis picked Gus and me up from the airport and we drove over. The first thing I did was run up the hill at the edge of town and sit up on top of it. I knew I must have done something right to have returned to my mecca, and the very next year! Gratitude overwhelmed me. Graeme, Harold, Gus, Craig, Michael, Dennis, Xander, Jim Hollander, and several famous Englishmen and even a member of the royal family of Spain had all come this year; our numbers had more than quadrupled. Cuéllar was becoming a thing. A very special thing that more people wanted to be involved in.

Gus and I ran the beginning stretch, El Embudo. I missed but ended up catching a suelto later on the course. The next day a television crew decided to follow me around. They were calling me "the Hemingway of Cuéllar." It was surreal. We went down to the pens where a local runner named Luis invited us to take part in hailing the animals after the pen gates open. It was nerve-racking. When the doors opened we bounced on our toes; the pack was afraid to exit. The steers in front stood tall, watching us. Then one steer ran out and we dodged to the side. We came back and hailed them again until finally the pack summoned the courage and charged. We dove out of the way. One bull careened to the side and disappeared into the cars. The pack evaporated into the misty pink haze. Terror exploded across the way; many people scampered atop their cars and pointed. There was a bull who was unrelated to the other animals. He was a replacement and as soon as he had the chance, he cut off to the side. I dashed after the suelto. Cut between cars and I saw a commotion ahead and people scampering to get on top of the vehicles. I came upon a woman screaming. She jumped out of a car and clutched her stomach where the bull had gored her. Blood streamed between her fingers. She ran to the ambulance. I kept pursuit of the bull but found several police officers on horseback blocking the way. Decided to let them handle it and ran back. We got in our car and drove to town.

Later I had a nice run up the hill at Hotel San Francisco. I was mainly beside the pack and went a long ways up the street with them. Then I had some time with the sueltos afterward. Ran the second-to-last suelto with Joséchu and the bull was right on me as we entered the arena. I cut to the right in the sand to the delight of the crowd.

The award ceremony for Xander and me took place afterward. It was at a nice quaint little bar near the Plaza de Toros. We gave a talk and Larry Belcher translated. It was fun. Dyango made the sculptures. They were these beautiful iron busts of a Toro Bravo mount. It was beautiful. Later Xander and I lounged around in these fancy chairs in pure bliss.

We drove to Sanse that afternoon. Checked into our hotel and went out and met up with Steve that night. He was tanked and we were very happy to see each other. Steve was down in the dumps about something and we tried to brighten his spirits. We hung out outside his Peña's clubhouse. Everyone was there. I was very grateful to Steve because he had kept his promise and gotten me to Spain again and very cheaply. But I also felt bad because he'd spent the whole day alone except for his Spanish friends. It might sound a little spooky, but there was this tall, skinny guy in his fifties with long white hair and sunglasses on and the whole getup, just like Bomber. Maybe I was hallucinating or maybe Bomber is still out there somewhere, who knows? But the guy seemed to be keeping an eye on Steve. He seemed to be looking at me disappointedly, like I was letting Steve down. The guys all wanted to go to Cuéllar again that morning. I thought about it, but Steve didn't want to go to Cuéllar. Thought, well, I can't leave him alone, not two days in a row. I decided to stay. Ran Sanse very badly and I found Steve at the curve afterward. I told him all the guys had gone to Cuéllar. He asked, "Why didn't you go too?"

"I stayed to be with you, man."

That made him happy and we walked all over town. Steve has a backstage pass around Sanse and I met all the heavies. We were at a bar when I turned around and saw David Rodríguez having lunch with his young daughters. Steve introduced me, and the girls pointed at my feet and talked excitedly. I said, "Si, mid didos," and wiggled my toes. I was wearing five-finger shoes. That delighted them, and David thanked me for my friendliness with them before they left.

Steve took me to a big cookout with all the Peñas. It was surreal. All the very best runners and pastores were there. I saw David Rodríguez. He recognized me! I wanted to apologize for pulling the tail with him in Pamplona so I fumbled through an apology. I don't think he knew who I was and asked, "Who the hell is this American hanging out at our party?" Some of the guys weren't so pleased and stared at me angrily. If I hadn't been with Steve I think they would have run me right out of there. Later I saw José Manuel.

"I am a student and I am in Sanse to learn," I told him.

He seemed to like that, and the better Sanse runners seemed to lighten up when the word got out that I was humble and trying to learn and not in Sanse to show off.

It was a great time with Steve. He was having some financial problems, and with Shrek, a longtime American runner and coworker of Steve's on house arrest in Brazil, it had put a real damper on things for him. It also made me very glad I'd stayed to look out for him and be with him when he needed a friend. I thought Bomber would be happy I did that. It made me glad to think about Bomber and what a good friend he was and how I wanted to be like him.

The guys came back to Sanse that night and we lived it up at Sanse's peppy party. I ended up going to Cuéllar the next day because Rick Musica and half the guys were with Steve now. We got to Cuéllar just in time for the run. We headed down to El Embudo again. There was no telling what would happen, and it ended up being quite spectacular.

The pack approached in all its glory, huge and wide and strung out. Two bulls galloped out ahead and one horseman got stuck in the inside line. He seemed to panic, and he cut his horse in front of the bull, and then cut to the side at full stride. As he did this, the lead bull clung tight to his horse's hindquarters and followed him in a long U-turn. The second bull followed as well, and the bulls were suddenly knifing though the halted horsemen. The rest of the pack approached us, and I was the final runner to leave the hill and lead the pack with steers out front down the hillside. Peeled off and walked back to the hill. I was afraid to walk up the hill. I was tired. Then something told me, *this is what you saw in your dreams*. I took a deep breath.

Hundreds of horsemen hailed the two bulls and tried to herd them back toward El Embudo. It felt like this had already happened to me. Slowly I walked up and it was as if I were watching from a bird's-eye view. I never lost sight of the animals as they roamed the thirty-degree plane of the hillside. Tremendous tension fluttered across El Embudo because there were hundreds of spectators all along the ridge of the hillside on foot completely unprotected. One bull found sanctuary in the small patch of pine trees; he even smacked his horns around in the branches. The other roamed the far hillside. The horsemen were brave and noble, attempting to lure the beast with their staffs, dragging them in the dirt behind their horses. Just when they were about to get the one bull to El Embudo it turned hard to the side and charged the weak wooden fencing that Padre sat on. He jumped off in the nick of time and the bull ran straight at him and smacked the wood as Padre considered his options. The second bull threatened to come through El Embudo as he slowly strolled down the gravel path. Finally the first bull got bored with the fencing and charged hard at El Embudo. I helped lure him down the path along with three other mozos. And he passed on up the street.

Finally the second bull approached. I was out of breath and worn thin with the adrenaline of the morning. A horseman tried but failed to lure him down the path. The bull was lost and confused and I wanted to help him on his way. I took a deep breath. The bull charged. A runner fell. The bull kicked up a white dust cloud, then charged the fencing and smacked it as the crowd receded from it. I hailed him and he charged. When I got to the bend I peeled off to the side and somehow he knew not to follow me. We'd made that deal and he soared up the street past me.

I jogged across town using the shortcut to the arena and climbed in, happy that there was still fear in the callejón, and that the final animal was still in the street. Ran out and found him there and I settled in to have a go. I felt a very strong and deep connection with this animal.

He nearly killed Xander when he slammed his horns into the fence on either side of Xander's chest, and I knew that he was merciful. The bull remembered me, and when I was in front of him he charged regularly and without deviation. Later on he refused to enter the arena, stubbornly holding his ground in the tunnel. I bent low, waved my paper along the ground. I called to him alone at the mouth of the tunnel and I knew he'd seen this place in dreams; that he somehow knew he would die there in the ring and he didn't want to enter.

By the time he finally entered the corrals, I felt an unbreakable bond with him. I bought a front-row seat for the bullfight. He came out first and displayed his bravery and was even more majestic and beautiful than I remembered. He died only a few feet from me on the whitish sand, blood streaming down his muscular shoulders, the blade of the sword sunk deep and true through his heart. I sat with Xander and Jim Hollander. They were observing and discussing the quality of the corrida. I fell into contemplation as I stared into the animal's black eye. A powerful agony consumed me. It was like a dear friend was taking his last breaths. Tremors rippled across his dark face as they severed his spinal cord with the dagger. I knew I couldn't look away. It was my duty to see it through to the very end. Couldn't help but feel that he looked me in the eye, and he was grateful I was there. I couldn't tell anyone about the emotions, the mourning I felt for the animal.

That night I went to the Hotel San Francisco and ate Rabo de Toro. I thanked the animal for his sacrifice, the same sacrifice his ancestors had made for centuries, a sacrifice which helped shape human society for millennia.

The next day I ran with Dyango at the hill at San Francisco. Ran a long stretch with the pack and I glided on the horns here and there before I tripped and fell.

We headed back to Sanse with two days left of encierros. We heard there was a second run going on. It was a new run that had been reintroduced after over a decade of absence. Miguel Angel Castander had organized it. It was in Alcala de Henares, about forty minutes away. I missed in Sanse as usual. We headed out there and slowly got the story of what was taking place. There was a brand-new Plaza de Toros built recently in Alcala. They'd erected a new course made of red metal and wood similar to the fencing at Sanse. As we waited, an older Spanish gentleman spoke to me in English. His name was Angel. He told me that Daniel Jimeno Romero was from Alcala de Henares. I asked him how Jimeno's family felt about the run.

"They were very sad but also proud. I visit the young men all over the country who have been gored and injured, some of them permanent. And they all say the same: it was an honor to run and I have no regrets or anger toward the animal. The families of the dead, they are proud too but sad. The bulls bring out very much passion in these people. And I always go to see them and to do what I can to ease their suffering. Daniel's father is here. He is very happy the encierro has returned."

As I walked with Angel, the who's who of runners streamed past. It was shocking. I don't know exactly what it was, but the atmosphere filled me with extreme joy. Terrible excitement rose through me when the rocket lifted up at the bend halfway. I watched it soar straight up the narrow channel between the trees, above the heads of all the fantastic runners, and then it burst up high there. But there was a delay in the bulls' release. Finally they came. I ran the horns of an early lone animal, then cut off to the side as he rocketed past and I dove flat on my belly. Got up and I ended up on the horns of a later bull. As he closed in on me I dove to the clean new asphalt. The locals watching along the barricades grabbed me and pulled me under to safety. They patted me on the back and I thanked them.

Afterward I was buzzing and talked to as many people as I could. It was the most exciting place I'd ever run. Mikael Anderson got a fantastic run that morning too.

The next day we ran both towns again. I missed at Sanse and we ended up at Alcala. The bulls approached and I was struggling to get out when Aitor smashed into me and the fencing. A lead suelto shot past, narrowly missing us both. I jostled out into the center of the street, and suddenly a pack of four bulls galloped into view. They were fifteen yards away and I turned and sprinted as hard as I could. There was no one near me. It'd completely opened. I ran the animals' horns for forty yards. It felt like I was running as fast as I'd ever run in my life. Then I felt something breathing on my thigh. I glanced back and the horn of the lead bull bounded right beside me. This terrified me. I gathered and cut hard and out. My long hair swung up in a big swoosh all struck bright in the sunlight as the four galloping black animals rushed past in the shadows.

It was a fantastic run, one of my favorite moments because I was part of something new, a rebirth of the encierro. That all made me very proud. Mikael Anderson and Aitor had run that same pack later up the street; it was like we were all just passing the lead to each other: one of us got out, the other got in. Gus had even run them around the bend with Aitor earlier.

Afterward we had a drink in the garden outside the Plaza de Toros, listening to the roars of the crowd as the bull leapers performed their magic inside. I was ranting and raving about how important this was to the encierro; thousands of people showed up for the event. It was an outpouring of support by the local community and that was truly fantastic. The gloom that this culture was dying cleanly erased from my spirit that morning. We were the only foreigners in town. This was truly the people coming out to support their culture. It was magnificent.

We got news that there was another run set to happen about thirty minutes away. We jumped in our cars. It was a place called Daganzo. This was an even more rural town, surrounded by agricultural fields. We found the course; Aitor and Joséchu were there near the plaza. I greeted them. Aitor was very friendly and jovial with me. It was nice to know he was there as well and it felt as if we'd been allowed passage deeper into the culture.

Gus and I walked the course and found the end, where there was a huge truck trailer containing the animals. The bulls banged hard into the metal structures of the truck and rattled it every few minutes. We sat in a doorway thinking over what we could do. We were very happy and excited to be there. It was so spontaneous and fun. Stern-faced herdsmen walked the course; the harsh sunlight cast shadows in the wrinkles of their weathered dark skin. Finally it got to be time for the run. The elder Angel showed up and explained that they were going to have five separate encierros over the course of about an hour. They would run one bull at a time with about five steers. Then they'd run the steers back to the pens and run the next bull until all of the five bulls were in the pens in the arena. That really shocked me because now we had the chance to run seven times in one day! That went beyond all my wildest dreams. We readied, and hundreds of mozos showed up, but not as many of the famous runners. These were mostly young mozos still learning.

I waited at the end of the long wide straightaway. Gus decided to start closer up the street. Mikael stood near him. As the herd approached the bull was out front hooking fiercely. The big bunch of runners cleared out and it was only Aitor and me. I looked at him; he grinned and shrugged and we ran together nicely up the narrow street approaching the hard turn. The bull closed on us. One local mozo ran his horns with Aitor and me on either side. As we turned the corner, the street cleared and we took the bull into the arena, the three of us sharing the horns.

The second run Mikael ran the horns of the bull and it surged and bellowed wrathfully and exploded toward him. Mikael peeled off to the side and it followed him and I swear its snout bumped Mikael's backside before he was cleanly out of harm's way. Again Aitor and I ran very near the horns of the bull around the bend and into the arena. In the arena I couldn't quite hit my highest gear of sprint and the bull was very near hitting me as I cut to the side and escaped.

The near goring shook Mikael and he decided to sit out for the next run. He offered me his elbow pads, which I took gladly. The next run I decided to run even later, letting Aitor go before me. Led the animal through the narrow channel before the bend when I realized the bull was much too fast for me. I ran hard but the fluid chaos of the beast behind me told me it was time to get out. I slid like a base-runner, feet first into the corner of the street; the elbow pads came in handy. The horn of the bull passed a few inches over my head hooking for me. The spectators' roars told me just how close it was as the wind of the animal gusted over me. I lay there, thoroughly winded. The huge doses of adrenaline forced me to consider quitting for the morning. Then Padre talked someone into letting him film from their balcony right over the final curve. He asked if I'd run there so he could film. I shrugged and said, "The hell with it, let's do it."

Waited near the curve and as the animal approached I ran around the bend. As I worked up the street toward the arena a runner cut in front of me and exited the center of the street. He pushed me toward the fencing and I angrily cut behind him and back into the street. The push made me lose my momentum and I probably should have just stayed on the fencing. When I looked back the bull locked on to me in full gallop. There was nowhere to go so I belly-flopped on the street. The bull surged toward me, stepped on my back, and kicked me hard in the back of the head. A powerful roar whooshed through my ears. I was sure he'd fractured my skull. I gripped my head and crawled under the nearby barricades. On the other side I lay on my back as all the onlookers stared down at me worried, just dark shadows in the midday sun. Then Steve Ibarra's voice eased through the barricades as if it were coming from down a long hallway.

"Bill, I'm here, Bill. I'm here."

I was glad he was and looked out and saw his worried face as I rubbed the back of my skull; it felt like it was made of putty. A runner came to my aid and kneeled beside me. Then another runner grabbed me and yanked at my shirt looking for a gore wound. I tried to explain.

"Solo mi cabesa, solo mi cabesa."

Then Aitor's face smiled through the barricades and I smiled back and Santi, a Spanish runner, helped me to my feet. I thanked everyone and climbed out. Steve and a medic escorted me to a little makeshift medical center where this beautiful woman examined me. I listened to the final run go by and regretted missing it, being stupid and getting myself hurt. Walked out into the bright light and a big cheer from the locals greeted me. The guys waved me over to a little food stand where they were giving out plates of great paella. I ate and felt better quickly, though I did have a minor concussion and was a little nauseated.

We finally called it quits for the day and I soaked in a bath the night before the final run. I ran into Aitor at the curve in Sanse and moaned "Duele mi cabesa..." and he cracked up. Tried to run Calle Estafeta but I had no plan. It was pretty stupid to think that I could pull it off on my own with a concussion to boot. The animal blasted past me with Aitor on the horns for more than a hundred yards. I was grateful though, to be on the course with the incredible runners at Sanse and so happy for Aitor. It seemed there was no challenge in the encierro that Aitor couldn't transcend and turn into pure art. Aitor was becoming something quite special and it made me proud to know him and to be on hand to witness it.

CHAPTER TEN:
MILLION DOLLAR WOUND
2014

When I got back to Chicago things went great at work. We took home a ton of money. I made $2,700 in one week, which was my all-time high. Our crew transformed into a machine. We worked together in complete harmony and all we did was laugh all day and make huge profits for the company. We just kept trying to break our own records for towers erected and beams jacked in one day. We cracked fifteen and thirty beams in one eight-hour day, which equated to over $100,000 of profit. We made the $750,000 profit we hoped for, and I saved $30,000. It was pretty ridiculous. I devised a plan to take out several huge ads for my novel and do some audacious publicity, which included a car wrap of the book cover on Enid's new white Dodge Avenger. Things were pretty cool. A series of full-page color ads ran in the *Chicago Tribune, Paris Review, Chicago Sun-Times, Newcity,* and several other papers. I bought a low-rider bike to use as publicity. Things were fantastic.

My novel released on April 10, 2014. The release event was at the Empty Bottle music club in Chicago and featured Irvine Welsh and artist Tony Fitzpatrick. Tony gave me an etching that he'd made of me beforehand; it was hilarious and cool, a blue bull with a hard-on chasing a red stick figure wearing a boxing glove. To own a work by a world-renowned artist like Tony just shattered me. I read from my low-rider bicycle. I'd been fighting with Enid the whole day and hadn't practiced and was a little off. At the end I brought the book down and looked into the crowd and as I did the book hit the chain-link steering wheel of the bike and gonged in this strange metallic echo, but I just rode with it and repeated the final lines of the passage.

"I'm gonna kill somebody I'm gonna kill somebody I'm gonna kill somebody . . . " The crowd went pretty nuts for it and we sold a whole bunch of books. I was happy and it was very surreal. Stayed up that night and thought maybe I should google my name to see if there was any coverage of the event when the *Chicago Tribune* review of my novel went live. It was the most incredibly well-written review I've ever read. The review was like an argument for the novel's merit. My life as an author began in that moment. I couldn't believe it and posted about it on Facebook and got 250 likes. It went bonkers, then the book hit the top 5,000 books on Amazon the next day, which equates to about 100 sales. That night I went to the Golden Gloves with Irvine and completed my interview for *Playboy*'s SFW site. It was a great night and we sold twenty-five more books. I rocketed toward becoming a best seller when the buzz went flat. There were no other print reviews for a long time. Then *Newcity* did a minor badly written review. The reviewer couldn't comprehend that the narrator was an adult looking back on his childhood, though it was a positive review overall.

I descended into a horrible depression, the worst of my entire life. Thought, *it's over, it's done, I won't sell any more books. My dream is dead.* The darkness I plummeted into was vast and powerful; it could have easily swallowed me whole. I wanted to kill myself very badly. I kept trying to pull myself out of it but it was so powerful, so incredibly strong. I lay on the couch for a month hardly able to get up. Enid kept yelling at me that I had to keep trying.

The summer before, I had come up with an idea for a Pamplona survival guide. I wrote John Hemingway, Joe Distler, Jim Hollander, and Xander about it. I wanted to collaborate with all of them and create a new guide to every aspect of fiesta and especially the encierro. They all replied promptly: yes, let's do it. But Xander began to argue against my ideas, and because I was so wrapped up with my novel it slowly but surely became his project. I was fine with it; I just wanted it done. But Xander's idea was to basically anthologize old essays we'd already published. It seemed like a weak idea, but I went along with it and combined my *Outside Guides* into one extensive guide. Xander edited it and sent it to us for final approval. The way Xander edited it was strange. He published several photos of himself running and one of me. Then he wrote a first person intro to my guide, which just flowed directly into my guide with no break signifying his writing had ended and mine began. In other words the reader would likely assume he wrote the entire bull-run guide. The only way to know I'd written it was to look in the glossary. The photos also seemed to exaggerate Xander's excellence as a runner while diminishing mine. Xander never really took the run seriously, it was more about the party and the friends for him. He was a bullfighter and that was what he brought to the group. It all felt wrong but I decided to just go with it. Jim wanted to change the name to *Fiesta: How to Not Get Gored by a bull*. I put my foot down with that one and said it has to be "Survive" because I could get gored at any time. Xander self-published the *Fiesta: How to Survive the Bulls of Pamplona* through Amazon and it went live that June.

Later, I somehow missed being included on the *Newcity* Lit Top 50. That disappointed me, but then Printers Row Lit Fest came up. They selected me for the fancy main opening event at the Union League Club, the most exclusive club in Chicago. I turned into the star of the show when it was revealed that I boxed in the room where the event was taking place: about ten years back at one of their cigar and fight nights. Then I partook in a main presentation with another Chicago writer named Alexai Galaviz Budziszewski. We had a blast and became friends. Then the *Chicago Reader* Best of Chicago 2014 list came out, and they called out *The Old Neighborhood* as Best New Book by a Former Chicago Golden Gloves Champ. A couple days later the *Chicago*

Sun-Times echoed the Best New Book award. I left for Pamplona flying high, but the good fortune ended somewhere over the Atlantic.

It all went wrong the minute we got off the plane. We tried to go to Cuéllar for a nearby run but it turned out that wasn't an encierro, just a run where they tie the bull up and lead it through town. I did get to meet Luis and we had Rabo de Toro from Hotel San Francisco; it was marvelous. I ran down the bull-run course to the bottom of the hill at the edge of town. It was pitch black. I was afraid, and it felt like the hill itself was a monstrous black bull with the gray sky hovering above. *Thank you*, I whispered, and then ran off to finish my sprints.

We arrived at Pamplona's Town Hall. When we got our bags upstairs in our place I looked for my leather briefcase. It was gone. My passport, computer, medication, and Gohonzon—all of it, gone. Somehow we'd misplaced it. In a panic I ran around everywhere, looking for it, the staircase, the doorstep, the plaza where we'd exited the cab. It was gone. At first we thought I'd left it in the cab. But after 24 hours of calling cabs we got hold of the cabbie we rode over with and he confirmed that he did not have it. We went to the police and the lost-and-found and it wasn't there. After two days, I gave up. We went to the emergency room and they gave us a similar medication to Seroquel, but it wasn't Seroquel. I was off my meds for the first time in eight years. The new medicine messed with my sleep and sunk me into a mild depression.

My first two runs went bad. The first I missed, the crowd pushed me off to the side. The second I fell in a small montón at Telefónica and an older mozo tried to leap it and instead landed a perfect flying knee to my mouth and busted my lip. Wandered around Estafeta that night. I brooded about my difficulties as the hundreds of faces blurred past in joyful revelry. I walked near my starting point on Estafeta trying to visualize my entry when a gravelly voice whispered in my ear, *If you want to stop getting the shit kicked out of you, then run the center of the street.* Convinced myself it was Carney's ghost and decided to run better the next day.

On July 9, I got up early to do a Skype interview with NBC's Esquire network, which was broadcasting the run live in the United States. It went well but I felt bad. I resigned myself to be hopeful. It was dark, cloudy, and raining off and on that morning. The cobblestones were extra slick. I warmed up on a side street watching the white and yellow stripe running down the center of the path. *Center of the street, kid . . . Center of the street, kid . . . Center of the street, kid . . .* Carney's mantra flowed rhythmically through my mind. As I watched the stripes slowly, a trail of fresh blood droplets spotted the paint lines. They were dark red and grew in girth with each step until they were big silver dollar-sized puddles. At the end there was a thick pool of red. *What the fuck is going on?* I broke off away from the line of blood to warm up in a small square. It was a clear omen. Still I tried to escape it and erase it from my mind as I chanted "Nam-myoho-renge-kyo . . . Nam-myoho-renge-kyo . . . Nam-myoho-renge-kyo . . . "

Tried to run the center of the street but the chaos easily pushed me aside. I stood near the tunnel into the arena, panting and frustrated.

First-time runners stood everywhere as the spectators on the barricades roared at something unfolding at the beginning of Telefónica. Ahead, the pastores' long willow canes poked above tourists. I crept toward the commotion when suddenly a suelto appeared in front of me. His name was Brevito from the Victoriano del Rio Ranch. He was tall, black, and immense—weighing over 1,200 pounds. He threw his horns at the dozens of scattering runners. Miguel Angel Perez and David Rodríguez ran masterfully in front of Brevito—using their bodies to guide him steadily toward the corrals.

With the arena at my back I stalked toward them, stepping past three British runners in matching blue shirts. The monstrous bull trotted toward me and I crouched, reaching my rolled newspaper into his line of sight. He noticed my paper and came to it as I stood tall and took a deep breath. He was magnificently enormous. His girthy horns stretched wide and long. Instantly he linked with me and we moved up the street as one. Miguel Angel Perez ran beside me, both of us at a forty-five-degree angle to the beast, master and student, mirrors of each other in the animal's vision. Brevito calmed for the moment. I reached my free hand behind me to let those nearby know I was approaching. Then one of the blue-shirted Brits screamed and pushed my hand, refusing to move out of my way. One of his friends gripped the barricades, screaming in terror just ahead. I was just like him my first run, frightened and dangerous.

They trapped me in a kind of triangle with no room to escape when the bull charged. I tripped over one Brit's feet as I tried to sprint past him. I felt the bull close in on me and tried to gather my momentum to make a cut when the third Brit in blue with blond hair slammed his hand into my stomach and propelled me toward the animal. I fell flat on my back in front of the charging bull—astonished at how the glory unraveled so quickly. Two of the Brits crisscrossed the animal. One of them knee-dropped into my chest. The collision made my right knee jerk upward. Brevito's right foreleg collapsed under his own weight as he dropped his head and swung his horn toward me. The point of his horn struck my inner thigh. I felt a needle prick then a vast universe of nothing. He lifted me into the air slow and graceful.

I grabbed my crotch. *Thank God it's not my balls. I want to have kids!*

No pain, just the slow majestic lunge upward and toward the barricades. My body twisted with him and my leg swung through the barricades narrowly missing the middle plank. Then I slipped off the horn and fell to the coarse zigzag bricks of Telefónica. On my back I grabbed the barricades, pulled and tried to scuttle under them. Bravito gored my leg again with a short jab. He looked me in the eyes and seethed so ferociously his horn resonated inside me. His viscious gaze told me he could drag me back out into the street and kill me. Then he chose to take mercy on me, plucked his horn out and vanished. Jesús my paramedic, grabbed me by my arms and dragged me under the barricades to safety. And for a moment I was alone.

I peered down at my torn pants and the deep baseball-sized, gaping wound—half expecting it to not be there. *What have you done to yourself?* My inner thigh bloated in a huge bubble. The hole at the center looked like someone reached in and scooped a whole handful of flesh out. The hole was a deep gouge with the skin torn in three triangular ribbons like undone wrapping paper. Blood streaked down the backside of my calf from the second hole and filled my shoe. I peered into the deep, mangled flesh—like a concave bloody eye—and a voice inside me calmly said: *Accept it. You knew this day would come.* I looked to the sky and then back at the terrible hole.

My god that's big, it had to have hit the femoral artery. Am I going to die here? Next to the Hemingway statue? I took a deep breath to calm myself and the blood slowed.

Dark red blood poured from the big, deep wound. *Dark blood is good, bright blood is the artery.* I tried to look at the blood coming out of the other hole and couldn't see it. The blood streamed fast down my leg from the back wound and trickled down my ankle. *Is this how I die? Do I die here?* I thought about the Hemingway statue. I saw his bearded face clear in my mind. *You got me into this, buddy.*

Suddenly Michael Hemingway appeared at my side, his camera around his neck. He looked into the dark hole.

"Bill! My god, you've been gored!" he said in his high-pitched voice.

"I know. Mike, go get somebody."

He went to leave.

"No, wait, just stay with me, man."

He knelt beside me and I reached my hand up and he took it in his.

"Mike, can you ask them if it's the artery?"

Mike asked them in Spanish.

"They said no. It's just the meat, the muscle."

I sighed. *OK. I'm going to live.*

"Mike, go find Enid, tell her I love her, and tell her I'm sorry."

Mike ran off.

A photographer stood on the barricade taking pictures of me. He had wild, curly black hair. He pulled his camera away from his face and I smiled at him. He smiled back.

A medic asked, "Esta bien?"

"Si, estoy bien," I replied.

Jesús, my medic, was there and they asked him, "Es el en estado de shock?"

"No, siempre esta tranquilo," Jesús replied. I laughed and smiled at the cameraman and gave him the thumbs-up. Realized that Enid might be watching on TV and that I should show I was OK and going to live and I gave all the cameras the thumbs-up and smiled. I thought of my family and all the guys watching and hoped they would understand that I was fine.

In the ambulance they asked me if I wanted painkillers. I said no because I was afraid I might pass out and I hated the idea of passing out and maybe not waking up. If I was going to die I wanted to feel it and know it, like I can only assume the Toro Bravo does.

A GUIDE TO THE BEST URGENT CARE FACILITIES IN PAMPLONA

When we got to the hospital they wheeled me into a big room in emergency. They transitioned me to a cold table, unwrapped my leg and took the stuffing out of the large hole. A young doctor observed it, then looked up at me.

"Dolor? Are you in pain?" he said as he slipped blue rubber gloves on.

"No, it doesn't hurt at all," I replied with a grin.

"OK." He hovered his blue-gloved hand over my naked wound. He pointed his index finger down at the hole. A couple nurses observed closely. He looked me in the eyes and said, "Ready?"

I watched him, wondering what he was going to do, and shrugged. Then he slowly pushed the tip of his finger into my open flesh. It felt like his fingertip was a sparking electrical wire. As his blue finger slid into the dark red abyss, my entire body convulsed. I screamed like a newborn baby being electrocuted. When his second knuckle disappeared inside me his fingertip hit bone or solid flesh which halted it. The pain exploded like a bomb. The finger hadn't sunk all the way in. He pulled his finger out looked at me and said, "No, es no cornada."

I gasped for breath, horrified. Then he changed to a more downward angle, the way the horn went in, and slid the entire finger in all the way to the big knuckle as my whole body trembled and contorted. He looked at me and said, "Si, es un cornada."

I could barely hear him through my screams. He pulled his finger out and they cut the rest of my clothing off, covered the wound and my naked body, and put an IV in.

The nurse asked, "Dolor?"

"Si," I replied and she nodded and shot morphine into my IV.

Enid walked into the room. She was crying and stood with her back to the wall near the door looking at me.

"Stop," I told her. "I'm fine, I'm going to be OK."

She cried harder and I waved her to me and she came and I held her as she cried. "I'm sorry," I whispered to her. "I love you."

"I was so scared and no one would help me. They wouldn't even tell me you got gored."

"It's okay . . . It's okay . . . I'm gonna be fine now. I love you."

As I held her, doctors and nurses came in and out through swinging doors. I noticed someone looking at me from the hall. Xander leaned against the wall in the white hallway with a stoic concern on his face. I kept seeing him through the swinging doors and I smiled at him and he smiled back. As Enid calmed I waved him in.

"How are you, brother?" Xander asked.

"I'm fine! It didn't even hurt!" I laughed.

"You're so stupid," Enid scolded me and slapped my foot, which shot bright pain to my wound. My laugh twisted into an agonized shout then folded back into a giggle as she apologized and they both laughed.

"Thank you for coming with her," I said.

"Of course," Xander replied. "Well, the *New York Times* called and a few other major outlets are looking for comment."

"I just want them to know that I'm very proud to have been gored by a Spanish fighting bull," I said.

"What happened?" he asked.

"I don't know, I fell. Somebody behind me was pushing me, I think. I just don't really remember."

I honestly didn't remember then. My memory of traumatic and

intense experiences are always marred and mixed up. It isn't until I see the photos that I can trust my memory.

They took me to surgery. The anesthesiologist was a young guy who spoke English.

"Did you eat breakfast this morning?"

"Yeah, I did."

"Well, we could put you to sleep but you might vomit. It could get complicated. We could also do an epidural but you have to sign off on it."

"I'll do the epidural. I don't want to go under."

Then they made me curl my back and they poked me in my spine. A swirling numbness flowed through my kidneys, lower back, and leg.

"How are you feeling?"

"Weird," I replied. "I got a question; can I talk to the surgeon?"

He called my surgeon over. He was a thin guy in his forties with bushy black hair, black-rimmed glasses, and a stern face.

"How long is the surgery going to take?" I asked. I just wanted to know what to brace myself for. The anesthesiologist translated.

Horrific outrage slid across my surgeon's face. His eyes bulged. He replied to the anesthesiologist angrily in Spanish and the anesthesiologist laughed and covered his mouth quickly as he chuckled. My surgeon gave me a dismissive wave and walked back to the other side of the small blue tent they'd put up on my stomach to block my view of the surgery.

The anesthesiologist tried to pull himself together and took a deep breath.

"He did not answer your question. He just asked if you know how serious this is?" The anesthesiologist grinned, nodded, and walked away. I'd clearly offended my surgeon and his entire profession.

They worked furiously on the wounds, pulling out pieces of horn and clothing. I couldn't feel it but my body jerked around like I was on a plane going through heavy turbulence. About halfway through, my surgeon pulled a particularly long sliver of horn out of my wound. Plenty of blood and gooey tissue clung to it. He showed it to me and raised his eyebrows. I assume he thought that would sober me but it only made me giggle. He gasped at my reaction, stuck his nose up glaring at me wide-eyed. He was like a cartoon or something. I really liked him.

The surgery took a little less than an hour. At the end I tried to thank my surgeon. I reached out to shake his hand; he took mine in his.

"Gracias, perdon a mi, señor," I said with a grin.

He just shook his head and sneered in his ultrastern demeanor and walked off to clean up.

They wheeled me into the hall. There was a waiting room beside the surgery room. A Spanish runner I recognized walked out looking at me, surprised to see me. He took my hand warmly and wished me well. I looked over his shoulder and four other Spanish runners huddled behind him. They muttered distraughtly and looked up to see me. Concern flashed on their faces. I looked around expecting to see my friends, Gus, Galloway, Gary, but they weren't there.

I thanked the guy for his warmth and asked, "Tu amigo, estas bien?"

"No se, pero . . . " He clasped his hands in prayer.

"*Suerte*, amigos," I said as they wheeled me away. They put me in this serene recovery room full of people sleeping off anesthesia. The stained glass windows colored the light into reds, browns, and oranges. I was the only patient awake. The others slept and the nurses just kind of disappeared. The silence grew until I honestly thought for a second that I was in the morgue or some strange stage of heaven, that my dead grandfather was going to walk in and explain to me that I died. Almost everyone in the recovery room was elderly. I wondered what it'd be like to grow old and sick. *Is that how I really want to die? Old, tired, and broken up by the world?*

They wheeled the other goring victim in. He was in grave condition. Brevito gored him in the vitals and his surgery was very complicated. I closed my eyes and prayed for him in a whisper: *Nam-myoho-renge-kyo . . . Nam-myoho-renge-kyo . . . Nam-myoho-renge-kyo . . .*

Finally a nurse walked up and wheeled me away. She crashed me into every single wall along the mile-long walk through a zigzag of tunnels to the other hospital as she texted with her free hand. She crashed me into the elevator and squeezed in beside me. Then she took a deep breath, put her phone away, placed her hand on my leg, and rested on it. I screamed. Was almost ready to choke her when she finally wheeled me into my room and crashed me into position.

Enid came in. I was shocked to find out not one of my friends was there with her. Xander was off talking to the world media but my other friends were nowhere to be found! We tried several times but the phones in the hospital rooms weren't capable of making outgoing calls. I asked Enid to go call my parents. My dad has a heart condition and I didn't want him to get some misinformation that I was dead or something and have a heart attack. Enid went to call them before they woke up to the television reports.

After she left a curly-haired guy with a camera walked in. He asked, "Do you remember me?"

I said, "Yeah, I do."

"I was the one on the barricades photographing you."

"Yes, yeah, I remember, thank you for coming!"

He introduced himself as Mikel and asked, "What do you need?"

"I don't know. I'm trying to reach my parents."

"What is their phone number?"

"No, no, it's too expensive."

He took out his telephone. "What is the number?" He looked me sternly in the eyes.

I sighed and told him the number. He dialed and handed it to me ringing.

My mom answered.

"Mom, I am fine. I'm in the hospital. I am OK." I took a deep breath and said those words every mother longs to hear from their child who's in Pamplona. "I got gored this morning."

My dad got on the phone. They were both remarkably calm. "Dad, I am fine. I'm going to be OK. I just got out of surgery. I'm fine.

"I'm using my friend's phone so I gotta go but I am done, I'm out of surgery and stable, don't worry about me. I'll try to call again soon. OK? I love you."

"I love you," my dad said back and I hung up, thanked Mikel, and gave him his phone back.

He explained that he had taken photos of the entire goring. He was directly above it. He showed me on the display screen on his camera. These photos would famously spread around the globe within the next few days and be broadcast on CNN's *Dateline*. I ran on the right center of the street. Not too close to the barricades, more than an arm's length away from them. Three British runners in matching blue soccer shirts stood in my path. How they all managed to be in nearly the exact same spot is remarkable. Not expecting a suelto, they suddenly found themselves in serious peril. The fattest of the three half climbed the barricades and screamed. The one closest to me ran in my path, we struggled, and our feet tangled. The final one absolutely stood his ground as the bull approached us. When I got close to him, trying desperately to simply run forward, he gathered his weight and pushed me in the stomach hard. My forward momentum stopped and I propelled backward and fell onto my back. The one who pushed me then, instead of running forward, toward the arena, chose to run directly across the street where he collided with an excellent Spanish runner and knocked him flat on his back then fell on top of the runner. The one who initially got in my path fell on me and the bull gored me in the thigh, picked me up, and sort of collapsed. He fell with me impaled on his horn into the fencing where the fat one still clung to the barricades and nearly crushed him also. The most bizarre thing of all was the sight of the horn entering my thigh. My skin just bulged like a balloon around its girth. The details of what happened were bull running at its worst, but it is nothing new for me. I'd been involved in much uglier awkward moments. The reason it was important for me to know exactly what happened was because I'd almost died in this particular mixup.

I thanked Mikel. A mother and daughter showed up. They were originally from California but now lived in Pamplona and always visited English-speaking runners who were seriously hurt at fiesta. The daughter was in school to become a surgeon. They let me use the internet on their phone. I checked my email. Irvine wrote me concerned and I assured him I was fine. That's when the phone starting ringing. Reporters from all over. Someone from CNN called and asked if I had access to photos. I said yes and asked how much they were going to pay, my friend Mikel had great photos. Mikel fielded calls for his photos and I helped get the bidding war going for them to repay him for what he'd done for me. The price ended up being $1,000 for the set. CNN broadcast them and they were printed in a variety of places internationally.

Dennis suddenly materialized. He was very concerned and I was so grateful to see my running mate. He asked me how I was and what I needed. He said NBC's Esquire Network, the show I'd been on earlier that morning, wanted a Skype interview. I said I'd love to but had no way of doing it, there was no internet in the hospital. Dennis, Mikel, the mother and daughter from California all brainstormed desperately to try and pull it off. One phone had Skype but was almost out of battery power. The other phone didn't have Skype; they downloaded and logged in but the TV show wasn't ready to do the interview and finally after a desperate couple hours I got through and gave an interview with one of the Esquire TV reporters. He was a nice guy. It was a good start. Everything calmed down and one of my friends who'd just gotten to fiesta that day loaned me her phone and I was able to start communicating with people via the internet. WGN TV called me in the middle of the night. I woke up and did a Skype interview while nearly completely stoned on morphine. I forgot the name of the femoral artery and called it my aorta which didn't make any sense whatsoever. I stopped and corrected myself but the aorta line made air in Chicago that day.

Enid was furious with me and we started fighting in the middle of the night. My roommate was an old man who was dying of cancer. It was three in the morning and we were screaming at each other. Finally out of nowhere the old man yelled "Ejo de Dios! Ejo de Dios!" and we finally shut up, and I held Enid in my arms until we both fell asleep.

The next morning Enid woke up and left and I drifted back to sleep. I knew the run was happening but I didn't want to see it. I just couldn't. I slept lightly. My surgeon stomped in and turned on the TV.

"Usted no ve el encierro!" *(You didn't watch the encierro!),* he scolded me. I was very sad and could hardly muster a smile.

Then he took scissors and sliced my bandage from ankle to hip and unfolded them until my sutured wound was visible. He lifted my thigh to his nose and took a deep inhale. Then he looked at me and said, "Bien" sternly and briskly walked out of my room. That made me grin. He's quite a character.

It was my first chance to see it since the surgery and I took a deep breath and opened up the bandages. It was like a morphed version of the Mercedes-Benz symbol. They tied the wound together with sutures but only five of them keeping the three flaps of skin connected. The wound was really still open. Three rubber tubes stuck out of it at the rounded points of the three lines which looked like little loops. Plenty of dried black blood caked all over it. It looked gross but the surgeon was happy, so it must be good. When a wound is as deep as mine, they have to allow it to heal from within. That's what the drains are for. They allow the wound to slowly heal itself from the inside. Over the next few days they'd slowly pull the tubes out of me with tweezers; the tubes were about seven inches inside me. Having someone to pull something out of your body is a very strange feeling.

Logged into Facebook, found out that I was trending, and not for a good reason. Mainly people were saying nasty things about me. Probably the nastiest commentary came from Huffington Post. They wrote "We swear we're not laughing . . . " on Facebook when they posted their article on my predicament. They found out I was a Buddhist because of my Facebook post about losing my Gohonzon and wrote that the bull delivered a tremendous force of karma when it gored me. There were other nasty phrasings. It was clearly written by a PETA-minded journalist. But to present hard news as a biased personal attack while poking fun at my religious beliefs was really disgusting and I immediately lost respect for Huffington Post, and I welcome calls from any lawyer who thinks I've got a case for defamation of character against them. The commentary on their Facebook feed was even more ugly and nasty than the article itself, hundreds of comments wishing I would have died and variety of other terrible things.

All the negativity enraged me and I began to battle with perfect strangers about their views of animal rights. I fought with them for about six hours on a variety of sites and articles. As I blasted them with equally nasty commentary, exhaustion overwhelmed me. Pain swelled in my leg. It felt like the infection was thriving and growing inside me. Doctors pumped powerful IV antibiotics into me to battle a nasty infection in my leg. The infection could easily kill me. The negativity was feeding my infection and finally I stopped the online bickering. I realized I had to forgive them all. There I was alone in my hospital room looking out into the rainy suburban horizon of Pamplona and I stopped. I took a deep breath. *I forgive you all.* I forgave them right then and refused to look at the comments anymore. Instead I looked at my Facebook feed, which was full of hundreds of friends and strangers wishing me well. I decided to focus on thanking them and reading their well wishes and being grateful that people in the world cared about me. These sudden swirling shivers rushed through my back and throbbed into my leg and I felt myself healing as I read their comments and replied with gratitude.

Then the phone rang. I picked up.

"Hello, is this Bill Hillmann?"

"Yes."

"I have your bag and your things."

"What?!"

"Yes. I am calling from the lost-and-found here in Pamplona."

"Are you fucking serious!"

"Yes. I saw you on TV and recognized you from the day you came looking for your bag."

"Oh my god. Thank you so much!"

"You are welcome. I have it here. Someone should come to get it."

"Thank you! Thank you so very much!"

This happened literally within an hour of me forgiving my internet trolls. Enid went to get my bag and when she'd brought it, the first thing I did was hang my Gohonzon on the triangular handle bar above my hospital bed and chant. Nam-myoho-renge-kyo . . . Nam-myoho-renge-kyo . . . Nam-myoho-renge-kyo . . . I prayed in gratitude that I'd survived, in gratitude for all the love and warmth, but most vigorously and sincerely for all the people who lashed out at me in such nasty ways. I prayed for their happiness. I prayed that they could find a more positive way to express themselves, that they could come to terms with whatever it was inside them that filled them with so much hatred and that they could find the truest happiness possible in their lives. Chanted for a long time even though my leg hurt to be out of bed. Finally I got tired and took my Gohonzon down and rested again. Within the hour Jacob Knabb wrote me to tell me the *Washington Post* wanted me to write an op-ed for them. This was the biggest outlet and payday for a print writing gig I'd earned in my entire life. NPR's *All Things Considered* also wanted to do an interview and *People* magazine did a profile on me which mentioned my novel, *The Old Neighborhood*. The NPR piece was fantastic. The initial response from the mainstream media was pretty strongly negative. I felt like Jeanne Moos backstabbed me in her CNN *Dateline* story. I bent over backward to talk with her via Skype and then she nailed me with a joke closing her piece by saying the bull "hit the bull's-eye of irony" when it gored me. During our interview NPR's Kelly McEvers asked, "You wrote a book on how to survive the bulls of Pamplona and you got gored; how is that irony sitting with you right now?"

"I don't see it as an irony at all. I am alive. I survived. Gorings are part of the run and if you run long enough you get gored."

Things were looking up and they only got better. Every time I got the chance to talk about my love and passion for the encierro, these amazing shivers would throb through my entire body, especially my thigh. I could feel the world was listening and I wanted to express that the encierro was a very special and beautiful thing. It seemed to be working as more outlets reached out to me. Because I had no way to hook a computer up to Wi-Fi, I dictated my edits for the *Washington Post* piece to Jacob by phone. As I expressed myself about the goring, I felt my body getting over the hump of the infection. I felt powerful again for the first time since the gruesome injury. It was a wild and exhausting time, but well worth it when I finally saw the piece on the cover of the Outlook section. Then to my astonishment, the *Toronto Star*, the biggest and most prestigious paper in Canada and the newspaper Ernest Hemingway was writing for when he first visited Pamplona, ran my essay as well. These were easily the two biggest print publications in my life. If I'd made a dream list of publications for my resume ten years back the *Washington Post* and *Toronto Star* would be on it. Dreams were coming true left and right, and *The Old Neighborhood* was finally getting the national and international attention I thought it deserved. Mentions of the novel appeared in *People* magazine, NPR, the *Washington Post*, and *Toronto Star.* The Spanish outlets also adorned it with outlandish attention. Antena 3 (a Spanish TV station) did a segment on *The Old Neighborhood* the day of my goring, and *El Mundo* wrote about it positively. Later *Cuarto Poder*, a major Spanish website, called me "One of the last and most serious Hemingwayites." It may sound corny to some, but I truly feel that my Buddhist practice gave me the tools to completely turn this powerfully destructive karma around and into one of the most incredibly positive experiences of my life. Through the goring, I became an internationally-acclaimed author with top shelf international print publishing credits. I wasn't just some dude trying to make it anymore. The door opened and I stepped through it and was on the inside. Pamplona had given me a Million Dollar wound when I needed it most. It was a major wound, but I could make a full recovery. It was one of the luckiest things that ever happened to me.

A lot of the great runners came to visit me. Joe Distler came in and did a fantastic impression of Xander and the way Xander had made the *New York Times* story all about himself and how he was a bullfighter. It was laugh-out-loud hilarious. Jim Hollander was particularly kind to me as well and Juan Pedro Lecuona came to see me, which was a tremendous honor. My visitors brought news that Aitor led Brevito into the arena. Juan José Padilla killed Brevito that evening and you could see my blood stained on his right horn the entire corrida.

I'd been on television in Spain and especially Pamplona pretty much all day long since the goring. The story there was all positive but around then it suddenly turned and the commentators began to talk negatively about me and make jokes that I didn't know as much as I thought I did. One commentator was making this sort of statement when he had Juan Pedro Lecuona on as a guest commentator. Juan interrupted the commentator in the midst of him talking derogatorily about me.

"I know Bill Hillmann, we have run together, he is a good runner. What you are saying about him is wrong. If he was gored, he was gored because he runs close to the bull's horns. He has many good pictures running with bulls. I won't listen to you talking bad about him. He is one of the runners who feels the encierro very deeply in his heart. He will come back to run again."

Iker Zausti, an owner of the Encierro Museum and nephew of Jokin Zausti, one of the legendary Pamplona runners, came to the hospital and told me about it. He said JuanPe talked about me with so much passion it gave him chills. It was a very beautiful thing. Couldn't believe it, I looked up to Juan so much, he was a truly iconic runner of the era and taught me so much and such vital lessons about the encierro. I just didn't know how I could repay him for that. Then JuanPe came back and visited me the next day, and I thanked him and he gave me a box of San Fermín candies. He told me if I need anything to call him and he would do it for me. If I needed a ride somewhere, anything at all, just call him and he would make it work. His generosity shocked me. His offer was truly heartening. It felt like a door opened, in not just of Juan's friendship, which was a wonderful thing, but to Pamplona itself.

So many people came to visit me. Julen Madina, Miguel Angel Perez, Aitor came twice, all the longtime foreign runners, Tim Pinks, Allen and Deirdre Carney. Mikael Anderson came and gave me his running shirt and said he'd retired it in my honor. I tried to give it back to him but he wouldn't take it. Tim Pinks told me about Mikael's son Lucas being a poet and that he'd written a poem about his father that nearly brought Tim to tears. I couldn't believe it. Lucas was nearly the exact opposite of Mikael in appearance and demeanor. Mikael was this tall handsome guy with long blond hair, extremely strong and athletic still even though he was in his fifties. He was outgoing and friendly. Lucas was shorter and very heavy. He was extremely quiet, there was a sadness to him, and he was almost painfully introverted. When Tim described the poem it really stirred me. Tim even almost memorized it. Mikael and Lucas came to visit very often and the next time I saw him I asked Lucas about the poem and he told it to me from memory, in English.

"A man proud as a lion,

brave as a lioness . . .

and for his kind he is strong as an ant.

this man always has an eye on me, looking after me . . .

with a roar so powerful it can set fear in anything.

I am proud to call this man my dad

and can never wish for anyone better . . .

he is my best friend."

It was clear his words were very powerful and I told him so. Mikael was having some pain in his leg and left my room to go to the emergency room to have it checked out. Several hours later he came back in very distraught and fell in to the seat beside me.

"What's up with you?" I giggled, astonished.

"I have a blood clot in my thigh. The doctors have told me to go home to have emergency surgery," he said, gasping for breath.

I couldn't believe it. I wished him *suerte* and told him I'd pray for him. Lucas and Mikael left for Sweden that day. The surgery went well and he wrote me via email that he still planned to run Sanse and Cuéllar that summer. It seemed unrealistic but Mikael Anderson is a very determined individual.

Joe Distler very graciously offered to let Enid stay in his apartment while I was still in the hospital and after I got out as long as I needed to. They finally released me eleven days after my goring and I went back to Joe's with Enid. Steve Ibarra got Eddie Blanco to give me a pass on Delta and Enid wanted us to go home right away. So we boarded a bus for Madrid. I didn't like the blood thinner I was on; it made me feel weak and dizzy. So I stopped taking it, but when Enid found out what it was and the danger of blood clots she made me start taking it again. But we couldn't get the one I was using in the hospital and I ended up with some nasty one that had very bad side effects. I felt terrible the second morning when we tried to board the plane flying standby.

The third morning in Madrid, I woke and my veins were feeling strange. This large vein in the big knuckle of my index finger throbbed and bulged and another one in my shoulder pulsed. I figured this was it, I was going to have an aneurism. I sat down and braced. Enid walked over worried and I grabbed her and told her "I love you." Then my whole body numbed and I went blind. My head filled with this incredible buzzing numbness and I thought, *OK I'm dead*. Then it slowly went away and my vision returned and I realized I'd just sort of passed out.

We went to the airport and tried to get on the plane and there wasn't room for us again. Enid finally confessed that she was just trying to get me home so she could divorce me and I'd have my family around me to help me deal with it.

I said, "If that's all we're going home for, fuck it I'm staying!"

We headed back to Pamplona and she left for France and Germany on her way home. But she had second thoughts about divorce so we decided to take some time separated. Gustavo and Santi were staying at Joe's and we ran around and had some fun together.

CHAPTER ELEVEN:
JUANPE'S GIFTS

My days in Pamplona at Joe's place were great. I started a friendship up with Mikel, the photographer, and a San Fermín reporter named Itxaso Recondo, then I reached out to JuanPe and Aitor to do an interview. It went fantastic. Aitor was a really fascinating kid. He was an excellent rally car driver. He was also an incredible outdoorsman who can dive into a deep, fast moving river and catch a three-foot-long trout with his bare hands. As I talked with both I began to realize that these two guys were the iconic runners of Telefónica. Juan had been the icon of Telefónica for the past twenty years and Aitor was the next in line. Realized I could never be like them. Not just because I wasn't as good athletically as them or as brave as them but because these were Pamplonicos; two of the finest Pamplonico runners ever. They were just friendly guys who loved it. My calling was not to go out and become one of the greatest runners of all time. My calling was to be a witness to these great runners. To observe them and to present their story to as much of the world as I could. It was a great honor just to get to know them as friends and be able to run beside them at times.

My first excellent run was also Aitor's first truly excellent run. He'd run nearly twice as long as me on the horns that morning. He went out and did it again and again and again, where I only was able to break through sporadically. I was good but not great. The seeds of greatness were growing in Aitor and it was a fantastic thrill to watch him strive into the light.

After the interview JuanPe asked me if I'd like to go with him to a couple runs to see some of the smaller encierros in Navarra. I said of course and that weekend he picked Gustavo, Santi, Emilio—Gustavo's five-year-old son who'd just arrived—and me up and we headed to Lodosa where we met his friend Miguel, an excellent runner who ran Santo Domingo in Pamplona. Their encierro was fantastic. It thrilled me to witness it. Afterward we ate a big and incredibly good breakfast. Then they brought us to meet the mayor and he presented us with a pañuelo and made a little speech welcoming me. Then *Diario de Navarra* interviewed me and *Noticias* did as well. Miguel was helping translate, and after my answers Miguel kept stopping me and saying "he's just like a Navarrese!" and slapping me on the back.

Afterward we went to a Finca owned by one of the pastores in Pamplona. When we pulled in, I saw it for the first time. It rose up a hillside and there were many pens and this sort of corral path that led up the hill and around the edge of the pens. I'd had many dreams about this place. It was very shocking to see it in real life. There were several German shepherds lounging around. Other than them, we had the place to ourselves. JuanPe took us on a walk up into the woods where a large pack of vaca huddled together. We watched them from the fencing when one of the German shepherds decided to give us a show and began driving them all over the large wooded pen. The way the dog cut and split the pack enthralled me. Sometimes the vaca got brave and tried to face and throw the dog but the dog's persistence overwhelmed them and drove them on. Gustavo's son Emilio was afraid of dogs and Gustavo was trying to help him get over his fear. I took a bunch of photos of him interacting with the dogs; they were very kind to him and treated him like he was their own child. I couldn't believe JuanPe had given us such a gift; he'd taken a huge chunk of his Saturday to show us these things. Then I was expecting to go home when he said:

"Now, we go to Estella."

I'd never even heard of it. JuanPe explained that it was where all the best Navarrese runners came as teenagers to learn to run with bulls.

Estella was a beautiful town. I loved it. We walked all over and way up on the mountainside to a cathedral where a large marching band was getting ready to play. Walking around with JuanPe was truly walking with a celebrity. People waved and recognized him and came up to him to say, "JuanPe, look at this wonderful photo of you" as they showed him photos on their phones. "You are an incredible runner!"

JuanPe just laughed. "Ha! Look how fat I am!" They'd laugh and he'd grab a chunk of his love handles and grin. Every single time someone complimented him, JuanPe immediately humbled himself in that way. The young runners looked up to him and all came up to say hello and show their respect.

One teenager in the marching band said hi to him. JuanPe grinned and introduced him to me as a "good runner." The kid almost fainted! It fascinated me to see the kind of person JuanPe is. The generosity displayed reminded me of the time he caught my arm as we ran side by side to keep me from falling in 2012. He was just like that all the time, a nice and giving person. I asked him about his work. He was a human resources person at his factory. He'd worked his way up from the very bottom to earn that position even though he didn't have a lot of schooling. His philosophy was he treated every single person he met equally. No matter how low a person was or how high they were. He believed that it was his duty to treat that person with dignity. Anytime we came across a deaf person in the street, they would approach him to converse and he always took time and care with them. Clearly they knew each other through his parents who were deaf but that sort of grace with everyone around him never seemed to leave JuanPe.

As the time approached for the encierro, JuanPe asked me if I wanted to run.

"I do but I can't," I replied.

"If you want, you can stand on the street to watch them run past and I will protect you if anything bad happens."

It was a tremendous offer. I knew JuanPe would do whatever it took to protect me, even if that meant getting himself hurt. I just couldn't put him that position though and declined. That was one of the moments I realized I had a new and very dear friend.

JuanPe brought us back to Distler's apartment and we thanked him heartily. The next day a couple big spread articles hit Spanish newspapers with photos of all of us with the bull monument in Lodosa.

Finally got my stitches out and the doctor said I was safe from any danger of infection and took the bandages off. This thrilled me and we bumped into Pamplona Man, an Irishman who lives in Pamplona, and he gave me a couple nice cigars. Gustavo, Santi, Emilio, and I posted up outside Masonave—a bar restaurant and hotel behind Joe's place—drinking, smoking, and playing baseball with my cane. It was a beautiful sunny day and I didn't realize it but I'd slipped into a manic phase and probably should have tried to calm it down but didn't. Enid and I started talking by phone and Skype and made up, and we suddenly were closer than ever. My joy kept me awake well into the night. I woke the next day groggy and pissed off. Got to Masonave and I found some video Owain Hoskins made that compiled a bunch of fiesta footage. There was a clip of the British guy pushing me down. I posted something on Facebook saying thanks to Owain because this video confirmed my memory of the guy pushing me even more and was helping me heal my psychological wounds from the goring. A creepy guy posted a comment in the thread. Xander had written a blog in defense of me but it sort of criticized my running, saying I shouldn't have been wearing the five-finger shoes and that I shouldn't have been running so close to the barricades. I didn't take offense to it because I'm way more knowledgeable than Xander and considered him a dear friend. But this creepy guy was using Xander's essay to criticize me. I began to destroy his and Xander's arguments and got really angry.

Then I started looking into who the guy was. I realized he was one of the Brits who I collided with that morning. He was the fat one who was screaming while half climbed up on the barricades. I asked him if he was one of the Brits and he replied. "We successfully evaded a Suelto on the ninth."

The implication was clear: they'd evaded the bull and I hadn't. So they must have done something right and me something wrong.

This reopened all the psychological wounds and I began lashing out at them. I wrote some unfortunate things blaming them for me getting gored. I didn't genuinely blame them but the guy's commentary just really enraged me. My posts caused a major backlash, mostly from the foreign runners. Their comments hurt me more than the strangers who'd wished I'd died. I went off and thought about it for a while. Lay in this park near Masonave looking up through a tree into the clear blue sky. *Am I really mad at these guys for being in my way and pushing me? I've panicked before. I've done stupid things. I for sure pushed people before. What if I end up pushing someone in the future and they get hurt? How would I look and feel then? It wasn't the guy's fault, it just happened. It's the encierro and if I didn't want to get gored I should have stayed out of the street that morning.*

Still the anger coursed through my chest. *I'm so angry, I could hurt somebody. What are you fucking angry about?* I sat up on the damp grass. *It's that he criticized me and using my own friend's words. This guy, who knows nothing about the run, he criticized me publicly on my own Facebook page. He goaded me into this and now I looked like a real asshole. He'd won. He'd outsmarted me by getting me mad.*

Felt a lot better about things after that realization and even laughed at myself as the children ran around on the playground. I went back, erased my post, and wrote an apology saying I didn't blame anyone. A lot of people applauded that and I felt better.

Then Xander started writing me creepy messages saying he was fielding dozens of emails from people complaining about my handling of things. I couldn't care less but then Xander started lashing out at me saying that he was 100 percent sure I was not pushed and that he wouldn't allow me to write that I was pushed in his ebook. I wasn't planning on writing anything about it for the *Survival Guide*; the way he was talking just didn't make sense.

That was probably the most hurtful moment in all of this. Xander was calling me a liar. My friend was calling me a liar when all I needed was a shoulder to lean on. I grabbed a screen shot of the incident from Owain's video and posted it on Facebook asking if people could see a man's arm pushing me to the ground. If not then I was clearly hallucinating and needed to check myself into a psych ward. This stirred another bunch of nasty commentary. I honestly just wanted to know what happened to me. People accused me of blaming the Brits again. One guy posted a screen shot of my previous post that I'd erased. It was really going bonkers. I left for Madrid before heading to England to start my tour with Irvine Welsh. When I got to Madrid Xander commented on the post saying, "This is a disgrace to the encierro."

I genuinely was seeking out the truth about what happened that morning. That is a key step in healing psychologically from a major trauma like I'd experienced. It felt like Xander had set me up, pushed my buttons to make me look bad. Xander's friend warned me about Xander's tendency to backstab people close to him. I didn't want to believe it but the evidence was stacking up. I prepared myself to split with Xander and the *Survival Guide*.

Xander also blamed me for the paltry ebook sales for the *Survival Guide*. His career was in a vulnerable spot; he hadn't been able to get his novel published yet. He is a very talented writer. *Into the Arena* is a brilliant book. I'd seen it happen with other talented writers before; he needed to stop expending his energy on petty squabbles and political infighting nonsense and focus on his writing. I wanted to tell him that but the rift between us was beginning to grow.

Before I pulled down the post I read a beautiful comment from Matt's son, Allen Carney. It was so heartening it nearly brought me to tears. He said that in the end I'd never know what really happened that morning, that it didn't really matter, that these things happen in the encierro and we have to accept them, that I just had to let it go.

Allen's words really helped me. Decided I wouldn't bring it up anymore on Facebook or talk about it with anyone for a long while. The wounds were just too fresh and I still had so much anger boiling inside me. It was then though after reading Allen's note that I finally started to let it go. Slowly, the anger started to fade away.

I left for London shortly afterward and ended up at Wilderness Fest, a big posh festival in the woods near Oxford University. It was a blast. I slept in a big event tent for free. The next day I met up with Irvine. People treat him like an actual deity in the UK. They were crying and cheering; it was impressive. Irvine introduced me to Elliot Jack, the head of Book Slam. He was a cool, calm, and collected cat. I vibed with him right away but we didn't have much time to chat. We performed to about 300 people. The host was this hilarious poet named Salena Godden. She'd read my book and called me "a Hubert Selby Jr. of today."

My head was spinning when I got on stage but it went over well. The producer of *Trainspotting* was at the fest and he invited me to eat with Irvine and his family and friends at this huge, long table. These were some really interesting people and some of the warmest I've ever had the pleasure to have a meal with. They were millionaires but very progressive-minded ones: one guy was from Africa and had some great stories about water buffalo; the producer's wife was also the costume designer for *Trainspotting*. She wasn't born into money and the sister-in-law was Jamaican. The Jamaican sister-in-law and I ended up having a nice talk about culture clashes and hair because of my sisters being adopted from the Dominican Republic. Then I ended up chatting about boxing with a teenager who was at the long table; he was a big fight fan. Some guys had mugged him and put a knife to his throat, and I talked with him about those Mexicans that'd tried to mug me and cut me all up. The incident had really shaken him. I'd had a rough time at his age too, getting beaten up and jumped. I could see angst all built up in him. I encouraged him to take up boxing just to learn to handle himself and get some of that anger out on the heavy bag. Boxing can be incredibly empowering for a kid that age. It helped me so much. I even showed him a few moves before Irvine and I took off.

The next day we headed to Blackpool and got there just in time to do our interview, which was a lot of fun. Then we took a train back to London. I did a storytelling show, USA versus UK with Mary Lockwood. The next night was the big event. The head of operations at Book Slam, Elliot Jack, booked legendary boxing venue York Hall, rented a boxing ring, and sold it out nearly instantly. I'd be reading to 800 people at the premier literary night in the UK and probably coolest literary night in all of Europe as well.

That morning I went into BBC Radio headquarters in London for my interview with a show called Outlook on BBC's World Service. It went really well and though the host was a little harsh with me, she was very fair in her editing and the story was broadcast around the entire planet.

Got to York Hall early and I bumped into former WBC world welterweight champion Junior Witter. I'd been a big fan of his from way back in his amateur days before he even became champ. He was a really friendly guy.

I was on first and figured the room would be half full but as soon as the doors opened the entire room filled. The host, Doc Brown, dressed up as a referee. He opened up with the best improvised humor skit I have ever seen. Doc Brown could host the Oscars and kill. I got up there and read the closing passage from my novel and every time I looked up from the page the people were hanging on every word. When I closed the passage they erupted into a huge extended applause and I just stood there waiting for it to end. I peered out into that sea of faces, 800 people from another country just roaring applause at me. It was quite surreal. Easily the greatest memory of my live lit career.

Junior Witter performed after me with a cool female dance troupe, then he sparred a round with this young prospect.

We took a break and they sold all twenty books instantly. I was signing books and fielding questions and laudatory comments; it was fantastic! The other performances were excellent and Irvine rocked the house last.

Afterward I met a guy named Jon. He told me what a great job I'd done and how he loved my performance.

"Wait, what's your name?"

"Jon Baird."

"Holy fuck! You're Jon Baird?" Jon adapted and directed Irvine's novel *Filth* and won a ton of awards for it.

"Yeah."

"Fucking *Filth* is amazing, man! I loved it!"

"Naw, no . . . but you, your performance. It was great!"

I couldn't fucking believe one of the hottest directors and screenwriters out there was complimenting me on my novel.

Irvine had done so much for me over the past few months. Not only inviting me to tour with him, but he'd also mentioned me in so many interviews in major outlets in the UK and Spain. I highly doubt I'll ever be able to repay the man but I sure plan to do my best.

Finally I had to go and headed up to Edinburgh for a performance the next day. Stayed up there with Daniel and Will for a couple days then I headed back to Pamplona. After twenty-four straight hours of travel, I arrived in Pamplona just in time for JuanpPe and his son Evi to pick me up and take me to Tafalla.

Felt busted up but I was so excited to be there. JuanPe positioned us on the barricades near the arena. It got really quiet before the encierro began. JuanPe had a great run around the bend on the horns and then Dani, another phenomenal Pamplonico runner, and Aitor sprinted past on the horns of different bulls. The perfection they ran with astonished me. I commented on it and realized the girl on the barricades next to us was Aitor's girlfriend. The man and woman on the other side of us were Dani's relatives and there I was with JuanPe's son. I took a deep breath. *Well, something pretty important has changed in your life as a runner, here I am smack dead in the center of the families of three of the very best runners in Navarra.*

Navarra opened its arms to me in a big way and I just tried to absorb as much as I could. We ran to the car and drove to Falces. As we got close, a trail of hundreds of cars trying to make it to the encierro stretched far outside town. JuanPe had to veer around traffic and tell a few cops that I was guest of the mayor so we could make it through. We made it just in time and got to the press box with Evi at the very base of the mountain. JuanPe ran up El Pilon just in time for the Falces encierro to begin.

The rocket went off and the entire mountain began to move, literally. The runners scrambled around and ran through the winding path. Then I saw them on the last steep straightaway. Aitor was on the horns of the lead vaca. Then about halfway down, he flung into the air and disappeared into the pack. *My god, was he gored?!*

After the vaca thundered past, runners yelled for medics near where I'd last seen Aitor. I ran up the mountain to find him. That was the first time I'd physically run since the goring. I didn't know I could. When I got to where he was, there was nothing, he was gone!

JuanPe appeared in front of me. He held his arm against himself, clearly in pain. Miguel was there and he said, "He's hurt, bad!"

We followed JuanPe down to the ambulance. He put on a calm face when Evi walked up. We waited outside the ambulance and then Miguel told me we should go watch the recortadores. So we went thinking JaunPe was fine. He wasn't. We watched the famous recortadore Javier PimPim work his magic turning the vaca. He would fall to all fours facing the animals as they charged only a few feet away and then he'd lead and turn them in circles. It astonished me. At one point he turned three vaca at once; it was like he'd hypnotized them. We met up with JuanPe afterward. He put on a stoic face and said he was fine. Went to breakfast with a bunch of JuanPe's friends. They were runners and photographers; they all had photos of me. They were kind of guarded with me and I was so tired from the long trip I couldn't understand a word of Spanish. I tried to talk but came off really dumb. Then we were walking around and ran into Victor, Xander, and Dierdre Carney. They'd run El Pilon that morning and we started talking. We all went up and met the mayor and had some drinks and got a pañuelo.

Afterward JuanPe asked me what I wanted to do.

I said, "I don't know, whatever you want."

"I am leaving, what do you want to do?" he said impatiently.

"What? Let's go. Where are you going?"

"I am going to the hospital," he said and winced so hard that he almost crumbled to the ground in pain. He'd dislocated his shoulder during the encierro and as the adrenaline from the run wore off the pain began to spike. He'd been trying to hide it from his son Evi because he didn't want Evi to worry about him.

"Let's go then!" I said urgently and we started for the car.

We ran into Dierdre and the guys again and she asked JuanPe, "Where's a good place to watch from on the mountain?"

JuanPe looked away from her, grimaced viscerally. He sighed and said, "Let's go, I will show you".

We started toward the mountain. I tried to stop him.

"No, we have to go." I pleaded but he ignored me. He put on a smile and, in astonishing pain, walked her not just to the base of the mountain, which was three blocks away but then he climbed with her up the switchback all the way up the adjacent mountain to show her the very best place to watch from. I wanted to shout, *Dierdre, he is hurt, we have to go to the hospital!* But I was so touched by the gracefulness of what JuanPe was doing I couldn't bring myself to tell her. I thought of Matt watching what was happening from above. Could only imagine Matt was feeling the same things as me, just pure pride and astonishment at JuanPe's grace.

I couldn't believe it. In the fantastic pain JuanPe was in, he took Dierdre Carney all the way to the top of the mountain, smiling and telling stories. I don't think he even knew Dierdre was Matt Carney's daughter. He just did it because she was a nice person and a friend of mine. I refused to go up the mountain because I was so distraught over what he was doing; the man should have been in the hospital, and here he was giving Dierdre a tour of El Pilon. This is the Navarrese people in their purest form, tough, generous, and honorable.

I tried to get JuanPe let me drive. He refused.

I told JuanPe, "Let's go straight to the hospital. I'll go with you."

He said, "No, I will take you home first."

Evi fell asleep in the back seat and JuanPe began to show his pain more. He nearly passed out at the wheel. I kept trying to get him to let me drive but he pulled himself together and drove me home. I really don't know what to say about the man, except he is something else, a very special and stubborn person in the most noble way possible. He invited me to Tafalla and Falces and part of that invitation meant taking me home afterward and Juan Pedro Lecuona is a man of his word.

Another article came out in *Diario de Navarra* about me. It was getting to be regular business. My friend Itxaso Recondo was working on an interview for SanFermin.com. She accompanied me with JuanPe back to Falces for the closing run. JuanPe's arm was in a sling but he assured me if San Fermín was on, he'd be running even in pain, but because it was only Tafalla and Falces he'd decided to sit it out. San Fermín was like that. It's like the Super Bowl—a star player would play in the big game even with a dislocated shoulder, but he might sit out a regular season game. JuanPe had decided to sit out Falces but still loved it so much he brought us out to watch. There we were sitting on the mountainside in the spot he'd shown Dierdre Carney a few days before. Two injured runners who just couldn't stay away from the encierro and a reporter who couldn't stay away either. From this perspective, Falces was even more magnificent. Thousands of people lined the fencing that snakes down the steep winding path. Other large groups gather on the adjacent mountains. The rocket went off and we spotted Aitor running in place near the last half of the course. From our perch we saw the runners scampering across the path. The vaca seemed huge and aggressive as they galloped behind the mozos. Then man and beast disappeared around a bend. The runners flowed down the mountain fast. A terrified roar swelled throughout the mountainside. A lead vaca exploded through the fencing at a hard bend. It gored a photographer and sprang into the air and they both fell off the mountain. Two other spectators tumbled down the cliff with them into a steep grassy hill and they all disappeared into a gully.

Aitor ran the horns of the rest of the pack down the last stretch like he was all alone with them on a slow morning stroll. Paramedics climbed down and helped the gored man. He was a *Diario de Navarra* photographer and when they carried him past, he looked very grave. They took the other two out on stretchers and then about a hundred mozos wrestled the vaca up and onto the course. She was tied up and blindfolded and still the runners struggled as they tried to restrain her. Afterward Javier PimPim put on another show. It was fantastic; his recortadore partner did quite well also.

I thanked JuanPe when he dropped me off. Itxaso did a great and extensive interview with me afterward and I finally got ready to say goodbye to Pamplona for the year. Thought a lot about what to give JuanPe as a gift.

I thought about all the things he'd given me. All the beautiful parts of Navarra I likely would never have seen. What it all had really shown me was I was only truly a guest in this place, an observer.

That I had struggled and strived all these years but only really ever been an inexperienced foreigner, who'd gotten lucky on the street a few times to run on the horns. I was not great. And I never would be a great mozo. The only thing I'd really done was position myself close enough to have a front row seat to witness these great runners of Navarra. JuanPe is a truly great runner. He could run in his magic way for another twenty years for all I know, but some day his time will fade. Aitor was a new figure emerging at the end of the course. JuanPe was fanning Aitor's flames and showing him the path to greatness. My deepest calling as a mozo was to witness this quite historic passing of the torch in Pamplona encierro history.

I found a photo at Foto Mena from that year. JuanPe is leading a bull into the callejón. Aitor is a few strides behind him leading another bull in the pack. They run in the exact same distance and position in front of the animals, their strides are in sync, it is like a mirror image, a repeated image, the tradition at its finest, the most recent passing of the torch, a gift and a responsibility given from one mozo to the next, a chain unbroken for centuries, hundreds of images of man linked with animal soaring up the way.

Got the photo printed for JuanPe and I wrote him a letter thanking him for all his gifts but telling him his greatest gift was giving me the honor of watching him showing Aitor the way.

I left Pamplona reflecting on something I'd said to Itxaso in our interview. I told her: "I wanted to thank the three Brits, because they pushed open a door to Pamplona that might have never opened for me. Inside I've found the most incredible warmth, deep and true friendship, the most beautiful people I've ever known in all the world, and now I love Pamplona more deeply than ever."

Arrived in the Madrid train stop and Al Goodman, the CNN Spain correspondent, picked me up. We walked around scoping out the scene. CNN International wanted a follow-up piece on me. Al was a great guy—we went all over getting press stuff together and he made his plan. Caught up with Gus, Mikael, and Steve Ibarra that night but called it an early one to be up for the CNN filming. We met up like we'd planned before sunrise and walked all over, and Al asked me some really tough questions and I began to worry that the piece might end up like the Jeanne Moos story with some joke at my expense but I toughed it out. We ran into some British nationals who'd just had their first run, and they were all amped up and asked me some advice. Talked with José Manuel, the Sanse Pastor who I'd run that long run on the horns stride for stride with in 2012, and he said some nice things about me for CNN Spain. The filming closed out with a nice talk over some coffee.

Ran into Steve on the way back to the hotel and he'd been drinking all night and started asking about the goring. I resisted but finally I let in. I told him, "You're one of the only people who could get me to do this." Then I told him everything that'd happened after the goring and the criticism I'd felt from the Brits and Xander. Steve had no idea that they'd goaded me into reacting, which confirmed there was a lot of negative talk about me going around with the regular foreign runners. I lost it a little bit and vented but finally we ended up just talking about Bomber and how Steve was becoming like Bomber or that he was doing Bomber's work now that Bomber was gone. I even told him Bomber was here with us because I believe that when you talk about the dead they come to listen. Steve broke down crying and I could feel Bomber with us and we hugged.

The CNN Spain segment was really beautiful. They'd done a wonderful job and I came across great. Then the CNN International segment came out and it was even better. I felt good, like it was some sort of final statement on everything that'd happened that summer and the final statement was positive.

We headed to Alcala de Henares with Angel. Mikael was limping badly as we walked up and I tried to give him my cane because he was limping worse than me. Mikael still chose to run. Then something marvelous happened as the herd approached; Mikael ran the horns of the lead bull for fifteen yards! I couldn't believe it but I had video proof. This man with a blood clot in his thigh, who limped up to the fastest run in Spain, ran the horns of the lead animal. I couldn't stop talking about it, it was such a spectacular moment. Back in the hospital we didn't know if he was going to survive and here he was daring to do what he loved and running the horns like it was nothing. Mikael Anderson is pure magic.

Mikeal's feat made me want to run, but I chose not to for Enid's sake. I just couldn't put her through worrying about me. Kept reassuring her that I wouldn't run, but I wanted to very badly.

We arrived in Cuéllar just before my book event. Dyango met Xander and me at Hotel San Francisco. We walked around to a few different Peñas. They greeted us warmly. They asked to see my scar. Dyango's scar from his goring was in almost the same place on the same leg as my bigger scar. We thought that was pretty funny. We got to Peña de Pañuelo. It was their fiftieth anniversary and they were to host my book event. The head of the Peña was a guy named Valentín. I was going to try to read a passage in Spanish but just wasn't prepared and asked Valentín to do it and he agreed immediately. As we set up for the presentation the regional TV station materialized with cameras and two reporters from different papers. Valentín read remarkably well. After the event, the books I had brought that had been translated into Spanish evaporated. They sold instantly. I did an interview with the local TV that was remarkably bad because I forgot how to say horse in Spanish. Just another reason why I'm back at school studying Spanish now.

That next day I was standing on the course with Dyango. His wife had been diagnosed with a serious illness and we started talking as the bulls approached town. I asked about his wife. He said she was okay, the news was good. Something somber came over Dyango's face.

"So many things have happened here on this street," he said, looking down the hill from where we stood next to Hotel San Francisco where a bull seriously gored him years before. "I spent so many years of my life trying to run in front of the bulls every single day. We know what we risk. You and I, we know so very well. Now, I think of my children, my wife. It's different for me now. It's so different now but here we are." He smiled, sort of astonished to find himself standing there.

I nodded, knowing exactly what he meant. I gave him a hug, a pat on the back, wished him *suerte*, and exited the course to watch from the other side of the fence.

Promised Enid and myself that I wouldn't run for the rest of the summer. Our love and my injury made it just an impossibility. There was something else though that I needed to do. I knew even when I sat there on that hospital bed after my surgery that I would go.

We are waiting at the corrals outside Cuéllar.

I've told them not to look for me and not to wait, that I will see them on the other side. The animals roar from the corrals into the horsemen and they all gallop into the paradisiacal forest and disappear into foggy, pink-orange haze. I jog fearful, fearless, and curious. I know that I might die there among the trees. *And if I do, I will be one of the very few lucky souls to die doing exactly what they truly love.* One last horseman gallops across the field, his long staff in hand, a gray apparition, both timeless and ghostly. The fog blisters through their long hair as they vanish. I follow, slipping into the ancient dusty aura struck bright in the heavenly morning light, into the pine forest to find out about life and myself and about us all.

POSTSCRIPT

I arrived home in September after my time in Europe. Finished a publishable draft of my memoir *Mozos* in early October and began work with my editor. The magnitude of everything that happened that summer settled on me. My opus *The Old Neighborhood* received acclaim from four different continents. More press appeared nationally as well. The attention astounded me, especially from Spain and the UK. The book was undeniably internationally acclaimed and I'd won the award from the *Chicago Sun-Times*. In my wildest dreams I wanted the book to become award-winning, internationally acclaimed, bestseller. I'd achieved all but one. There were still 500 unsold copies left of my 2,500-copy first run sitting in my distributor's warehouse. I wanted a second printing to show off all my blurbs and awards so I reached out to every literary night and storytelling event in Chicago and started ordering books from my distributor by the hundreds. My motto was "Sell All The Books." I even made it into a hashtag: #sellallthebooks. I sold forty copies one night at the Green Mill Uptown Poetry Slam. Some nights I only sold a few but others I did great. Several nights I even offered to show my scar as a reward to the crowd if I sold all the books I brought. In November I sold seventy-two books in three days, including twenty at a big event down in Mexico City with Irvine. That was pretty much what initiated the second printing. I've already sold well over 200 copies of the second edition.

I could have given up back in April of 2014 when all my luck and momentum grinded to a halt and I fell into the worst depression of my life. I could have killed myself, or just let go of my dream. I didn't though. I tried and made a great effort and things happened. But if I didn't have the love in my life in the form of my wonderful wife Enid, I never would have made it this far. It's so easy to be blinded by the darkness of this world. Sometimes the light of a true and deep love is the only thing that can guide you through the darkness. Enid saves me from the darkness on an almost daily basis. I would be a pathetic mess, if not dead or in prison, without her love, which fortifies my life.

Things continued to progress with the press attention. I told a story on NPR's *Snap Judgment* about the goring, which ignited a bunch of interest in *Mozos*. Sadly the growing rift between Xander and me swelled. I decided to part ways with his *Survival Guide* Ebook and told him to take my writing out of it. I chose to include my Outside bull-run survival guide in *Mozos* instead.

An American student named Benjamin Milley received several horrific gorings in Rodrigo that winter. CBS This Morning with Charlie Rose contacted me and brought me into the CBS station in Chicago to give comment for the national broadcast. They showed a picture of the cover of *Mozos* in the segment. Later that day NBC's *Today* show asked me to give comment on Milley's goring. They sent a black Cadillac to drive me to the station and broadcast an image of the cover of *Mozos*. Major outlets are treating me as the expert American journalist on the encierro, which is quite humbling. It's a responsibility I hope I'm ready for. My duty is to present the encierro as it is, a beautiful art form with deep roots in Spain and in humanity as a whole, a tradition that transformed my life and made me a more humanistic person.

HOW TO RUN IN THE MODERN ERA OF THE RUNNING OF THE BULLS IN PAMPLONA

For eight consecutive mornings in July, six half-ton Spanish fighting bulls and several bell-oxen rampage through the streets of Pamplona. There's more to the ancient tradition than just surviving it. At its most pure form, this is daring street art, a dance with death and majesty, a chance to come into harmonious contact with one of nature's fiercest monstrosities. At its worst, it's a bunch of panicked tourists falling all over each other in an idiotic stampede. Whether it's your first trip or you're an experienced runner or even just someone interested in the tradition, this passage will guide you through the running of the bulls in Pamplona as it is today. We will go step-by-step through the morning's events and walk the entire course from beginning to end. This is your practical information on how to survive it, do it right, and what to look out for. I'm going to break it down in tips for beginners, intermediates, and experts. Pay close attention to the rules, because if broken they have colossal consequences. Also for beginners, you cannot run a very long distance with the bulls. They have four legs. They're faster than you. You'll only keep up for a short distance in the crowded street. So you must pick one of the following six sections to run.

A LITTLE PHILOSOPHY BEFORE WE GET STARTED:

The duty of all mozos bull runners) in the encierro (bull run, enclosure) is to help transition the herd from the pens at the edge of town to the corrals inside the arena in the swiftest and safest way possible. Runners are meant to lead the herd with their bodies and create a moving human enclosure around the pack. The experts do this by running on the horns (running just inches in front of a bull's snout and in essence leading the animal), but I don't recommend that if this is your first fiesta. For beginners your goal is to run beside the pack, for intermediates the goal is somewhere between running beside and on the horns.

The absolute worst thing a bull runner can do is to interfere with the herd and cause an animal to separate from the pack. As we've seen in the past, interference often leads to the severe injury or even the death of a runner. The Spanish do hold a grudge, even after they've beaten you bloody. That word of warning out of the way, when done correctly, running with the bulls can be an exhilarating experience.

BEFORE THE RUN:

The hour before the run is a tense time for any mozo. The run starts at 8:00 a.m. sharp. The first stick-rocket signifies the corral gates are open. The second rocket signals the last bull has left the pen. You can hear the rockets from almost anywhere on the course except for sometimes near the arena when there are too many loud runners.

Beginners: Be at Town Hall by 7:00 a.m. If you can see the clock at Town Hall and you are in the street between the barricades, you're in the right place.

If you are standing anywhere between the police line on Mercaderes and the bull arena, you're in trouble. A second police line forms behind the first; this police line begins a slow methodical walk along the course to the arena. They pick their biggest, craziest, and most sadistic police officers for this task. There's always around a thousand uniformed tourists standing in the wrong place, foolishly expecting to run. The police push all of these would-be runners back with their huge, glossy black nightsticks. Any bigmouthed tourist who protests gets an abrupt wake-up crack to the skull. Those who continue to resist get beaten exponentially harder and then dragged off the course by their ankles. A gate swings open at the two intersections along Estafeta Street and they push every single tourist off the course. How do I know? This happened to me in 2005, my rookie year.

The stationary police line at Mercaderes breaks at ten to eight, and you can walk up the course to any starting position you want.

Rule: Don't be a Drunk Idiot

Aside from the obvious reasons for not being inebriated, here's another one. Police remove the visibly drunk from the bull-run course. Other things they don't like? Ridiculous costumes and hats. So, yes, leave the giant banana outfit and foam pirate hat at home.

Intermediates: Grab a newspaper at Carmelo's Bookshop (36 Estafeta) and look for photos of your friends and yourself from the run the morning before. Don't be a sardine at Town Hall. Go down to Santo Domingo to sing the blessing to San Fermín and hang back in the less-crowded stretches of Santo Domingo until the police line breaks.

Experts: You've been around long enough to know people. Find an apartment with a door that opens onto the run. Relax on a couch. Take a nap. Watch the previous day's run on TV. Then at ten minutes to 8:00 a.m. and the beginning of the run, walk down and enter the mass of soon-to-be runners on the street.

SECTION 1: SANTO DOMINGO

This is the beginning of the course. The terrain is fairly steep, which can be dangerous. You probably run slower when moving uphill, but the bulls run faster. Plus, they're fresh and rowdy. This is their first experience with a crowd of people. There's no telling how an individual bull will react.

Beginners: Position yourself an arm's length away from either wall. After the second stick-rocket explodes run like you've never run before. The herd will likely be tight and out in the center of the street. Stay to the side but keep your head on a swivel. In 1971 a bull scraping the wall here nearly disemboweled Pulitzer Prize-winning author James Michener. Sometimes bulls just decide to break from the herd and start hooking. If that happens, hit the deck.

Intermediates: The most popular chunk in this section for years was the Suicide Run but it seems that with the new regulations that run doesn't exist anymore. Pick your position about halfway up Santo Domingo where it tends to be fairly empty. As the herd gallops forward at speeds approaching 35 mph, run hard. Keep your head on a swivel and stay in the center as long as you dare. At the last second, dive off to one of the sides as the herd barrels up the center of the street.

Experts: In the old days the Butcher's Guild would gather here in their white cloaks. Like our suicidal intermediates, run downhill at the herd. Yet at the last possible moment, stop, turn around, and sprint up the street just before the tips of the lead bull's horns. Legend has it that the Butcher's did this to ferret out the most aggressive animals in order to make their job of selecting which bulls they'd cut that evening a little easier.

SECTION 2: TOWN HALL

Town Hall is a technical section but tends to be fairly quiet. That said, a bull gored Matthew Peter Tasio to death here in 1995 after he fell and stood up in the path of the herd. The bull gored him in the heart and threw him twenty yards. He bled to death within seconds.

Rule: If You Fall Down, Stay Down

The death of Tasio further cemented the rule, if you fall down stay down. The bulls see best under their snout where they eat. They also have an instinct that tells them to jump over debris while they gallop. If you stay down and cover your head, there is a good chance the herd will step and leap over you. Even if they do step on you, it's a better option than being gored in the vitals. Stay down and if you have a few moments, roll toward the barricades.

Beginners: Start before Town Hall. Stick to the left side of the street and stay an arm's length from the barricades. Wait until the cameramen on the balconies above start to take photos and pan, following the herd. The ground will begin to rumble with the tremendous weight of the stampede. Then run. Keep your head on a swivel; the herd might be out in the center of the street and one bull might be hugging the barricades. If you end up in front of a bull, dive under the barricades. Always expect the worst on the course—that mentality will protect you from the unexpected.

Intermediates: Running either side is fine, though sometimes the herd swings wide right and hits the barricades. When the herd is close, the street opens up. Stay away from the beginners on the left as they will suck you into the barricades and ruin your run. When it opens up, go for it!

Experts: Wait it out. Your entry can be from either side but needs to be timed perfectly. This is a fast section. A thirty-yard run on the horns here is an accomplishment.

SECTION 3: LA CURVA

The Curve, Hamburger Wall, Dead Man's Corner—it has a lot of nicknames because, after so many years of accidents and mishaps, danger is almost guaranteed on this section of the course. The herd flies into this hard-banking turn at full go. They crash and fall and chaos ensues.

Beginners: Don't even think about it. If you are a beginner and you run La Curva most veterans would say that you deserve whatever horrific wound the bulls give you. Beware, you may attempt to run Town Hall, but if you leave that section early guess where you'll end up? Pancaked under a half-dozen fallen bulls with a horn inserted into your ass.

Intermediates: There is an old technique popularized by American Joe Distler that the Spanish have been using for an eternity. Stand in a doorway on the left side entering The Curve. After the herd hits the wall, break into a sprint. Catch up with the pack as they rise to their hooves. Run them up the street as far as you can. But beware; there may be a straggler or two.

Experts: Scotsman Brucie Sinclair created a modified version of Distler's run. He started halfway up Mercaderes in a doorway on the left.

After the herd passes, sprint right up to their backs. When the bulls hit the wall, swing around them on the inside of The Curve and onto the horns. Take them up the street. Another Scott, Angus Ritchie, has made a name for himself doing just about the same in his yellow Partick Thistle jersey.

Note: Deaf and mute Spaniard José Antonio has spent decades at The Curve doing the impossible. He stands nearly in the center. As the herd passes, he picks up any straggler bulls, quiets them, and leads them up Estafeta. But you probably don't want to try this: José's superhuman sensory perception and insane courage are the only things that keep him alive year after year.

Rule: No Cameras

Last year I was running beside a guy who was filming with his fancy new chrome-cased iPhone, when a tall bulky Spaniard ran past and smacked said instrument right out of his grasp. The expensive device splintered into a dozen pieces, then clattered on the cobblestones. I doubt he was able to put that back together.

Look Out for Sueltos

A suelto is a lone bull that has separated from the herd. The bull loses his herding instinct. It looks around and sees all runners as predators. Just like a Cape buffalo attacking a pack of lions in Africa, the bull goes in to kill.

Beginners: This one is simple. If you see a lone bull on the street, run. Not further down the course, but to immediate safety. Run as fast as you can to a barricade and dive under the bottom rung. If you try to climb over you will be a slow and easy target for the suelto.

Intermediates: You know how dangerous it is but this is one of the places where you can gain incredible experience. Wade in slowly. Keep your distance. Be sure not to trip anyone up. Aim your shoulder at the animal and keep your hand feeling for runners behind you. This is a team action. Wade as close as you dare but know if you get too close it might be the last thing you do.

Experts: Attract the animal with your newspaper or hand. Remember that the bull sees better broadside. If he is facing you, make your motions low where his vision is OK. If a suelto is goring a fallen runner, dash up behind the animal and grab hold of his tail. Do not yank but apply a steady, heavy pressure. The animal should stop. Try to turn him with low or peripheral motion. Then lead him toward the arena.

SECTION 4: ESTAFETA

This is a long straightaway. James Michener said that if you're in Paris and someone is trying to tell you how to run bulls in Pamplona, tell them you always run Estafeta and the conversation will end as they look at you in awe.

Beginners: There are four exits on Estafeta at the two intersections. Use them if you need to, but note that you are usually safest on the street while running toward the arena. Start about halfway up Estafeta. Get an arm's length away from the wall. It is vital that you wait until after the second rocket. It will take over a minute for the herd to reach you. A series of waves of panicked runners will flood past. Don't run with them. Wait until the cameras on the balconies 20 yards/meters from you start to flash and pan with the herd. Then run.

Intermediates: The stones on Estafeta are very smooth and slippery. It's like sprinting on a slip-and-slide. You can't accelerate quickly or cut side to side. Start running early and fight for the center of the street. Do whatever you must to stay on your feet.**Experts:** The legendary David Rodríguez dominates this section. He does it with iron will and courage. That said, even he still falls from time to time. Start running early and hold the center of the street. As the herd gets close to you, the crowd will thin. There is a bubble of space before the herd. Sprint full speed inside that small bubble. They're fast here, so you better move quickly or they'll use you for traction.

Look Out for Pastores
These guys are like the bull's little, green-shirted ninja bodyguards. They carry long, elastic willow canes that draw blood in bright, explosive splatters.Pastores are stationed all along the course wearing green, three-button, collared shirts with PASTORES written across the back in white. Pastores translates roughly to cowboys on foot.

Rule: Don't Touch

If you touch an animal during the run, that includes swatting one with your newspaper, the pastores will not hesitate to swing that cane down and splay your hand wide open. Unfortunately, that probably won't be the end of it. It isn't unheard of for every Spanish runner in the general vicinity to stop, turn around, and beat someone down to the cobblestones. This is their tradition. You are a guest at their party. The bulls are sacred to these men. Respect the bovine.

Beginners: If you think it will be a lot of fun to run up, grab a steer's tail, and pull on it for no reason, then you are asking for trouble. Some tourist tried this a couple years ago. A pastor ran up beside the tourist and swung with all his might and broke his cane across the tourist's nose. The tourist wasn't laughing as his blood splashed on the cobblestones.

Intermediates: Don't touch and don't break the pastores' line if they're halting runners due to a suelto or you'll end up another notch on their willow cane.

Experts: The pastores' job with a suelto is to keep the crowd in the street back. It's your duty to help lure the suelto toward the corrals.

SECTION 5: TELEFÓNICA

At Telefónica the street widens and it becomes more difficult for all of the participants to keep the herd of bulls together. Sueltos are a problem here and controlling them is made more difficult by the fact that lots of intermediate runners pack the street in this section. Capuchino of the Jandilla ranch killed Daniel Jimeno Romero at Telefónica in 2009.

Beginners: Though its width seems inviting, its location at the end of the run makes it hazardous. If there is a suelto on the loose he will likely cause the most havoc here due to exhaustion and frustration. You don't belong at Telefónica. If you leave Estafeta early and end up here with bulls in the street, dive under the barricades and take cover.

Intermediates: Telefónica is a great place to push your boundaries. You can make a lot of mistakes here and still pull off a decent run. Fight for the center of the street but keep your head on a swivel. Juan Pedro Lecuona will fly through here, leading the herd. Stay clear of him. He is the top dog at Telefónica. Try to fit in where you can and roll all the way into the arena with the bulls. The arena's embrace is about as close as you'll ever get to being a professional athlete who's just won a championship.

Experts: The stones are drier here and your maneuverability is better. Run the center of the street. Watch for fallen runners and maneuver around them. The herd will find you. If you spend a lot of time looking back, you'll drift to the sides of the street where other runners will trip and tangle you up. When the herd finds you, accelerate into the open pocket. Say hi to Juan. Now that you're on the horns, the problem is staying on them. There will be a wall of tourists ahead of you. They will slowly crumble around you. You'll need to leap them and slash around them all while maintaining your connection with the animal and not interfering with Juan and his protégé Aitor. Do your best and remember this is a team. It takes a team to create an encierro. Be good to your brothers on the street.

Rule: Don't be a Valiente

Valiente translates to Brave One. The Spanish are being ironic here. If you really want to run with the bulls you have to wait till they get to you. Depending on where you are along the course it could take up to two minutes for the herd to reach you after the rockets. Run too early and you'll end up entering the white sand bullring minutes ahead of the herd. There the enormous crowd in the 20,000-seat arena will pelt you with hunks of bread and vegetables and shower you with mocking laughter. As the crowd chants "valiente," you'll understand that the Spanish have a brutal sense of humor. And you will have failed to run with the bulls.

SECTION 6: CALLEJÓN (THE TUNNEL)

Callejón is known for the deadly montóns (pileups) that occur here. One runner falls, the next falls on top of him until there is a stack of bodies five high and the width of the tunnel. The herd arrives at full speed. They buck, gore, and stomp their way through the pileup. The injured fill the local hospital beds to capacity.

Beginners: You don't belong here. This section is even more hazardous than La Curva. If you are approaching the tunnel with the herd still in the street, say a prayer and get through the tunnel as fast as possible.

Intermediates: If you're in good position ride through the tunnel with the pack and get out to either side. If you fall in the tunnel don't forget about the small openings at the floor. Crawl in as quickly as you can to avoid causing a pileup.

Experts: Roll through the callejón—into the tunnel and through to the bright, explosive pandemonium of the packed 20,000-seat arena. Sprint straight into the center of the white-sand bullring and hand the animals off to the dobladores with their pink luring capes. They'll get them into the corral at the back to the arena. If there is a pileup, you need to keep your wits. There will be runners crushed to near death at the bottom. Pitch in to break the pile and if you find someone not breathing at the bottom like I did in 2013, help carry him to the infirmary inside the arena; that's where he can get the swiftest help. Pray that they survive.

AFTER THE RUN:

This is a time of unparalleled euphoria. Hemingway said that the most exhilarating feeling a man could experience was being shot at and missed. That is the joy of running with the bulls and surviving unscathed.

Rule: Clean the Wounds

If you are scathed, even in a small way, you need to clean the wound. There are dozens of Red Cross medics stationed in between the double barricades outside the course. Wait in line if you have to; they'll spray your abrasions with peroxide. If you don't take care of any scrape or cut caused by the street, it is guaranteed to infect. Trust me, I learned this the hard way. Going to the hospital with a knee swelled up like a watermelon isn't how anyone wants to spend four hours of their fiesta.

Beginners: The herd has passed you by. Go for it! Run toward the arena. Beware, there may be a suelto; but if there is, you now know what to do. Run into the arena (beware there may be a loose bull there) so get out over the bullring wall. Once the final rocket goes off and the arena starts singing, climb back in. They release vaca (wild Spanish fighting cows) into the ring after the run. Hemingway used to pass vaca with a cape here. Go to the corral gate and kneel with the other maniacs. The vaca will leap over you—hopefully, but she is guaranteed to land on somebody. Then run around like a lunatic. Don't pull the vaca's tail or the Spaniards will lump you up.

Intermediates: Get over to Bar Txoko and figure out if your friends have all made it out safely. Talk about what happened and try to contemplate how to get better. Ask the experts questions—most accept drinks as payment. Have a beer or two. You earned it.

Experts: Stroll to Bar Txoko and spread the wealth of your knowledge and experience. Don't be cocky. It's bad karma and will mess up your next morning's run. If you're lucky and someone invites you, go to the Runners Breakfast. It's one hell of an honor.These are the basics. They will help keep you safe. But beware, these are wild animals in an incredibly volatile and spontaneous environment. Anything can happen in an encierro, especially in Pamplona's overcrowded streets. Also Pamplona plans to impose strict and steep fines on bull runners who break the rules. We'll see how effective they are, but this further enhances the fact that there are rules and you should respect them. I'll close with this. The things that will protect you in the encierro are:

knowledge (which you now have a strong chunk of), a plan (which you have a few to choose from), and fear. Fear will keep you alive. I've run eighty-seven individual encierros to date and I was nearly killed when a bull gored me on July 9, 2014. Most of the great Spanish runners who I've mentioned in this guide and in my memoir: David Rodríguez, Juan Pedro Lecuona, Julen Madina, have all been severely gored. Serious injury is part of the encierro. This guide can't keep you safe. It is only a road map to safety. You can die doing this. Only run if it is vitally important to you. If it is, *suerte.*

BILL HILLMANN is the author of the award-winning, internationally-acclaimed Chicago novel *The Old Neighborhood*. He's run with the bulls of Spain for a decade and acts as an expert guide to the course for English speaking tourists in Pamplona. Excerpts of his memoir *Mozos* have appeared in the *Toronto Star*, *Washington Post*, *Chicago Tribune*, NPR, PRI, and *Outside* Magazine. Hillmann famously survived a near fatal goring July 9th, 2014 in Pamplona. In the aftermath, his story spread around the globe. Hillmann is a former Chicago Golden Glove Champion and a Union Local 2 Construction Laborer.

| **ALSO AVAILABLE FROM CURBSIDE SPLENDOR**

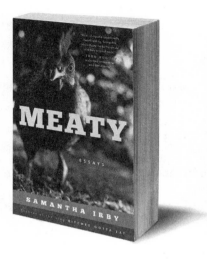

MEATY
ESSAYS BY SAMANTHA IRBY

"Raunchy, funny and vivid . . . Those faint of heart beware . . . Strap in and get ready for a roller-coaster ride to remember." —*KIRKUS REVIEWS*

Samantha Irby explodes onto the page with essays about laughing her way through a life of failed relationships, taco feasts, bouts with Crohn's Disease, and more. Written with the same scathing wit and poignant bluntness readers of her riotous blog, Bitches Gotta Eat, have come to expect, *Meaty* takes on subjects both high and low—from why she can't be mad at Lena Dunham, to the anguish of growing up with a sick mother, to why she wants to write your mom's Match. com profile.

CRAZY HORSE'S GIRLFRIEND
A NOVEL BY ERIKA T. WURTH

"Gritty and tough and sad beyond measure . . . Contains startling, heartfelt moments of hope and love." —*DONALD RAY POLLOCK*

Margaritte is a sharp-tongued, drug-dealing, sixteen-year-old Native American floundering in a Colorado town crippled by poverty, unemployment, and drug abuse. She hates the burnout, futureless kids surrounding her and dreams that she and her unreliable new boyfriend can move far beyond the bright lights of Denver that float on the horizon before the daily suffocation of teen pregnancy eats her alive.